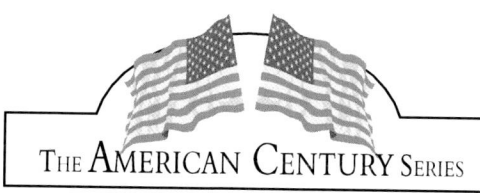

The American Century Series

Rails through the Hanover Hills
The Morristown & Erie Railroad

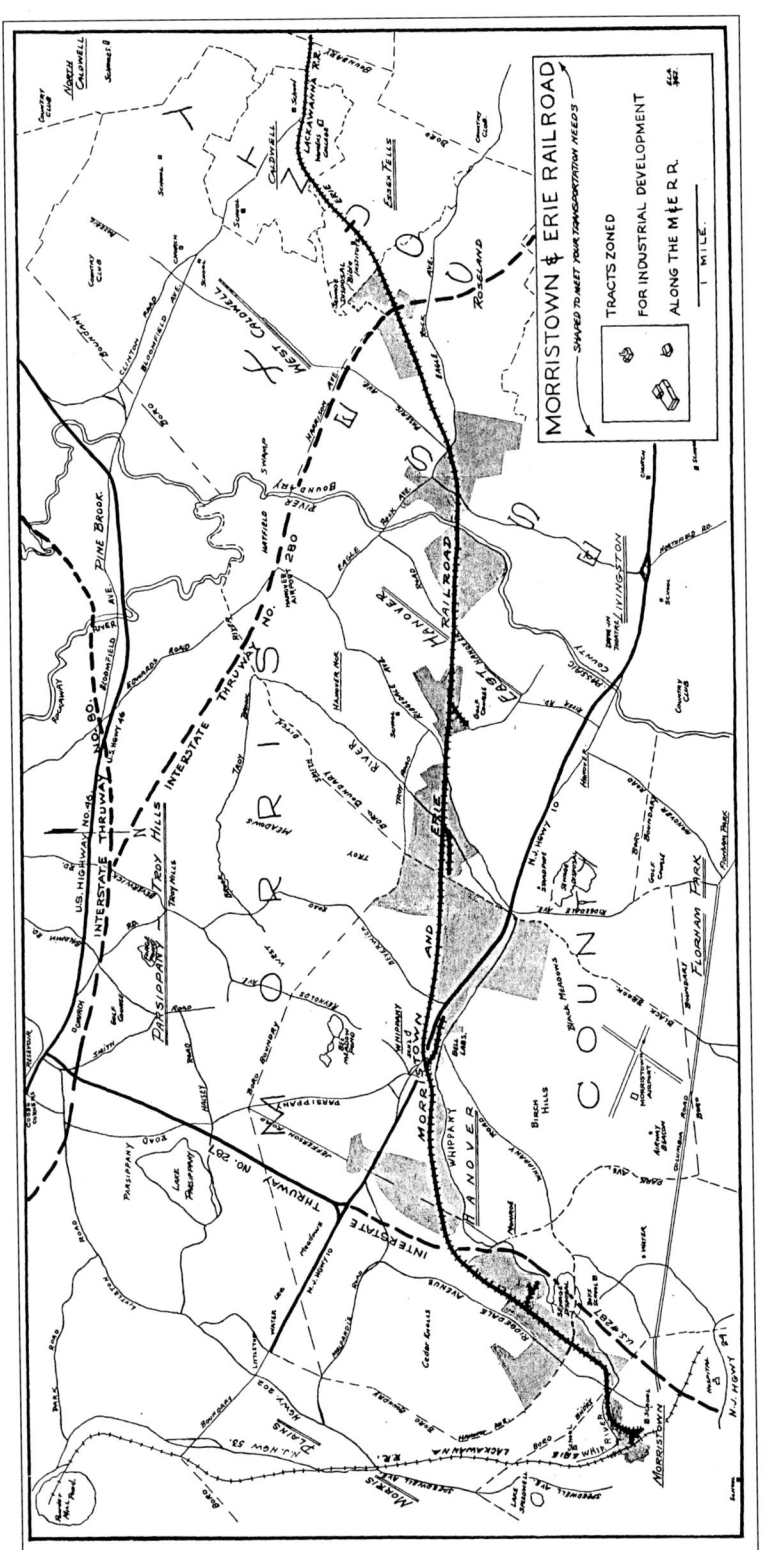

This March 1962 map was provided to potential shippers who were considering locating their industrial concerns along the busy right-of-way of the Morristown & Erie Railroad (M&E). At each end of the 11-mile line, connections were made with the Erie-Lackawanna Railroad. (Collection of Steven Hepler.)

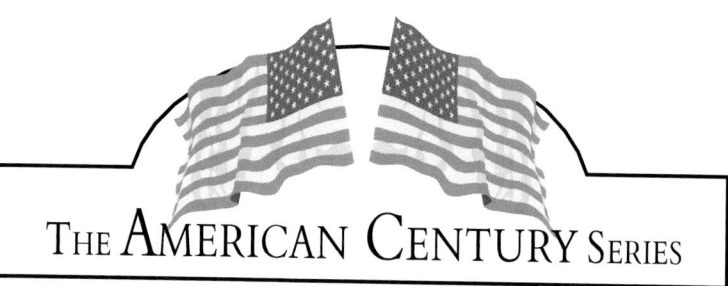

THE AMERICAN CENTURY SERIES

RAILS THROUGH THE HANOVER HILLS
THE MORRISTOWN & ERIE RAILROAD

Steven P. Hepler

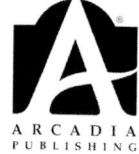

ARCADIA
PUBLISHING

Copyright © 1998 by Steven P. Helper
ISBN 978-0-7385-9702-7

Published by Arcadia Publishing
Charleston, South Carolina

Printed in the United States of America

Library of Congress Catalog Card Number: 98-89165

For all general information contact Arcadia Publishing at:
Telephone 843-853-2070
Fax 843-853-0044
E-mail sales@arcadiapublishing.com
For customer service and orders:
Toll-Free 1-888-313-2665

Visit us on the Internet at www.arcadiapublishing.com

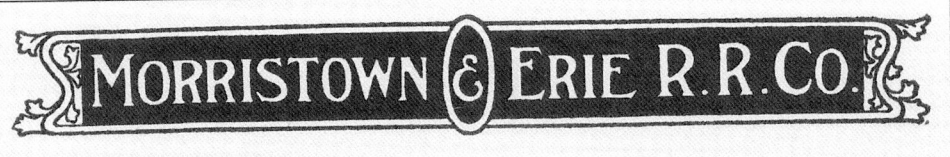

This book is dedicated to the memory of Benjamin J. Friedland, President and General Manager of the Morristown & Erie Railway . . . a kind and generous man.

Contents

	Acknowledgments	6
	Introduction	7
1.	The Whippany River Railroad	9
2.	The McEwans and the Morristown & Erie Railroad Company	13
3.	Locomotives, Equipment, and Structures	25
4.	Coal Smoke Along the Whippanong	43
5.	Workin' on the Railroad	57
6.	The Steam Era Passes	75
7.	The Diesel Era . . . 1950s–60s	81
8.	"Ride the Whippanong Trail": The Morris County Central Railroad	91
9.	Rebirth . . . The Morristown & Erie Railway	105
10.	Historic Preservation at the Whippany Railway Museum	119

Acknowledgments

The publication of any author's work is usually a time of satisfaction and celebration, but, as production on this book was entering its final stages, tragedy stuck. Benjamin J. Friedland, president and general manager of the Morristown & Erie Railway, passed away suddenly on August 3, 1998. The shock of his death has stunned his friends and associates, and the thought that we will never see him again is unfathomable. Ben's support of historic railroad preservation is well documented, and New Jersey's many rail historical societies have all benefited from the kindness of this singular individual. Today, because of his dedication and personal sacrifices, the Morristown & Erie survives, ready to meet the growing challenges of the 21st century.

In a way, this book was being written for Ben, to thank him in some small way for 18 years of friendship and for his continued support of the Whippany Railway Museum over the last 15 years. Ben was truly unique, and I was most fortunate to have known him. Thanks for everything, Ben; we miss you.

Additionally, I would like to offer my thanks to the numerous individuals and organizations that provided photos, recollections, and assistance:

Thomas Townsend Taber III's outstanding 1967 publication, *Morristown & Erie . . . People, Paper & Profits*, now long out of print, is a valuable reference as were countless old newspaper clippings, magazine articles, annual reports, and company files.

Homer R. Hill of Bernardsville, New Jersey, is one of the legendary photographers of the railroad scene in the Garden State. Homer's finely crafted images are remarkable contributions to any published work.

Donald Van Court of Madison, New Jersey, provided many of the day to day "working scenes." Don's photos, along with his documented anecdotes, compiled as a teenager nearly 60 years ago, help to bring the M&E of old to life.

A special word of thanks goes to Paul Tupaczewski . . . through the use of his computer, he was able to enhance a significant number of scenes that otherwise would not have been included.

Thanks also to American Locomotive Company (ALCO) Historic Photos, Schenectady, New York; Edwill H. Brown; California State Railroad Museum, Sacramento, California; Mike Del Vecchio; Jeanette Dimovski, for proofreading and setting up the manuscript on her PC; John Durkota; Hanover Township Landmark Committee; Alan J. Holleuffer; Robert F. Krygoski; the estate of Richard W. McEwan Jr.; The Morristown & Erie Railway; The Joint Free Public Library of Morristown and Morris Township; Bob Pennisi's "Railroad Avenue Enterprises Collection"; Railroad Museum of Pennsylvania (Pennsylvania Historic Museum Commission), Strasburg, Pennsylvania; Edward J. Ruland; Tony Russomanno; John Terry; and, finally, the Whippany Railway Museum for the use of its M&E Historic Collection.

Introduction

In an age before railroads spun their ribbons of steel across mountains, valleys, and streams, many towns and hamlets began to develop. As communities grew, so too grew their need to transport their citizens and the materials they produced.

One such community was Hanover Township, situated in the heart of Morris County in northern New Jersey. Within Hanover's boundaries is Whippany, located along the banks of the winding Whippany River. Named "Whippanong" centuries ago by the Leni-Lanape Indians living in the vicinity, the river's name means "place of the willows," or "many willows," indicating the trees which line this waterway. The river supplied power to the community's mills, including three paper mills which were continually growing. It soon became clear that a railroad was needed to haul the booming daily output of paper products.

Over 100 years ago, construction began on the 4-mile-long Whippany River Railroad (WRRR). The tiny road was destined to become the present-day Morristown & Erie Railway, which proudly continues its century-plus tradition of providing personal service to its customers and is an important link in Morris County's transportation network.

The creation of the Whippany River Railroad in 1895 was the climax of several years of talk by the owners of the paper mills around Whippany and the tradesmen in Morristown. In late 1894, James E.V. Melick turned his interest from building and operating the nearby Rockaway Valley Railroad to that of connecting the Whippany mills with the Lackawanna Railroad, 4 miles away at Morristown. Before the Whippany River Railroad started operating, nearly 40 teams of horses were required daily to pull huge wagons loaded with freight to Morristown.

Construction commenced on April 22, 1895, near St. Mary's Cemetery in Whippany, and, on August 16, the WRRR opened for freight traffic. A special passenger train was run on September 2, 1895, to celebrate the opening of the line. Regularly scheduled passenger service between Morristown and Whippany began on December 4, 1895.

Despite all the work done by Melick, his railroad was very cheaply and poorly built. The 4 miles cost approximately $25,000, including land, minimal grading, and track. Melick had promised to pay back all construction loans, but this proved to be impossible. By November 26, 1895, the WRRR was in the hands of a receiver.

At this time, the McEwan brothers, owners of the paper mills in Whippany, agreed among themselves that the railroad, properly managed and maintained, could become profitable with a bright future. They decided to acquire control of the line from Melick. By settling Melick's loans, they received stock control and ownership in 1897, and eased him out of the company. Over the next several years, the entire railroad was relocated on a new roadbed, and the 3-mile Malapardis Branch was constructed to the Moore Brick Manufacturing Company (later the Hanover Brick Co.).

Following the rebuilding of the line, the McEwans realized that it would be in their best interest to have a connection with a second large railroad in addition to the Lackawanna.

The McEwan brothers organized the Whippany & Passaic River Railroad to build a line from Whippany east to Essex Fells in Essex County where it connected with the Roseland Railway, a branch of the Erie Railroad. Construction on the 7-mile extension was started in the spring of 1903. On August 28, 1903, both the Whippany River Railroad and the Whippany & Passaic River Railroad were consolidated to form the 11-mile-long Morristown & Erie Railroad Company. The final spike was driven on May 3, 1904. On that day, the first M&E passenger train arrived at Essex Fells.

For nearly 75 years, the railroad operated successfully under the direction of the McEwan family. During their era, the McEwans created a paper "dynasty" and provided community residents with respectable employment that was passed on from generation to generation. For many years, a large sign not far from the Whippany station proudly stated: "Whippany Makes Paper; Paper Makes Whippany." Undeniably, paper made the Morristown & Erie.

Despite its small size, the M&E was always considered to be one of the most profitable railroads in the country. Indeed, in September 1940, the McEwan-led stockholders proudly announced that they were paying off their last bond. The M&E was the only United States railroad to rid itself of all debt during the Great Depression. Unfortunately, the railroad's fortunes changed drastically when the management of the mid-1970s caused the company to fall into bankruptcy. Through the efforts of a court-appointed trustee, the railroad was reorganized and appeared on January 1, 1982, as the Morristown & Erie Railway, Inc.

Today the Morristown & Erie continues to move forward in a vastly changing world, and, just as it has for over a century, the railroad and its people continue to provide essential and friendly service to the many communities along the "Whippanong Trail."

Steven P. Hepler
September 19, 1998

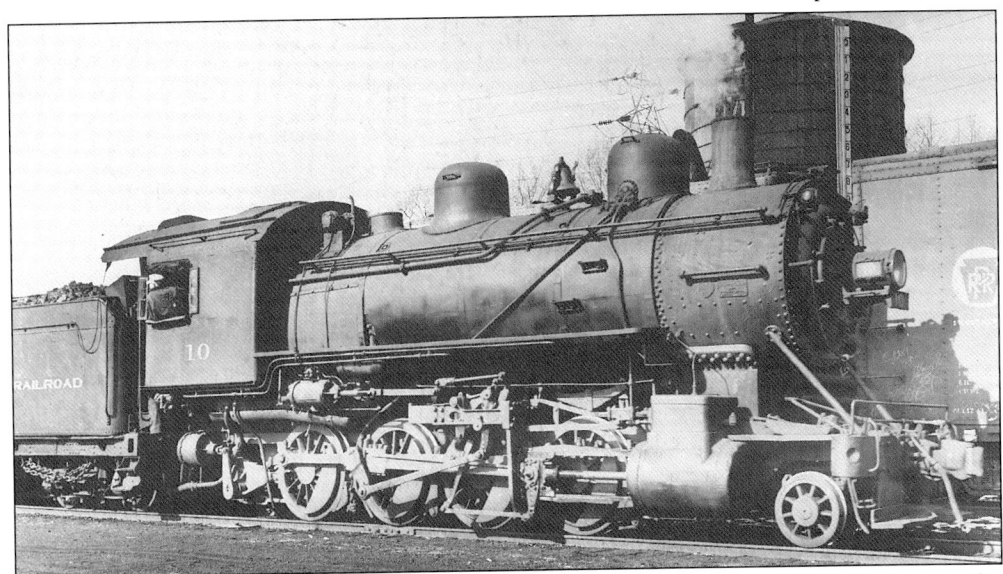

In a scene enacted countless times, No. 10 switches the "house track" adjacent to the Morristown & Erie's Whippany, New Jersey station and general office. Three of these heavy "Consolidation"-type (2-8-0) locomotives were purchased second-hand from the Monongahela Railroad in 1944 and 1946. Numbered 10, 11, and 12, they became the main freight power on this unique New Jersey shortline throughout the 1940s and early 1950s. Throughout this volume, engine wheel arrangements will be given for the various steam locomotives; in this case, "2-8-0" refers to the two small leading wheels beneath the pilot (or "cowcatcher"), eight large driving wheels, and no trailing wheels under the firebox. (Photo by Tony Russomanno; collection of Steven Hepler.)

One
THE WHIPPANY RIVER RAILROAD

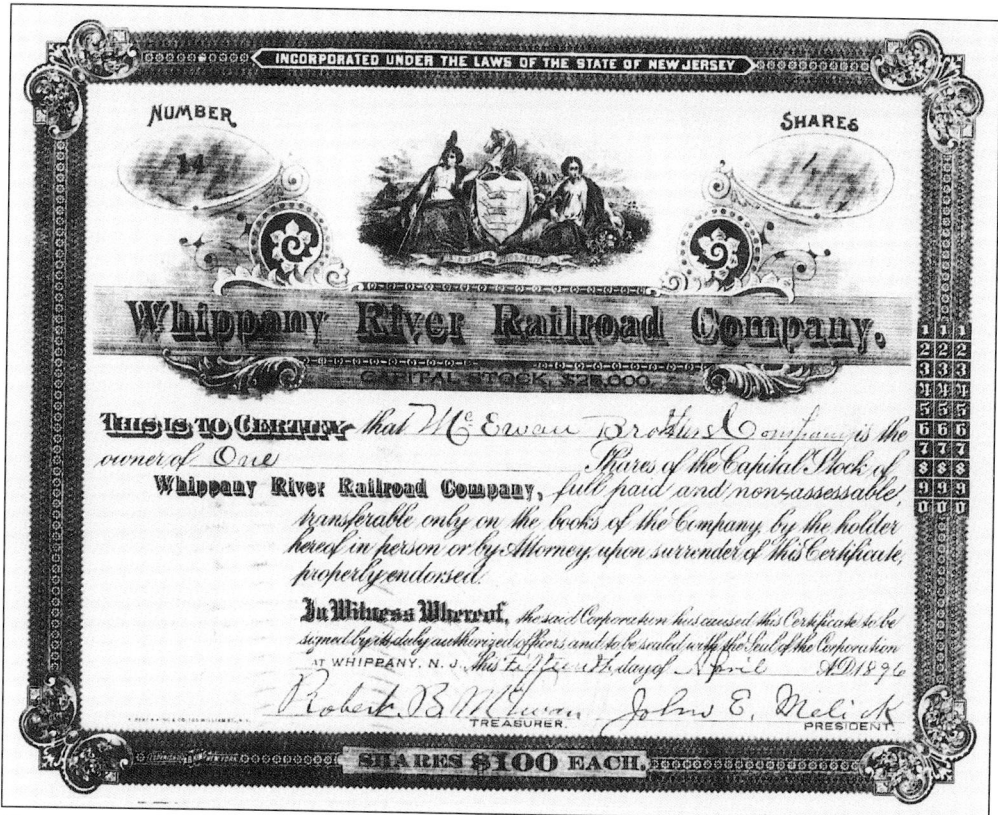

Construction on the Whippany River Railroad commenced on April 22, 1895, near Whippany's St. Mary's Cemetery. On August 16, 1895, the 4-mile line was opened for freight traffic. This c. 1896 WRRR stock certificate includes the signature of Robert B. McEwan, a member of a powerful, Whippany-based family who eventually controlled the destiny of the WRRR and, ultimately, the Morristown & Erie Railroad. (Collection of Steven Hepler.)

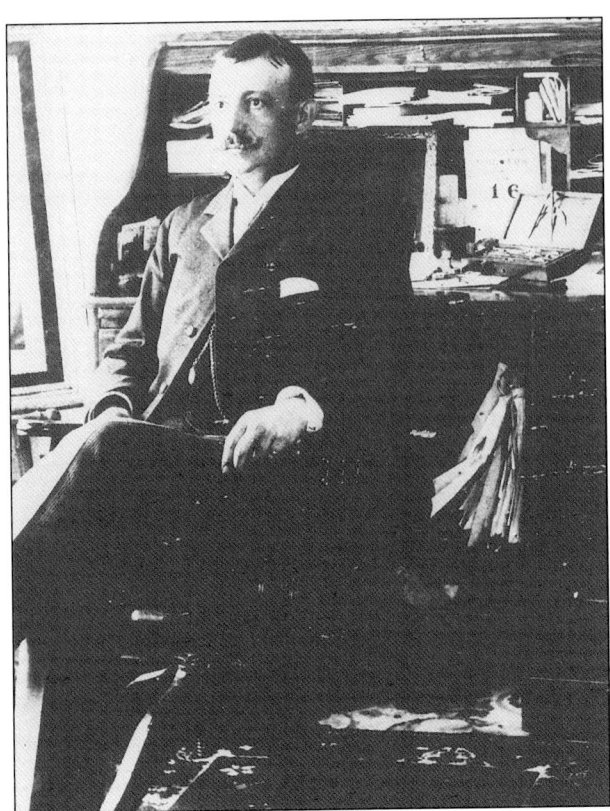

The Whippany River Railroad was built in a cheap and haphazard manner by John E.V. Melick, who built the Rockaway Valley Railroad between Morristown and White House, New Jersey. Melick's strategy was to lay his rails down first and secure permission later. He created a twisting, turning road, often laid on freshly cut trees instead of hewn crossties. (Courtesy of Railroad Museum of Pennsylvania (PHMC) Collection.)

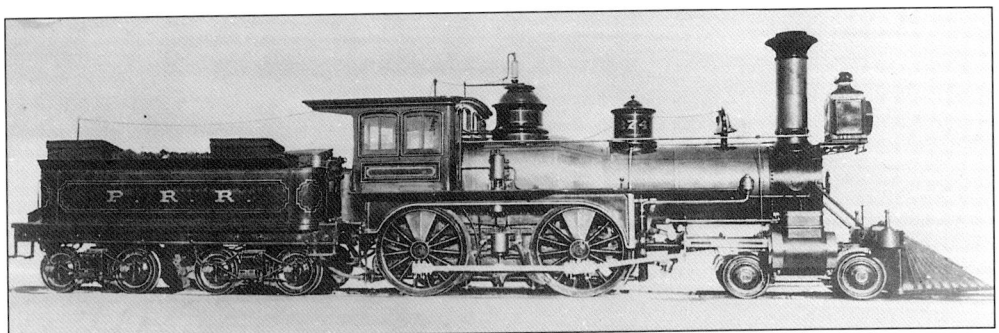

The Whippany River owned only one locomotive, which originally was a Pennsylvania Railroad (PRR) C-class (later, D-3) 4-4-0 No. 137 built in December 1874. An example of No. 137 is shown here in the form of PRR No. 274. When the classic "American"-type locomotive arrived at Morristown in June 1895, it was numbered "1" and named "Whippany." (Courtesy of Railroad Museum of Pennsylvania (PHMC) Collection.)

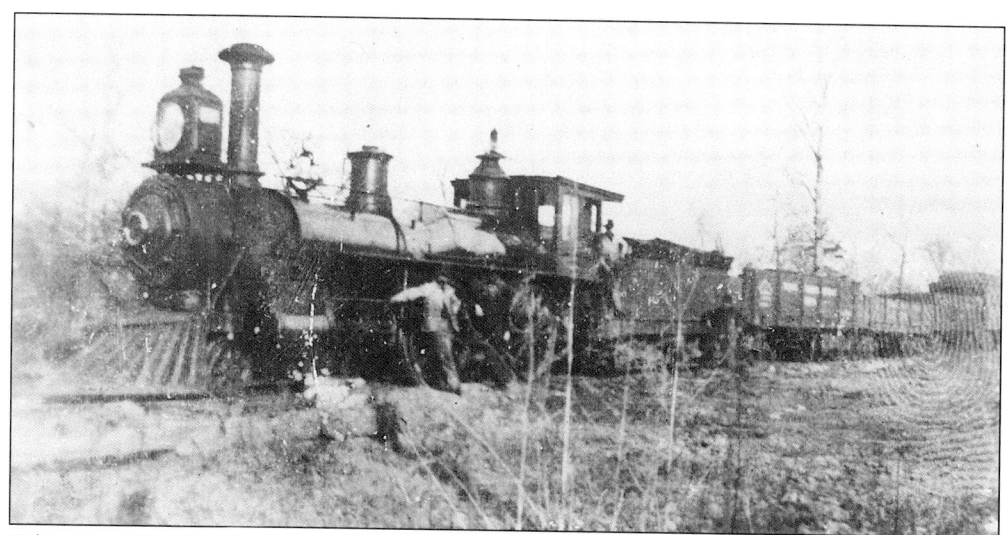

Whippany River No. 1 is seen near Whippany c. 1898. It is said that John Melick deferred paying his board at the U.S. Hotel for a month in order to make a down payment on the locomotive. Payments were made in 25 monthly installments of $100, plus 6 percent interest. In 1903, No. 1 was stored at the end of a siding at Hanover Mill in Whippany. In 1908, the engine was towed back to Morristown and scrapped. (Courtesy of Hanover Township Landmark Committee.)

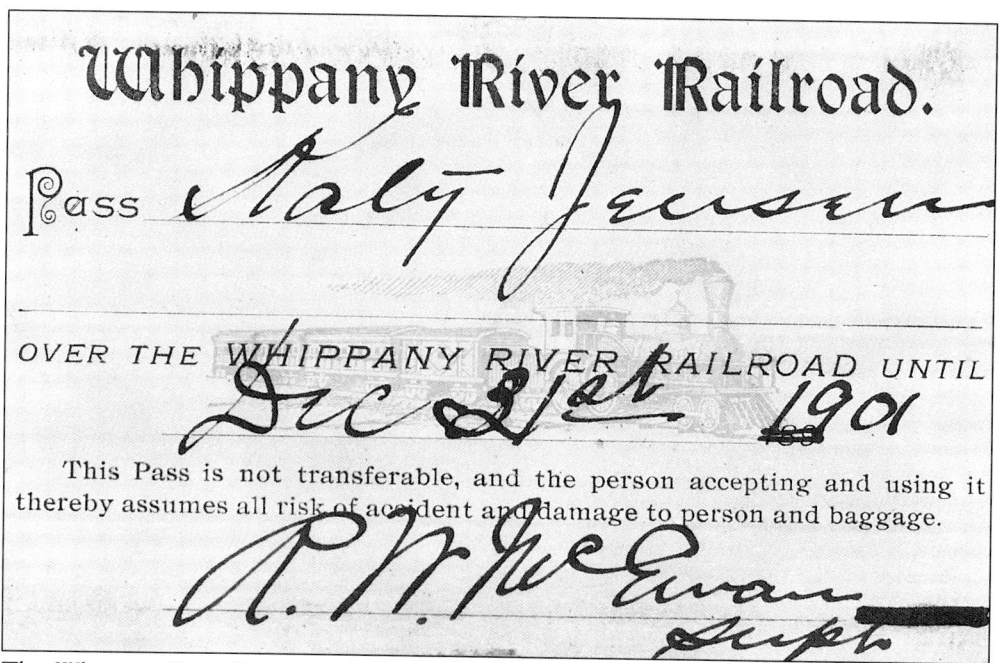

This Whippany River Railroad pass was issued to Katy Jensen and was in effect until December 31, 1901. It was signed by Superintendent Richard W. McEwan and provided the bearer free transportation over the line between Morristown and Whippany. (Collection of Steven Hepler.)

Despite all of Melick's efforts, he was unable to pay off his construction loans, and, by November 26, 1895, the Whippany River was in the hands of a receiver. The McEwan brothers agreed among themselves that the railroad, properly managed, could become profitable. In 1896, they acquired stock control of the line from Melick by settling his loans and then eased him out of the company. (Collection of Steven Hepler.)

When the McEwans brought the WRRR out of its financial difficulties, Jesse L. McEwan became president of the line. Under his leadership, the railroad developed its freight and passenger services. In 1896, work was started to completely relocate and rebuild the road. This balance sheet from January 1, 1903, shows the net worth of the McEwans' tiny railroad. (Collection of Steven Hepler.)

Two
The McEwans and the Morristown & Erie Railroad Company

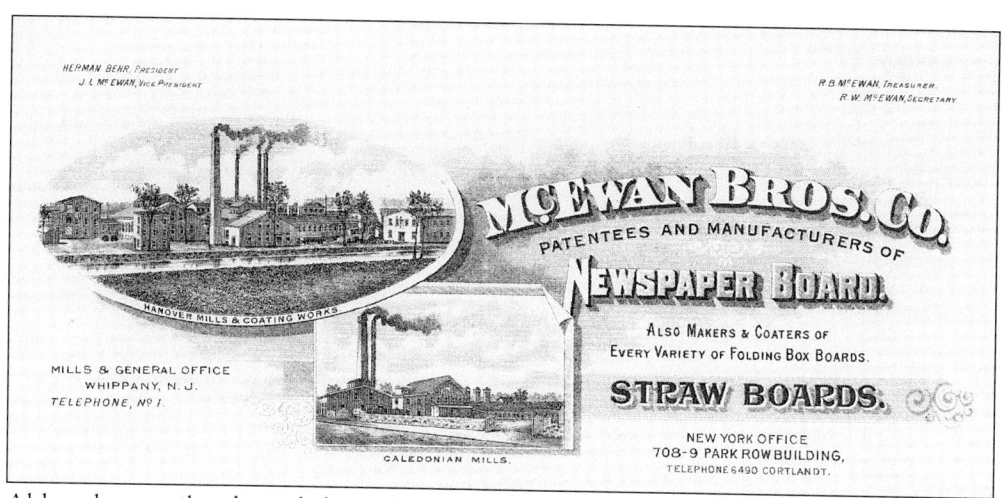

Although not railroad people by tradition, the McEwan brothers had great faith in the future of the Whippany River Railroad. From late 1896 to the close of 1900, the entire 4 miles of road were rebuilt and placed in as straight a line as possible. The cost of doing this work had been financed from operating profits and money advanced by the McEwans. (Collection of Steven Hepler.)

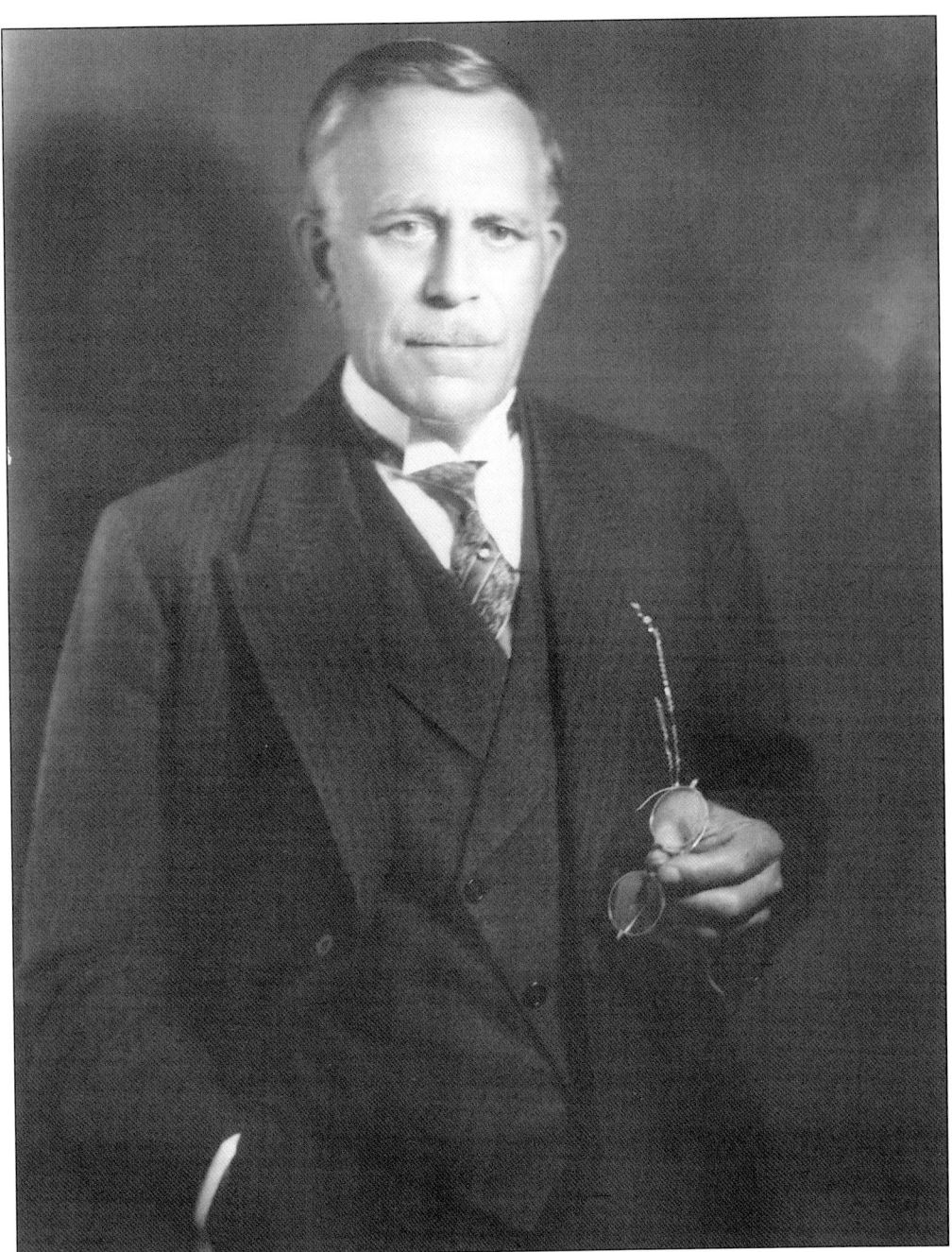

Of the seven McEwan brothers, Richard W. McEwan had taken the most energetic interest in the operations of the Whippany River. In 1896, Richard was made general freight agent. In 1897, he assumed the title of superintendent and secretary and oversaw most of the rebuilding of the WRRR. When the Morristown & Erie was formed in 1903, he became its first president and promoted the new line whenever he could. During Richard's administration, the railroad continued to grow and prosper. On the evening of April 14, 1936, Richard passed away at the age of 70. In future years, the M&E would come to miss his guiding hand. (Courtesy of Whippany Railway Museum Collection.)

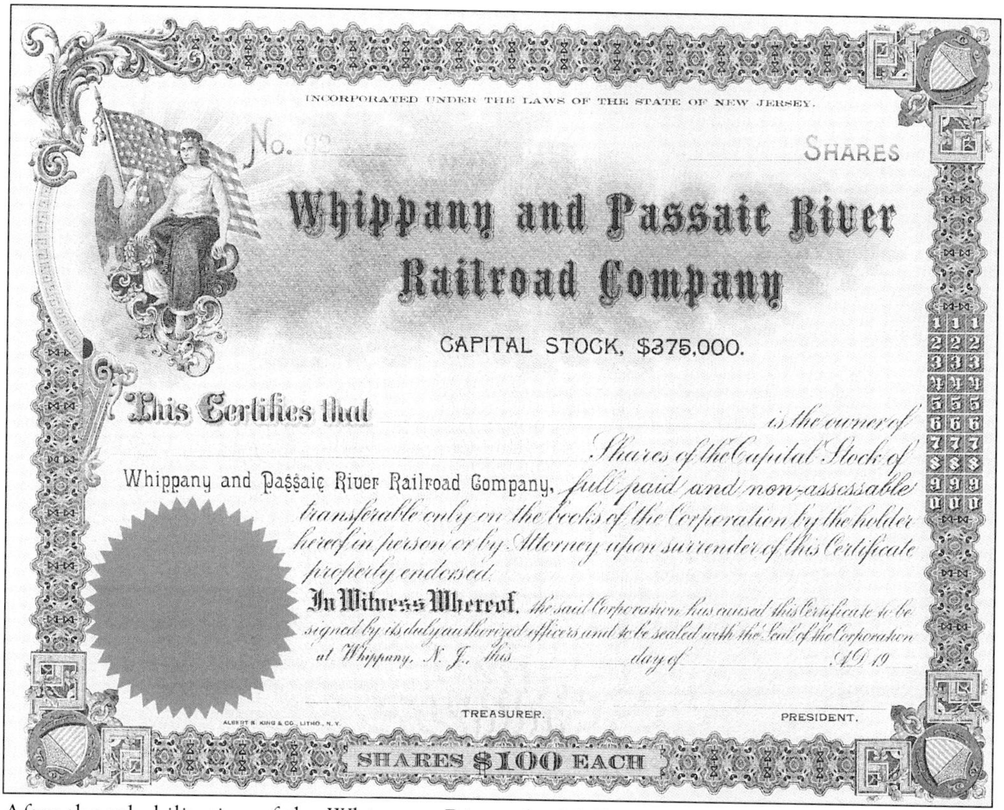

After the rehabilitation of the Whippany River, the McEwans, aware that it would be to their advantage to have a connection with a second large railroad in addition to the Lackawanna Railroad in Morristown, organized the Whippany & Passaic River Railroad in October 1902. This company would build a 7-mile line to Essex Fells where it would connect with the Roseland Railway, a branch of the Erie Railroad. (Collection of Steven Hepler.)

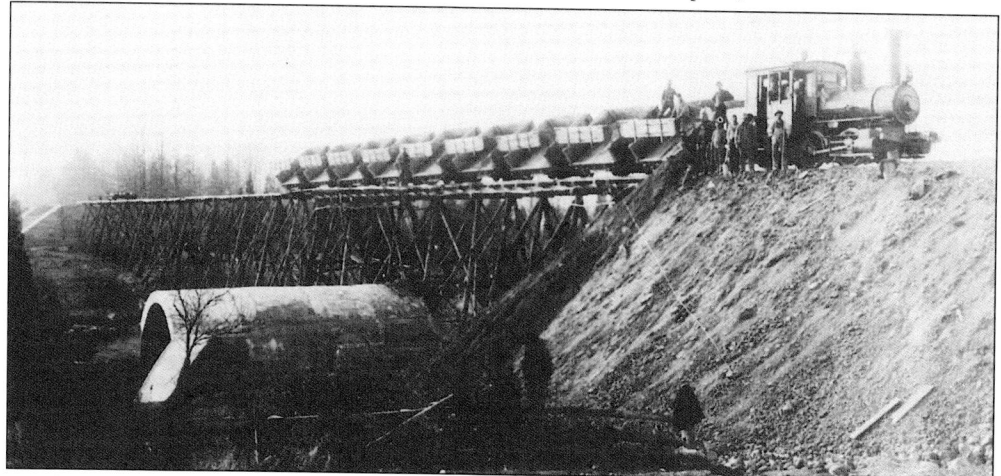

Work on the Essex Fells extension began in the spring of 1903. The route would require a large trestle and fill at Roseland. This photo shows the construction of the Beaufort Fill between Beaufort Avenue and Roseland. The overpass for Eagle Rock Avenue can be seen at the left of the image. (Collection of Steven Hepler.)

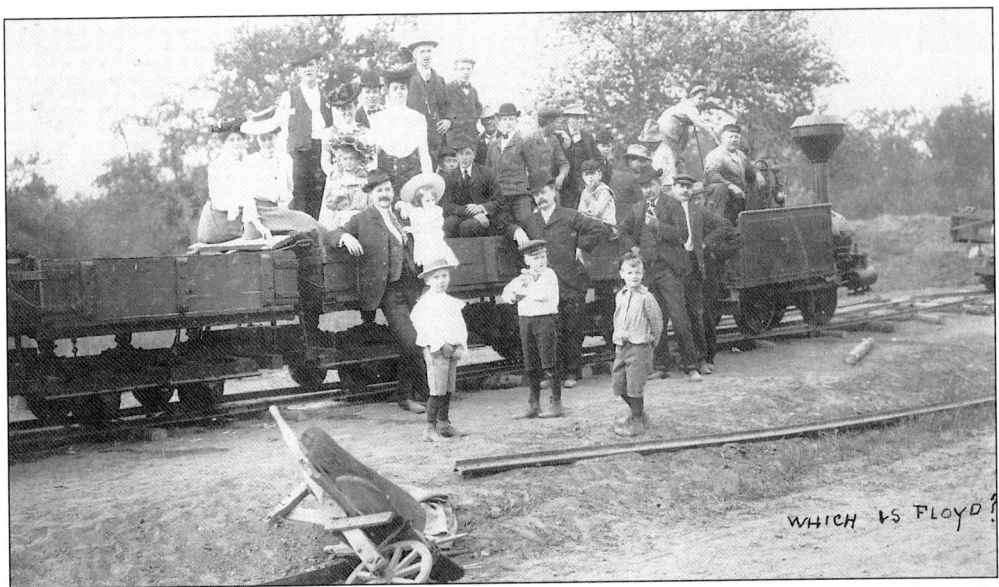

This photo of a Whippany & Passaic River Railroad construction train was taken in the early spring of 1903 near Harrison Avenue in Roseland. A burly engineer named Seymour is at the controls of the contractor's diminutive locomotive while children and adults in Victorian attire crowd around the train for their portrait. (Courtesy of Whippany Railway Museum Collection.)

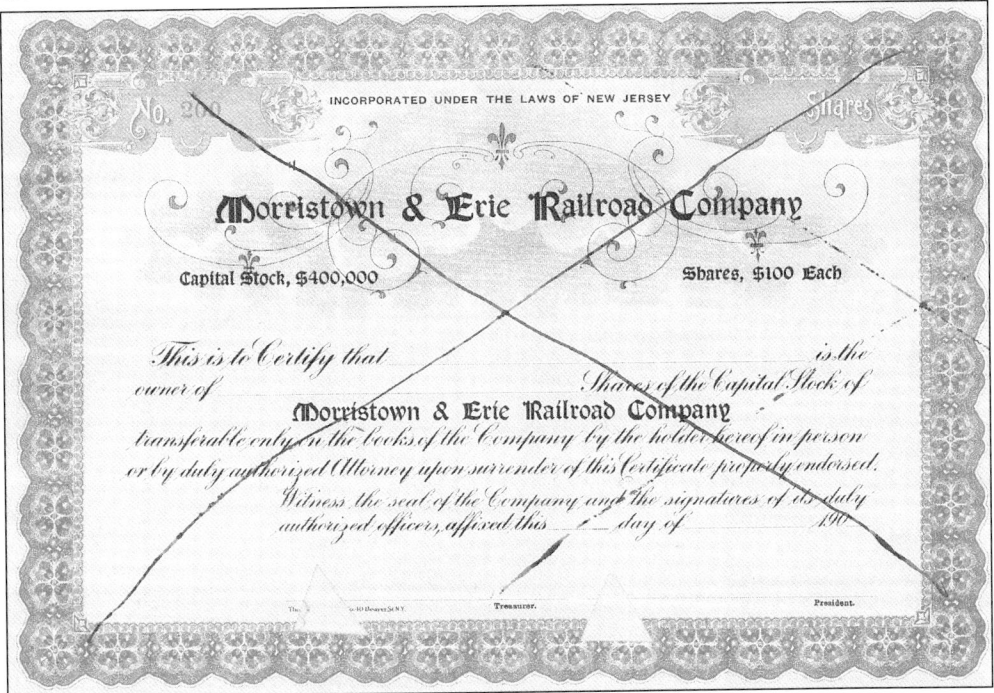

On August 28, 1903, both the Whippany River Railroad and the Whippany & Passaic River Railroad were consolidated to form the 11-mile long Morristown & Erie Railroad Company. The final spike was driven on May 3, 1904. On that day the first M&E train carrying railroad officials and local dignitaries entered Essex Fells. This stock certificate is from the newly formed company. (Collection of Steven Hepler.)

The first special passenger train operated over the new road on August 3, 1904, when the Methodist Sunday school ran an excursion over the M&E and Erie, connecting with the Pennsylvania Railroad west of Jersey City for Asbury Park. The PRR supplied the coaches used on the train. The doubleheaded seven-car train is rolling eastbound at Whippany and is passing Eden Mill on the left. (Courtesy of Hanover Township Landmark Committee.)

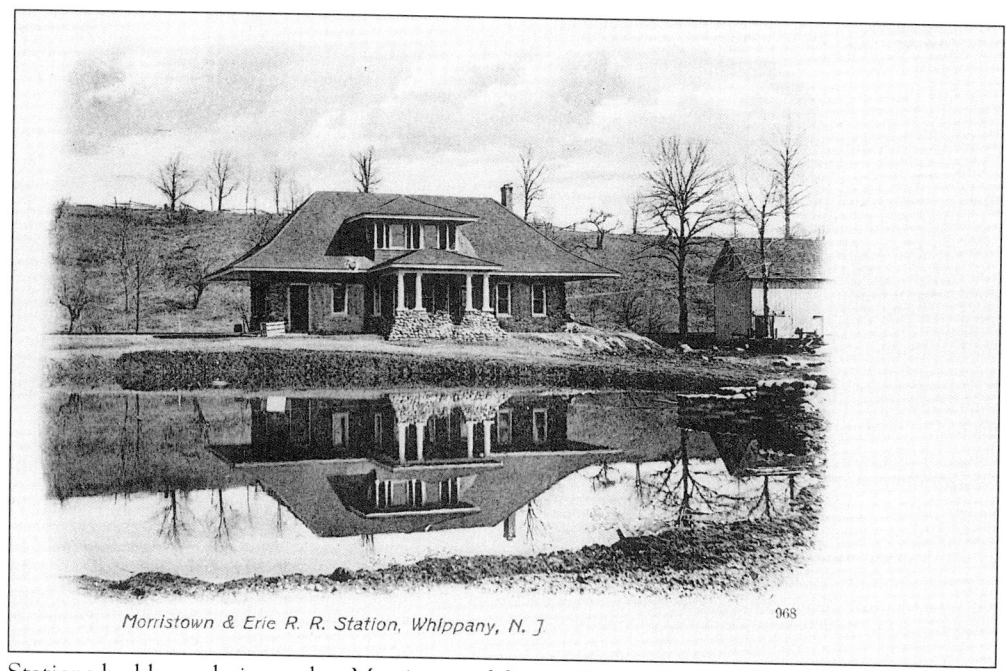

Stations had been designated at Morristown, Monroe-Cedar Knolls, Whippany, and Hanover in Morris County, as well as Beaufort Avenue, Roseland, and Essex Fells in Essex County. At Whippany, a large fieldstone passenger station and general office was erected. Today, it is still a community asset and a true local landmark. This postcard shows the station late in 1904. (Collection of Steven Hepler.)

1909

MORRISTOWN AND ERIE
RAILROAD COMPANY

Pass Mr. D.L. Gray,

Asst. Genl. Frt Agent, E.R.R.Co

UNTIL DECEMBER 31, UNLESS OTHERWISE ORDERED

No. 107

This is a M&E company pass for 1909 that was issued to Mr. Gray, the assistant general freight agent for the Erie Railroad at Jersey City, New Jersey. The 2 3/8-by-3 3/4-inch blue stock card with red and black ink could be shown to M&E trainmen and would guarantee free passage over the line at any time for an entire year. (Collection of Steven Hepler.)

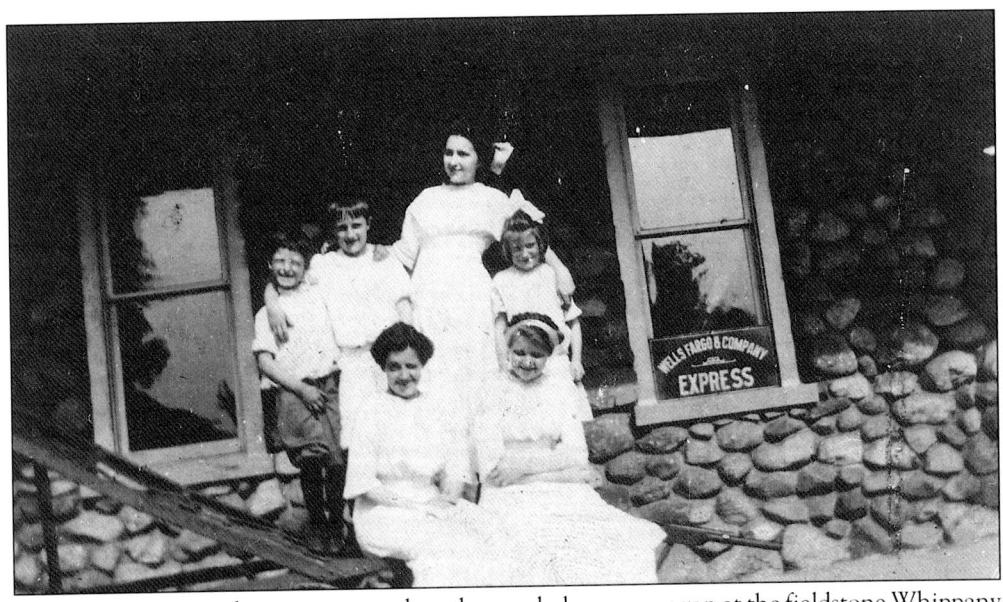

A group of happy residents are seen gathered around a baggage wagon at the fieldstone Whippany station in this c. 1910 photo. They are no doubt awaiting the arrival of a loved one who may be onboard a passenger train en route from either Morristown or Essex Fells. (Courtesy of Hanover Township Landmark Committee.)

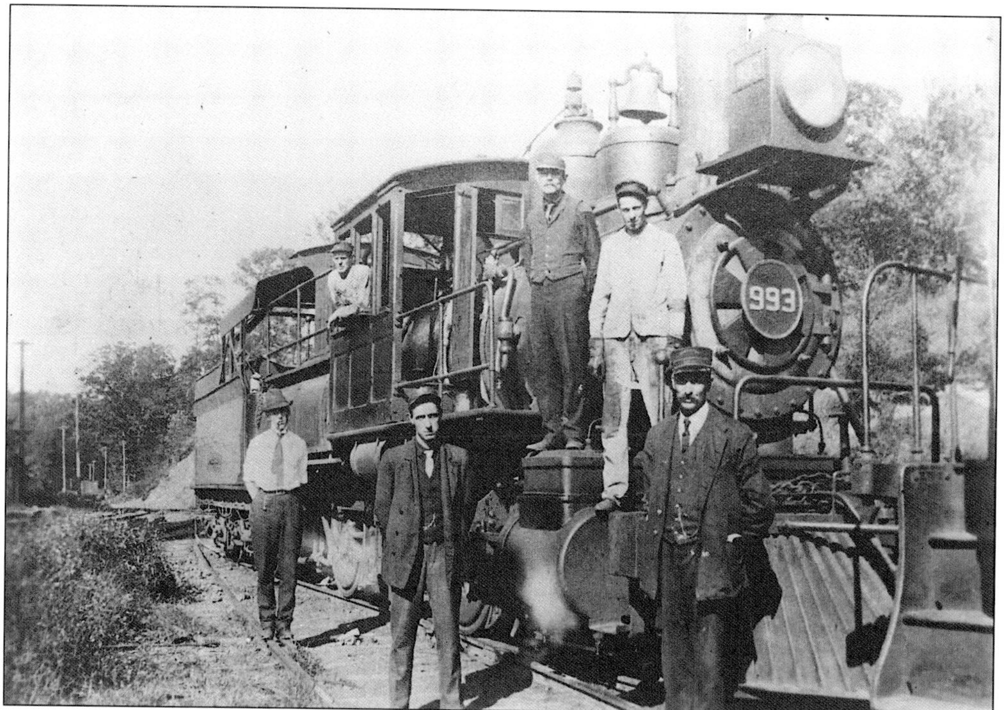

In the summer of 1905, a M&E passenger crew poses with leased Erie "Camelback" No. 993 at Morristown. The "Camelback" moniker refers to the placement of the locomotive cab over the center of the boiler, resembling a camel's hump. Throughout 1904–06, the M&E routinely leased two engines from both the Erie and the Lackawanna to supplement their own engine, the former Whippany River No. 1. (Courtesy of Hanover Township Landmark Committee.)

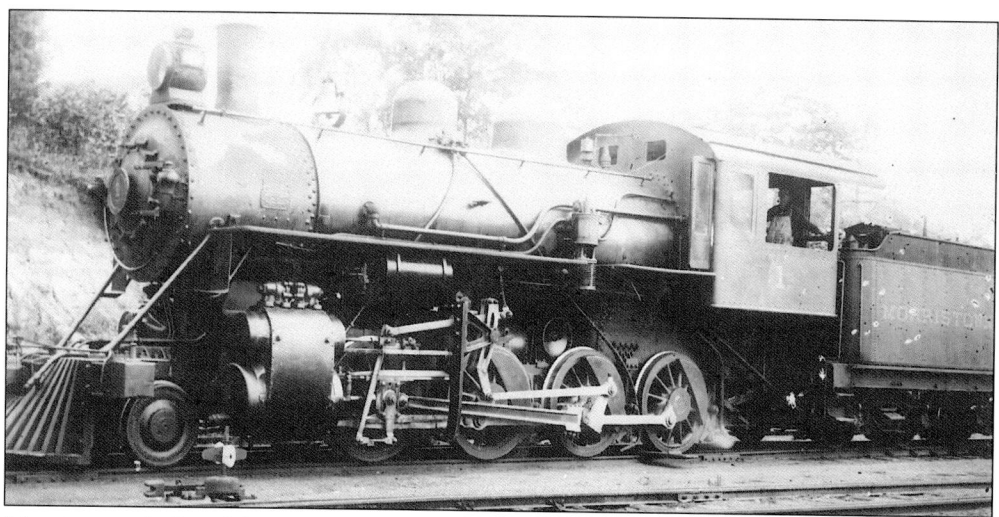

Morristown & Erie No. 1, a 2-8-0 "Consolidation"-type locomotive is viewed c. 1911 at Morristown. Built by the American Locomotive Company's Rogers, Paterson, New Jersey plant in February 1908, No. 1 was intended for the M&E's Essex Fells freight run. No. 1 had the distinction of being the only locomotive purchased new by the M&E until the arrival of diesel switcher No. 14 in 1952. (Courtesy of California State Railroad Museum, Gerald M. Best Collection.)

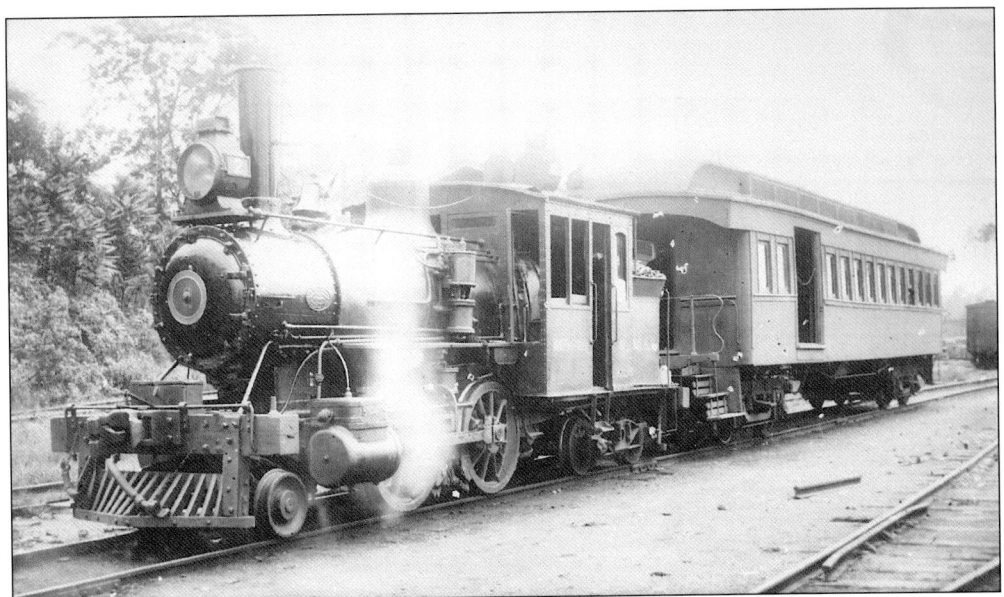

M&E No. 2, nicknamed "The Dinky," takes a brief respite at Essex Fells in this c. 1912 view. The pint-sized passenger train is ready to receive its homebound commuters who will soon arrive via their Erie Railroad connecting train from Jersey City. Once aboard the familiar old wooden combine and underway, they will relax as the shrill whistle echoes throughout the Hanover hills. (Courtesy of California State Railroad Museum, Gerald M. Best Collection.)

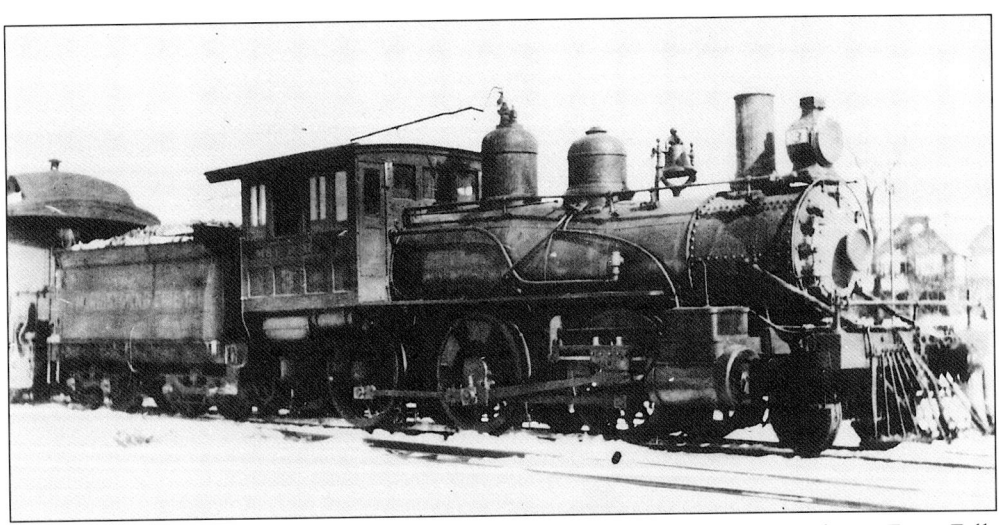

M&E No. 3, an ancient 2-6-0 "Mogul"-type engine built in 1870, is ready to depart Essex Fells c. 1915. No. 3 was considered a spare passenger locomotive and usually filled in when No. 2 was at Morristown in the shop being repaired. (Photo by Walter A. Lucas; courtesy of Railroad Museum of Pennsylvania (PHMC) Collection.)

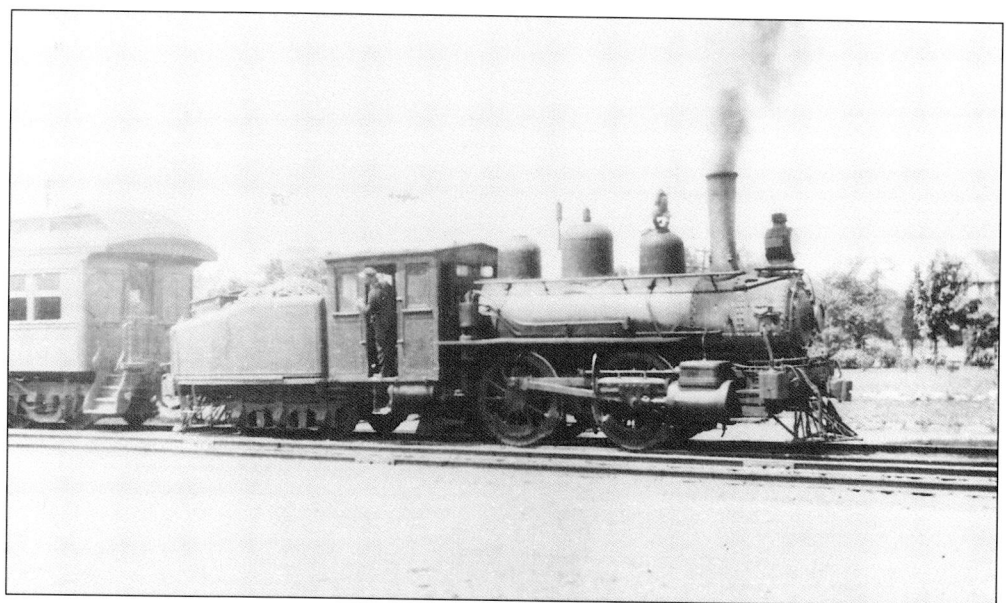

The engineer peers back from the cab doorway of M&E No. 4 as he awaits the conductor's highball at Essex Fells on June 11, 1915. The fireman has just tossed several shovel loads of coal onto the grates in an effort to build up a last minute head of steam for the run ahead. (Courtesy of California State Railroad Museum, Railway and Locomotive Historical Society Collection.)

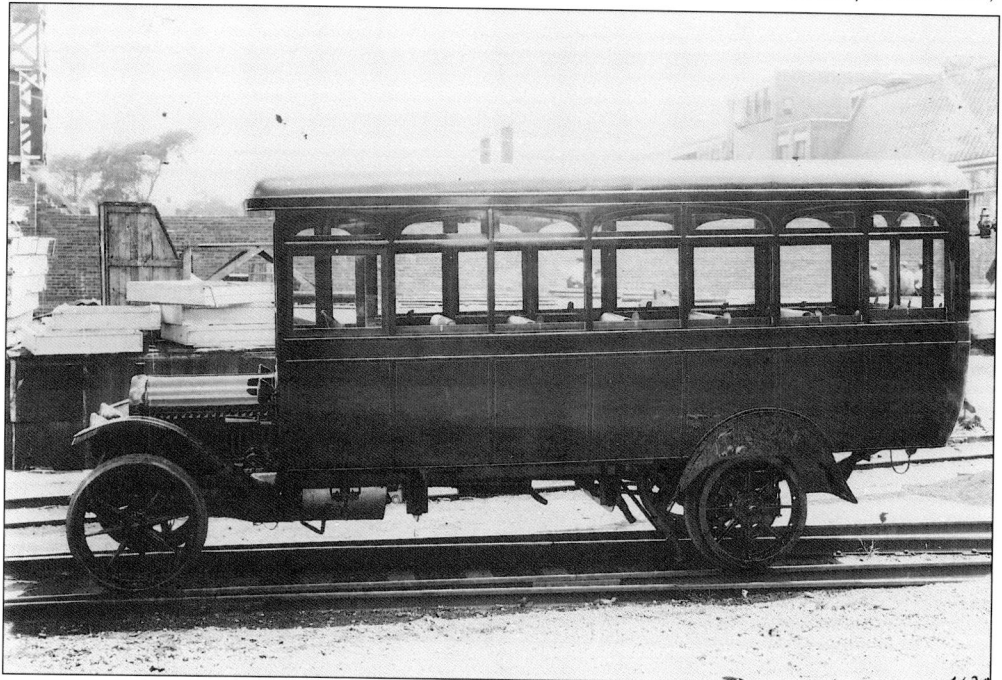

Early in 1906, M&E president Richard McEwan began to consider replacing his steam-powered passenger trains with railbuses. It was not until 1917, however, that the White Company of Cleveland, Ohio, succeeded in selling McEwan a Rail Motor Car. This unit, seen at the Cleveland plant, was sent to the M&E on a trial basis and ran until Bus No. 10 arrived at Morristown in June 1918. (Railroad Museum of Pennsylvania (PHMC) Collection.)

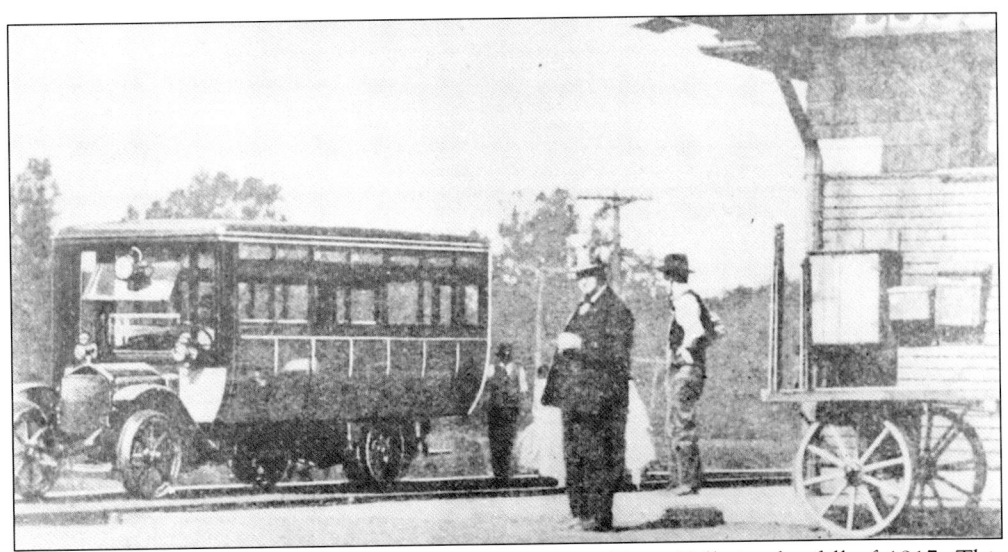

The White Company's trial Motor Rail Car is seen at Essex Fells in the fall of 1917. This particular unit carried 28 passengers and proved to be popular. The bus that the M&E would ultimately purchase, No. 10, would be slightly smaller, carrying 22 passengers and traveling at 35 miles per hour. (Courtesy of California State Railroad Museum, Railway and Locomotive Historical Society Collection.)

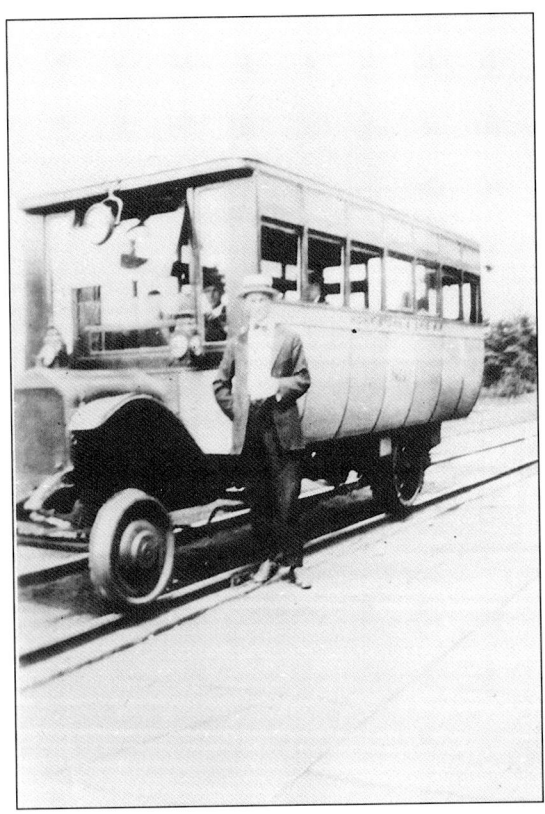

In June 1918, Railbus No. 10 arrived on the property and was placed in service between Morristown, Whippany, and Essex Fells in mid-July 1918. The bus was a 45-horsepower unit that cost $6,042. From all accounts, it appears that No. 10 performed admirably and fulfilled all of President McEwan's expectations. No. 10 is seen at Essex Fells shortly after delivery. (Photo by W.R. Hicks; courtesy of Railroad Museum of Pennsylvania (PHMC) Collection.)

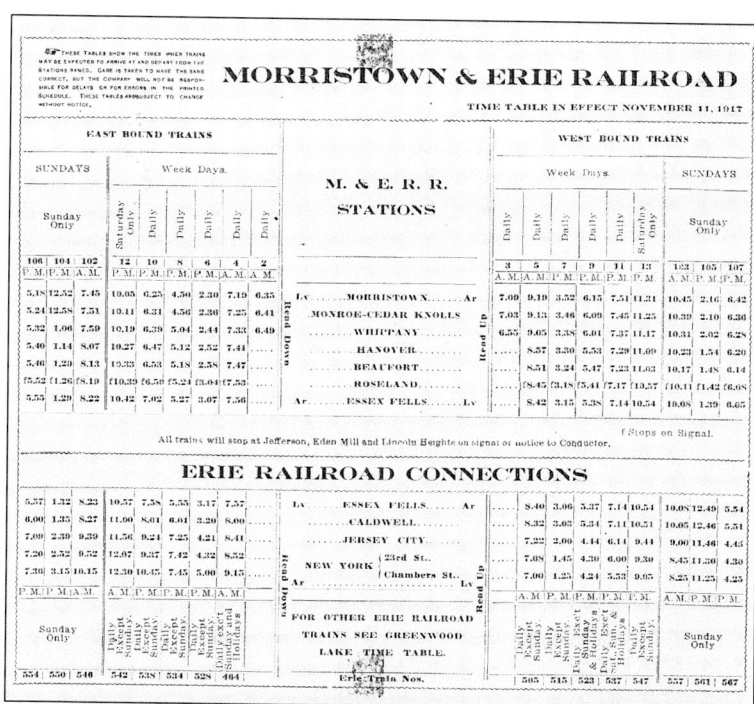

This Morristown & Erie public timetable from November 11, 1917, allowed just 37 minutes for most trains to make the run over the 11-mile line between Morristown and Essex Fells, including station stops. The lower section indicates the connecting services provided by the Erie Railroad to Jersey City and Manhattan via the Caldwell Branch. (Courtesy of Donald Van Court.)

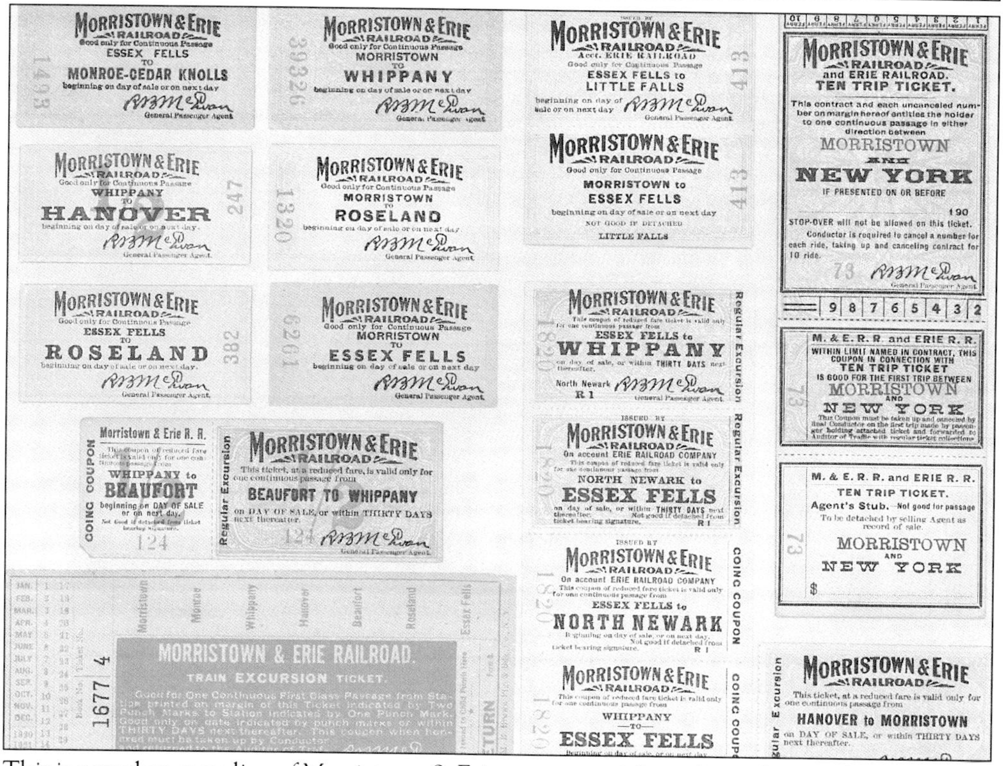

This is a random sampling of Morristown & Erie passenger tickets. A nearly complete collection of original tickets in all styles can be seen today preserved and displayed at the Whippany Railway Museum. (Collection of Steven Hepler.)

The Whippany depot is seen in the distance in this 1914 postcard. The "tin lizzie," whose growing popularity led to the demise of the M&E's passenger service, is crossing the mill raceway and will soon travel over the tracks leading to the Hanover Mill. The iron truss bridge over the Whippany River is just ahead, and, at the intersection, is the Newark and Mt. Pleasant Turnpike. (Courtesy of Robert F. Krygoski.)

NOTICE

PURSUANT TO AN ORDER OF THE BOARD OF PUBLIC UTILITY COMMISSION DATED JAN. 19, 1928, PASSENGER TRAIN SERVICE ON THE MORRISTOWN & ERIE RAILROAD WILL BE DISCONTINUED ON AND AFTER APRIL 29TH, 1928.

Morristown & Erie Railroad Company

R. W. McEWAN, Prest.

This 11-by-14-inch placard was tacked on walls and affixed to windows in all stations along the M&E throughout the winter and early spring of 1928. Its short, terse statement indicated that the era of local commuter service along the "Whippanong Trail" would soon come to an end. (Collection of Steven Hepler.)

Three

LOCOMOTIVES, EQUIPMENT, AND STRUCTURES

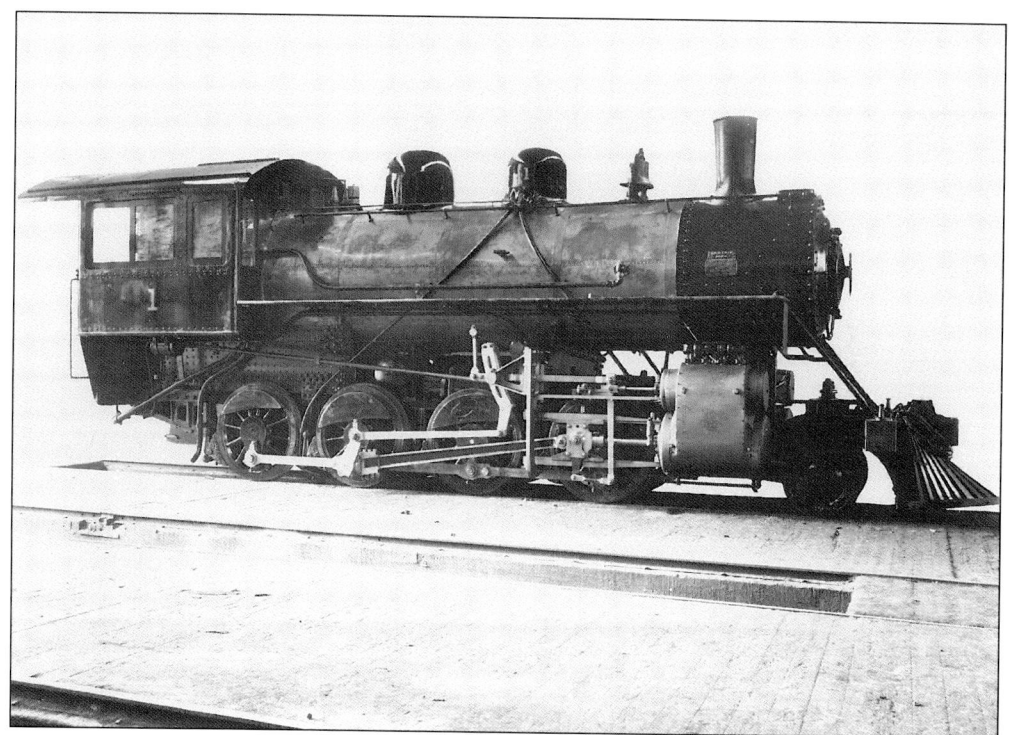

This American Locomotive Company builder's photograph of Morristown & Erie No. 1 was taken at the Rogers Works in Paterson, New Jersey, shortly after construction was completed in February 1908. The locomotive cost $14,899.55, and it arrived at Morristown on February 26, 1908. On December 6, 1917, No. 1 was sold to the Toledo, St. Louis & Western Railroad when that line offered $5,000 more than the engine cost new nine years prior. (Courtesy of ALCO Historic Photos.)

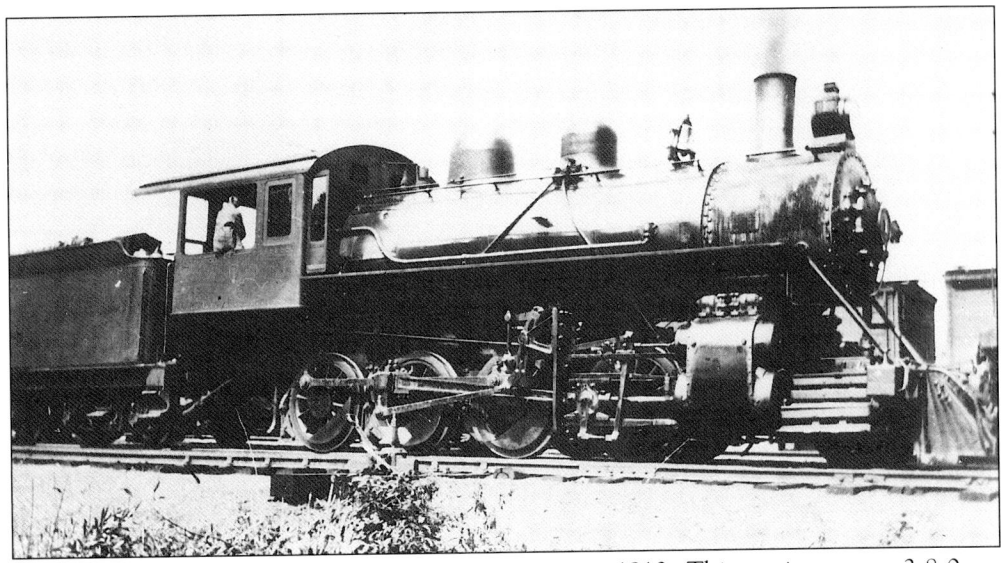

M&E No. 1 is seen switching cars at Morristown, c. 1910. This engine was a 2-8-0, or "Consolidation"-type locomotive. (Photo by Lloyd Gertz; courtesy of Railroad Museum of Pennsylvania (PHMC) Collection.)

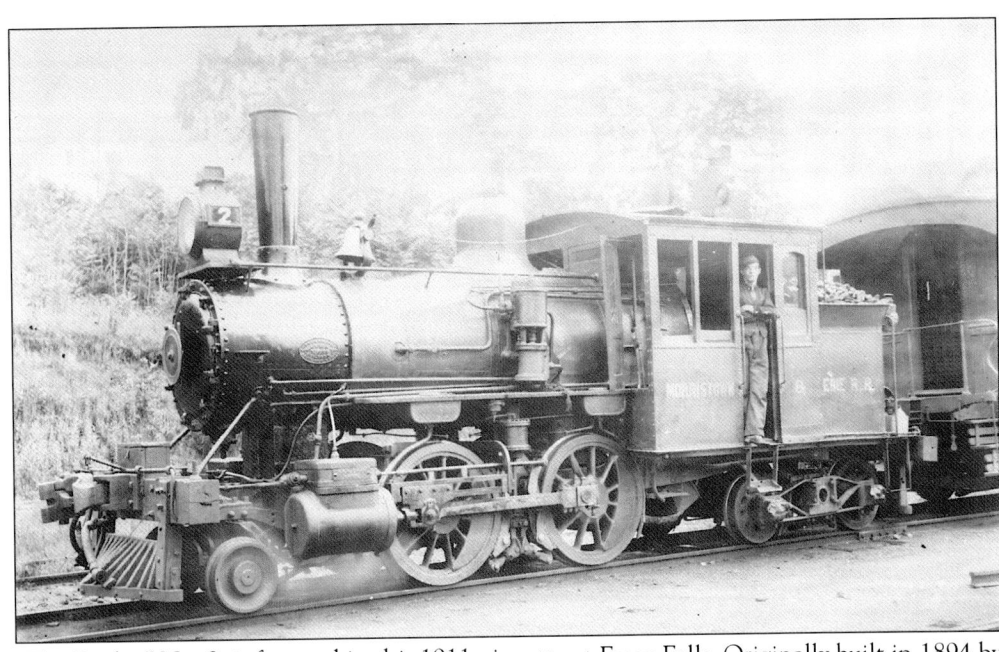

"The Dinky," No. 2, is featured in this 1911 vignette at Essex Fells. Originally built in 1894 by ALCO's Rhode Island Works for the Chicago Southside Elevated, this unusual "Forney"-type engine came to the M&E in February 1908. Sold in January 1922 to the Hanover Brick Company, it operated there until the plant closed in 1931. The little engine was scrapped at Morristown in 1936. (Courtesy of California State Railroad Museum, Gerald M. Best Collection.)

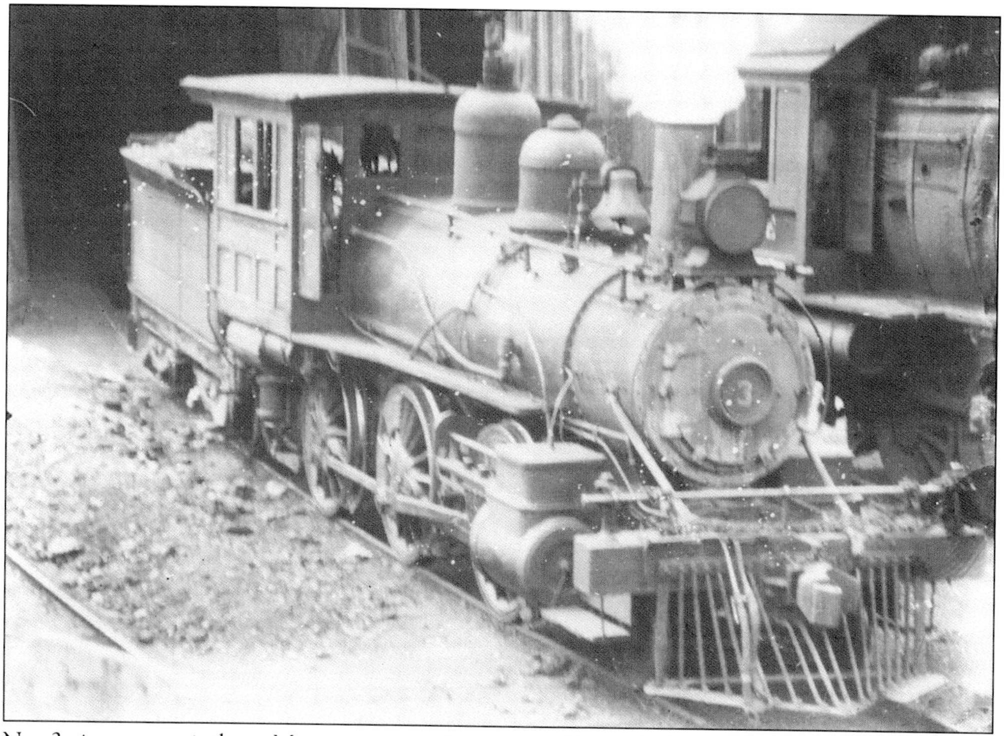

No. 3 simmers quietly at Morristown on August 19, 1920. Built by ALCO's Dickson plant in 1870 for the Lackawanna, the M&E acquired this engine in March 1908. Mainly used to work the paper mills at Whippany, No. 3 occasionally filled in on a passenger run. When the locomotive was scrapped in November 1927, its boiler was used to heat the Morristown Enginehouse until 1952. (Courtesy of California State Railroad Museum, Gerald M. Best Collection.)

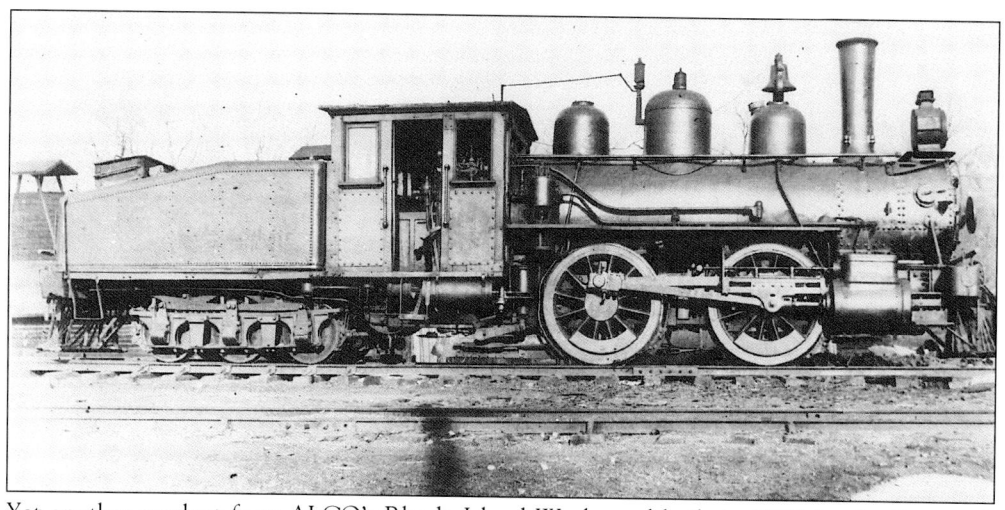

Yet another product from ALCO's Rhode Island Works and built in 1885 for the Boston & Providence Railroad, this unique 0-4-6T (the "T" refers to the coal and water tank attached to the rear of the cab) became M&E No. 4 in June 1911. Working for the road only a short while, No. 4 was sold off in December 1915 and scrapped. It is seen here c. 1912 at Morristown. (Courtesy of Railroad Museum of Pennsylvania (PHMC) Collection.)

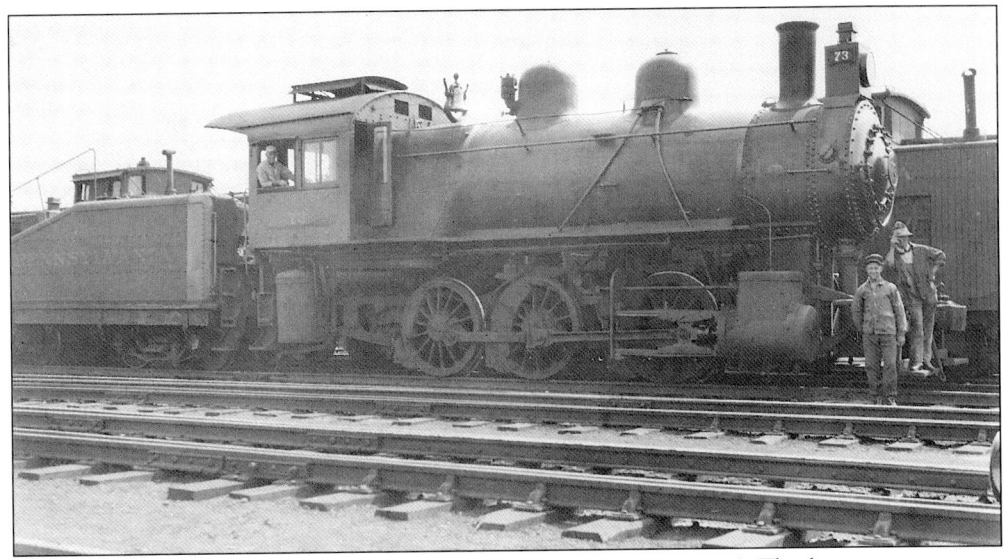

This photograph of Pennsylvania Railroad No. 73 was taken in 1916. The locomotive is very similar to M&E No. 5. Built in the mid-1880s, No. 5 was purchased in November 1913 from the PRR and was known to be defective. Upon arrival at Morristown early in 1914 and after careful inspection, it was decided to scrap the locomotive without delay before any pictures could be taken. (Courtesy of Railroad Museum of Pennsylvania (PHMC) Collection.)

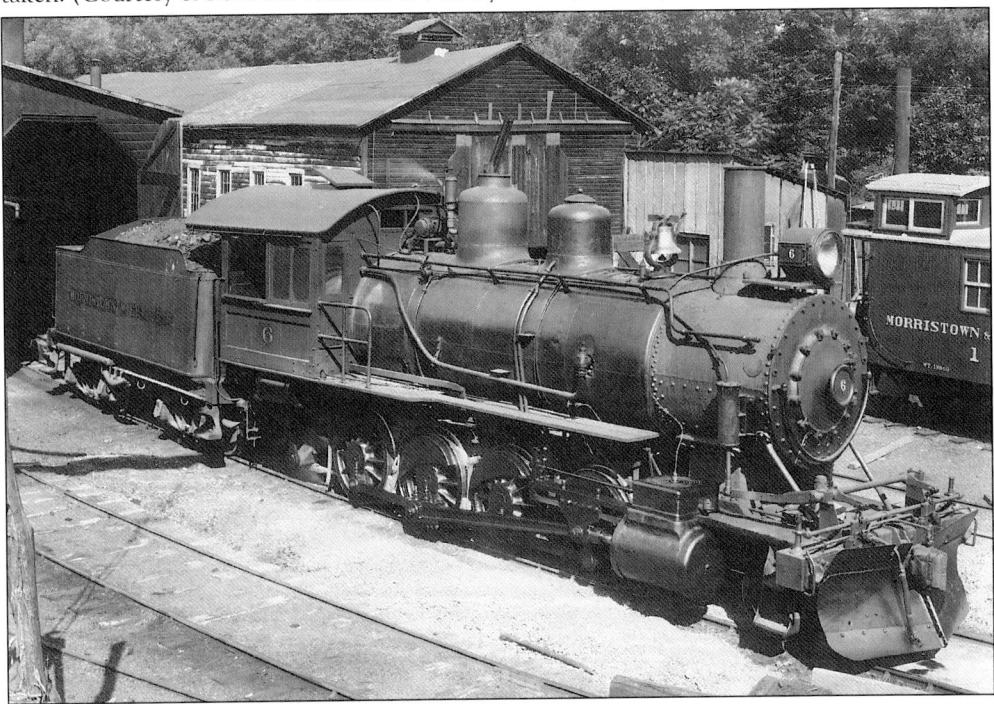

M&E No. 6 was a handsome 2-8-0 built in 1898 for the Pittsburg & Lake Erie. Acquired by the M&E in 1915, she was pressed into freight service and used until Nos. 10 and 11 were delivered in 1944. Scrapped in 1948, a bit of No. 6 is preserved today. In 1992, the estate of Richard W. McEwan Jr. donated the bell from No. 6 to the Whippany Railway Museum where it is proudly displayed. (Courtesy of Mike Del Vecchio.)

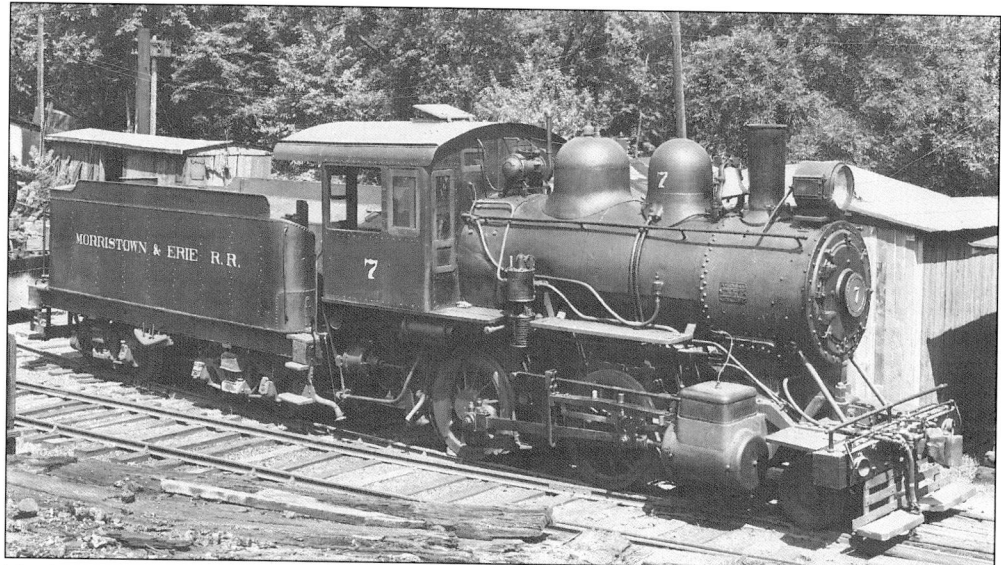

No. 7 was produced by ALCO's Schenectady Works in 1905 for the Lake Champlain & Moriah Railroad. Purchased by the M&E in 1917, she was rarely steamed up. Her demise came in 1952 and is documented on pages 77 through 80 of this book. M&E president Richard W. McEwan Jr. thoughtfully saved 7's bell and whistle, and his estate presented them to the Whippany Railway Museum in 1992. This picture is c. late 1930s. (Courtesy of Donald Van Court.)

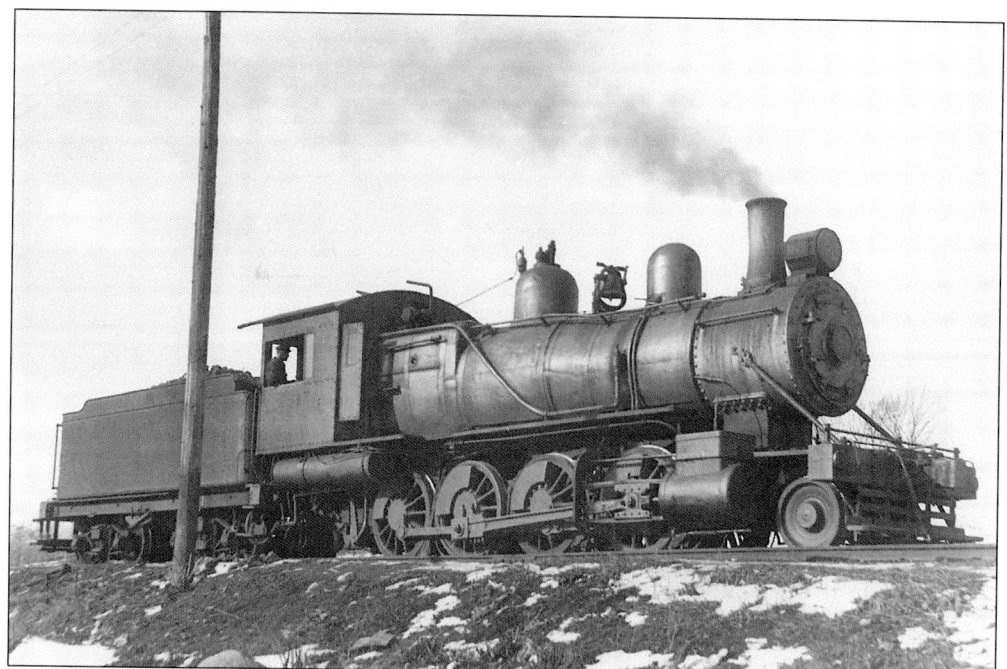

No. 8, another 2-8-0 "Consolidation"-type engine, was built in 1902 for the Hocking Valley Railroad by the Baldwin Locomotive Works. The M&E acquired No. 8 in May 1920, and she worked on road freights until she was retired from service in 1933. In 1936, the scrapper's torch ended her existence. (Courtesy of Mike Del Vecchio.)

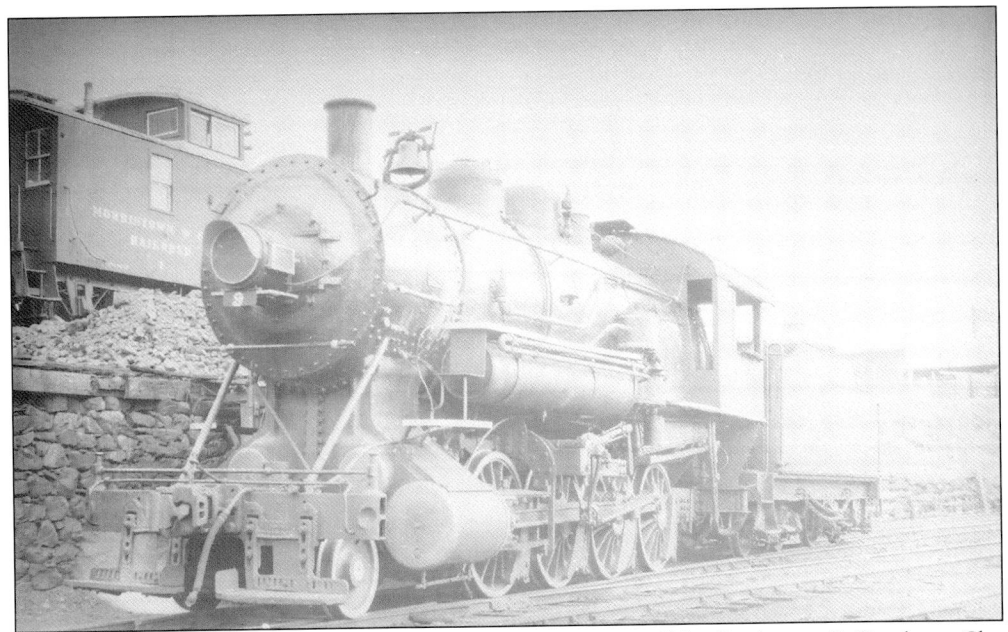

No. 9 was built by ALCO's Brooks Works in 1904 for the Buffalo, Rochester & Pittsburg. She arrived on the M&E in October 1927 and provided reliable service until she was scrapped in January 1947. No. 9 had the distinction of leading the first passenger train over the M&E in 11 years on July 9, 1939, when the Railroadians of America chartered an excursion over the line. (Courtesy of California State Railroad Museum, Gerald M. Best Collection.)

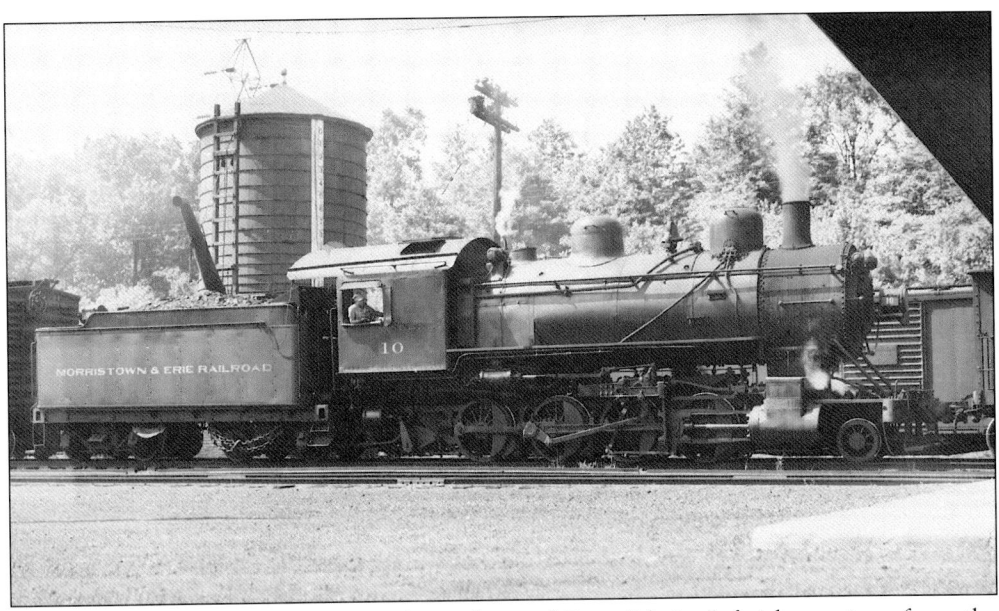

In August 1944, the M&E acquired two heavy "Consolidation" freight engines from the Monongahela Railroad that effectively replaced old Nos. 6 and 9. Numbered 10 and 11, these big engines were rotated in service on a monthly basis until 1946 when it became necessary to work two freights over the line each day. No. 10, seen here at Whippany, was built at the ALCO Brook's plant in 1909. (Courtesy of California State Railroad Museum, Gerald M. Best Collection.)

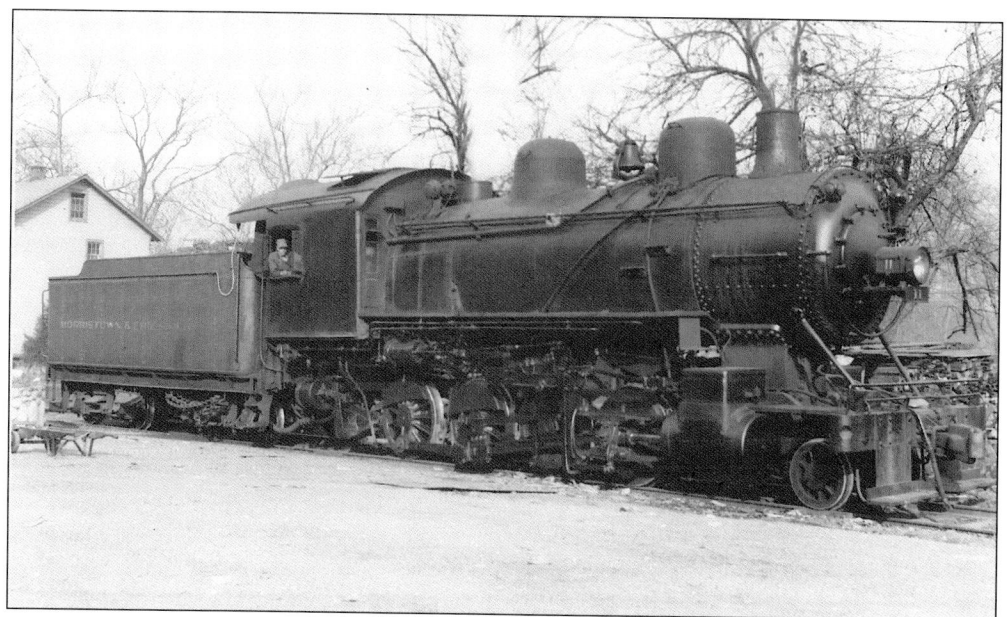

No. 11 arrived on the M&E from the Monongahela Railroad along with her sister, No. 10, in August 1944. This was a product of ALCO's Pittsburgh Works and is seen working the branch to the Hanover mill of Whippany Paper Board at Whippany in December 1946. (Courtesy of Mike Del Vecchio.)

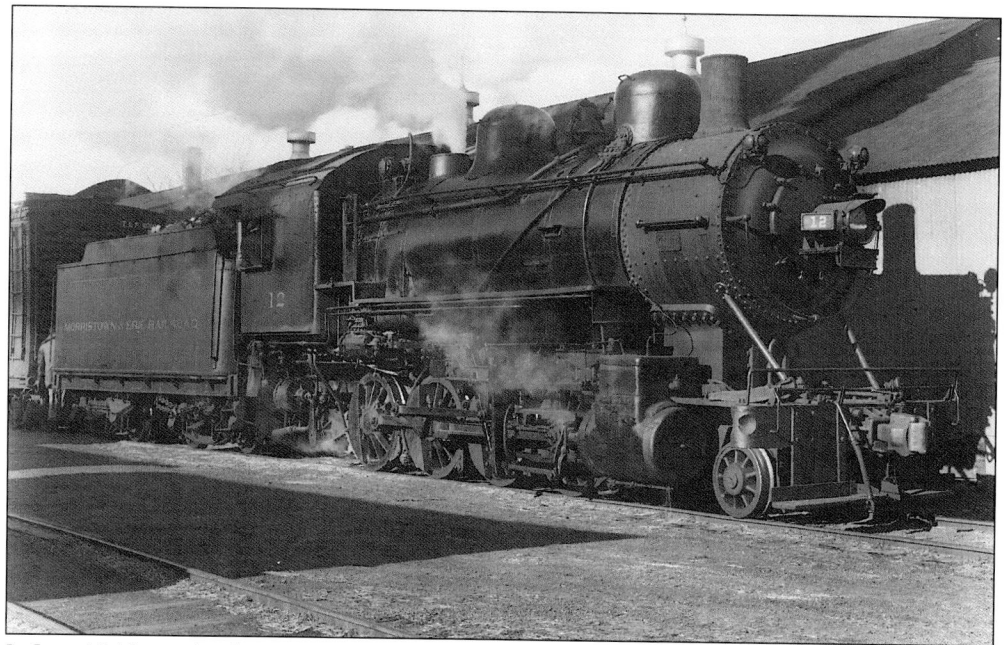

In June 1946, another big 2-8-0 was purchased from the Monongahela Railroad to work alongside Nos. 10 and 11. The 12 was another 1912 Pittsburgh-built ALCO product, and once she joined her stablemates at Morristown, the three sisters quickly became well-known representatives of the prosperous Morristown & Erie—an image of industrial power that remains today. The photo was taken at Morristown in 1952. (Courtesy of Homer R. Hill.)

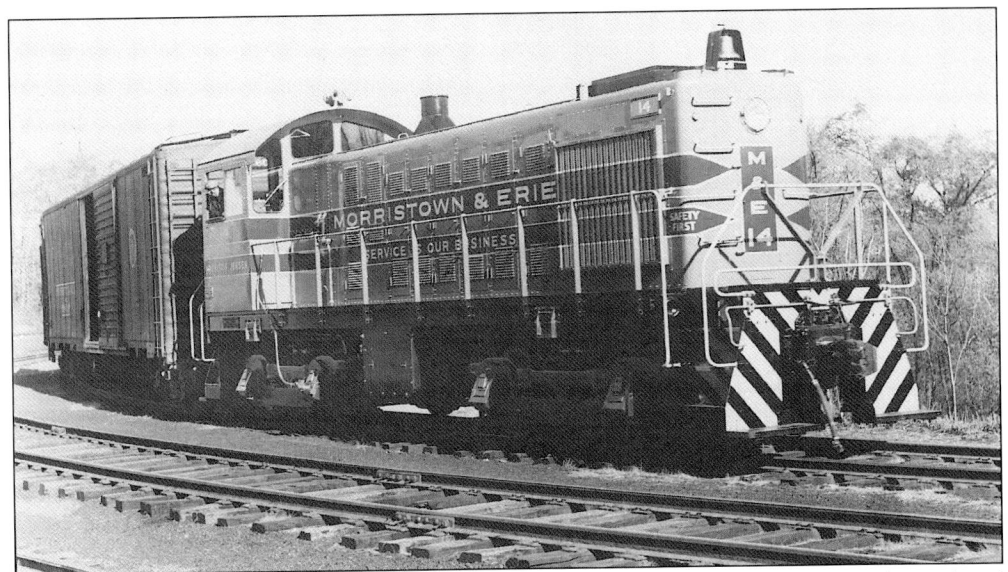

When the M&E purchased a brand-new diesel from ALCO in April 1952, the railroad superstitiously skipped the "13" slot by numbering the engine "14." It was painted in a handsome red, blue, and gold scheme designed by Roseland dairy owner Henry Becker and was named for M&E vice president Mauritius Jensen. The photo shows 14 at Morristown on its second day of service, April 29, 1952. (Courtesy of Homer R. Hill.)

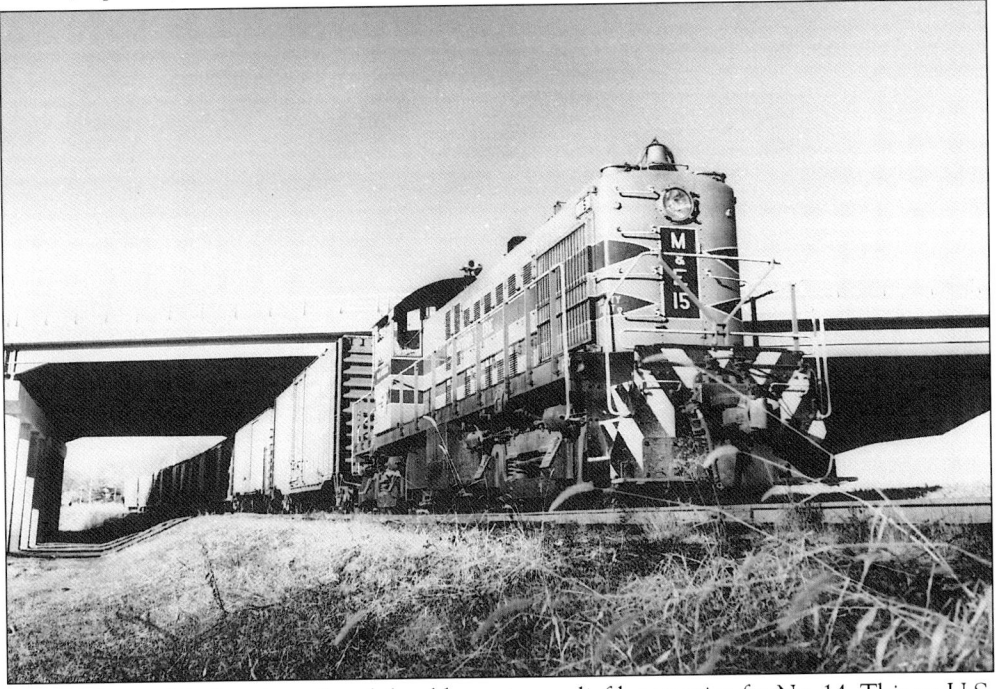

In 1963, it was felt that the railroad should acquire a relief locomotive for No. 14. This ex-U.S. Navy diesel built by ALCO in 1944, arrived in October 1963. Like No. 14, it featured the railroad's slogan, "Service Is Our Business," on its side and was named for former President Richard W. McEwan Jr. No. 15 is seen here at the Route 287 overpass in Cedar Knolls, c. 1970. (Courtesy of of Morristown & Erie Railway.)

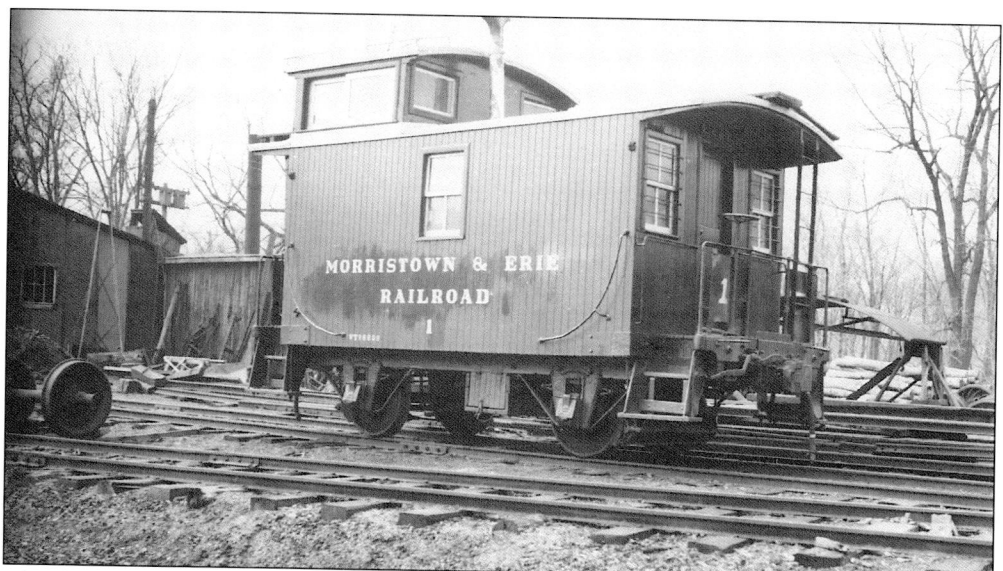

This former Lackawanna four-wheel, wooden "bobber" caboose, built in 1899, was acquired by the M&E in 1933 and was the delight of its crew right up until 1952 when it was retired from service. In 1960, old No. 1 was sold to the Black River & Western Railroad and was displayed at their Flemington and Ringoes, New Jersey sites for over 30 years. (Courtesy of California State Railroad Museum, Gerald M. Best Collection.)

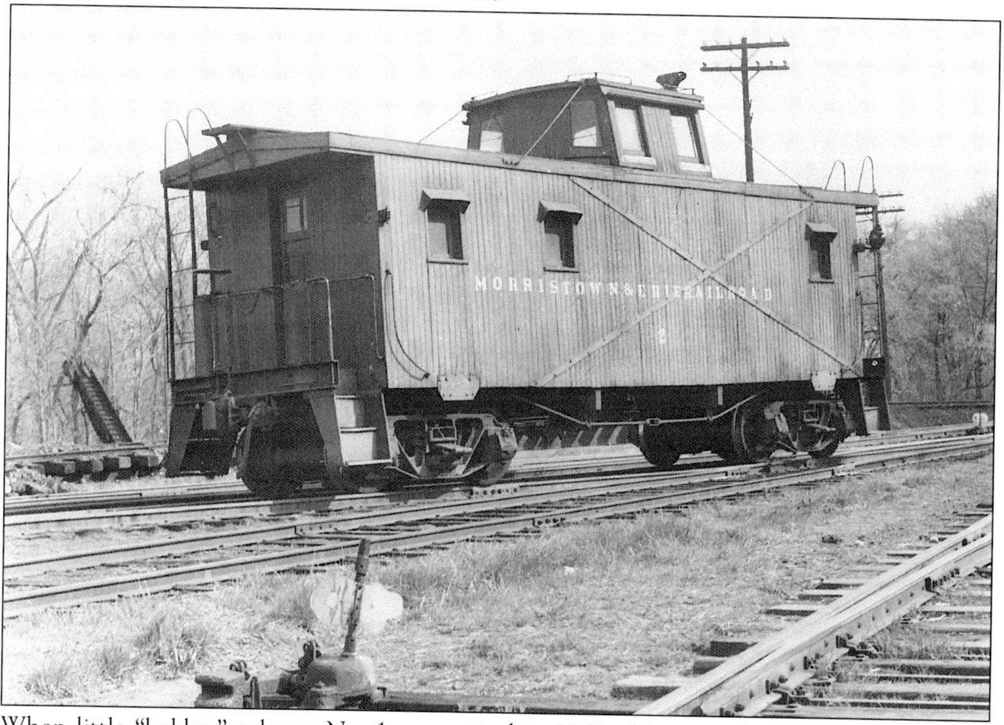

When little "bobber" caboose No. 1 was retired in 1952, this ungainly wooden replacement was purchased from the New York, Susquehanna & Western Railroad. Caboose No. 2 was used until February 1962, when it was destroyed by an accidental fire started by its overheated pot-bellied stove. This photo was taken at Morristown, c. 1952. (Courtesy of Homer R. Hill.)

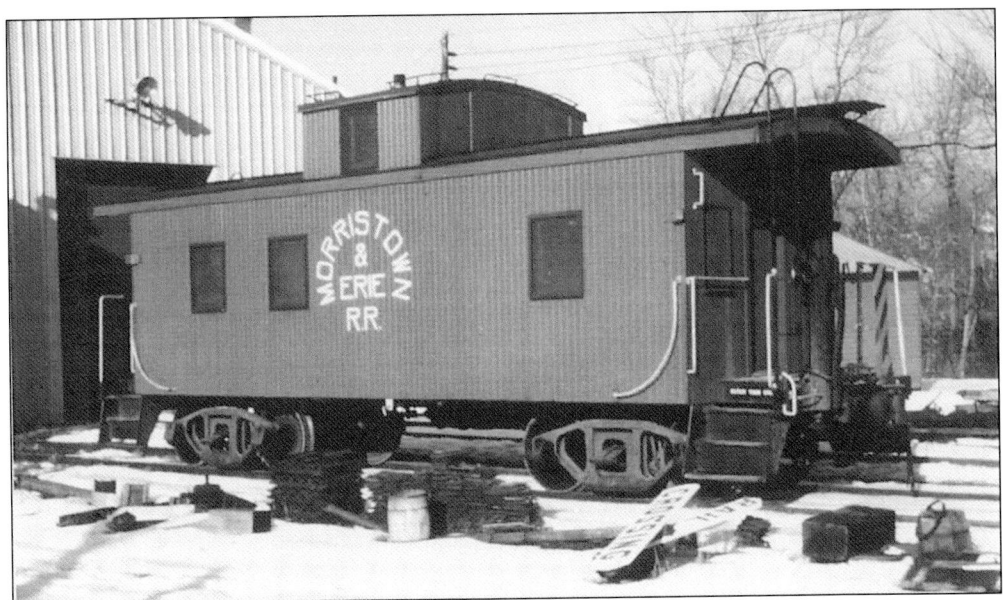

M&E caboose No. 3, a wooden car originally built for the Erie Railroad, was procured from the Erie-Lackawanna Railroad in the spring of 1962. It was used until the mid-1970s when it was withdrawn from service. Acquired by the Whippany Railway Museum in 1980, the car was unfortunately scrapped due to its advanced state of deterioration. (Photo by Earle H. Gil; collection of Steven Hepler.)

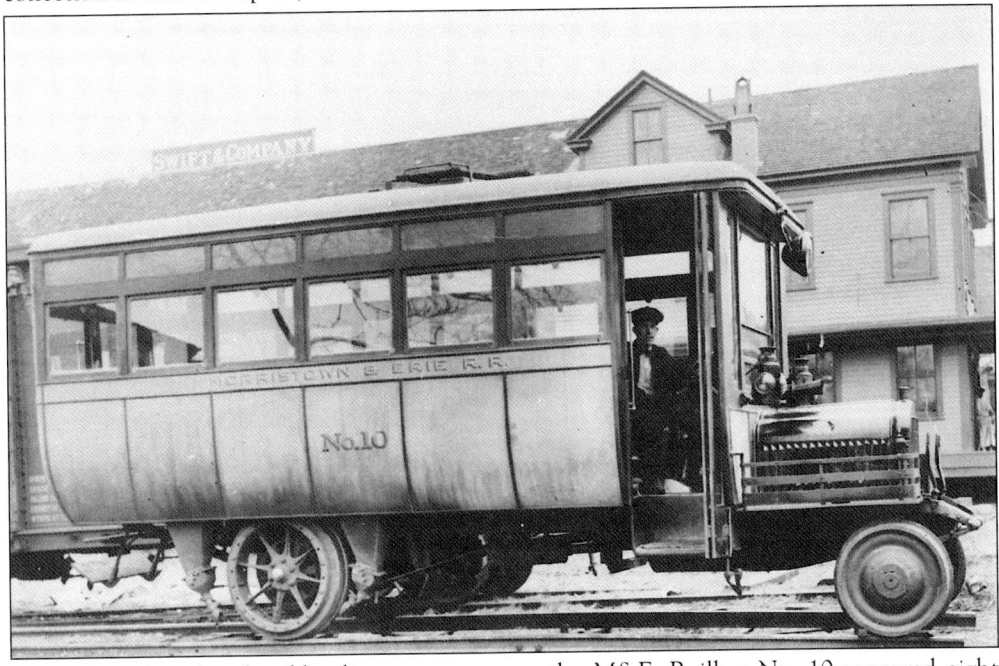

Throughout her decade of hauling passengers on the M&E, Railbus No. 10 averaged eight trips over the 11-mile line each day. Although patrons seemed to like the service provided, continued and aggressive competition from automobiles and motor buses eventually put an end to the railroad's passenger service in 1928. This view of No. 10 sitting on the Morristown bus turntable was taken in 1921. (Courtesy of Morristown & Erie Railway.)

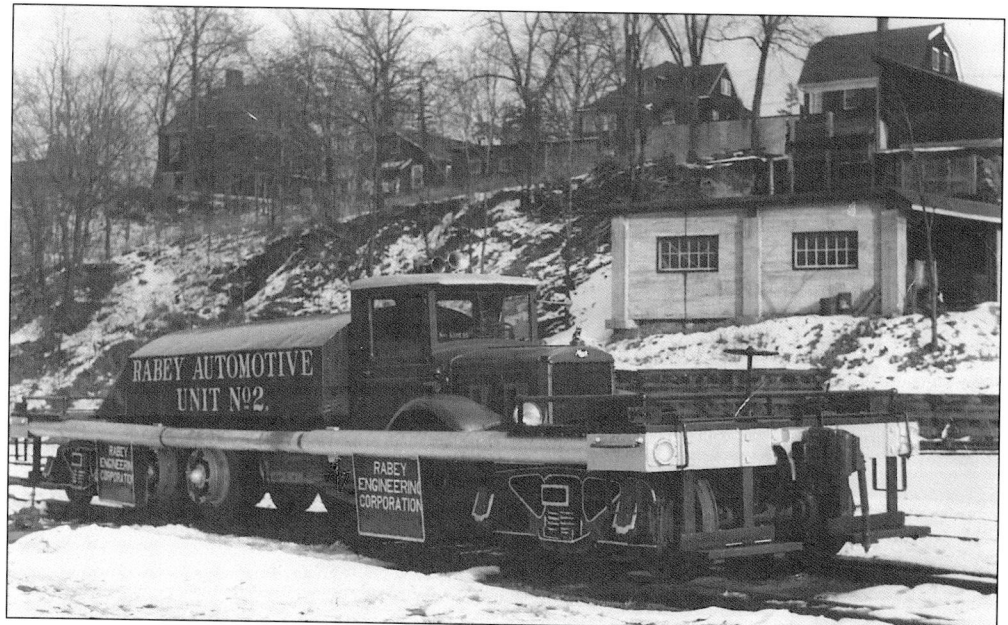

This unusual vehicle was designed as a light-duty railroad switcher. A highway truck was placed inside the light-colored frame (fitted with railroad wheels), which helped to keep the vehicle's tires on the rails for traction. The unit was tested on the M&E on October 9, 1940, but was too light for the heavy grades and traffic on the railroad. It was scrapped around 1946. (Courtesy of Homer R. Hill.)

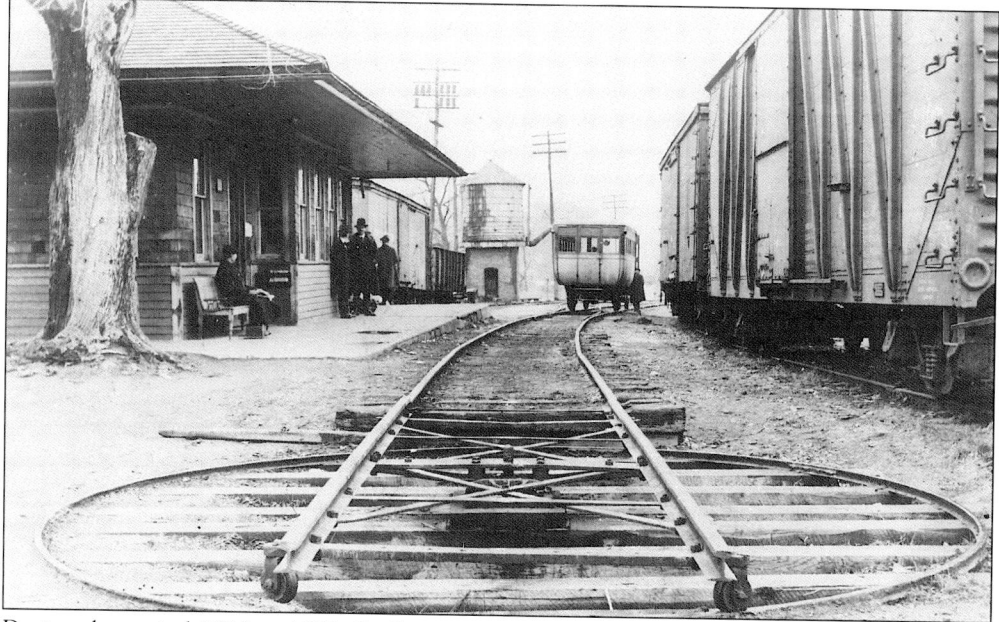

During the period 1918 to 1928, Railbus No. 10 operated in passenger service; the M&E had two small, specially built turntables installed at Morristown and Whippany. At Essex Fells, the bus was turned on the Erie's large locomotive turntable. This 1918 view shows No. 10 backing up to the Morristown station. The bus turntable is in the foreground. (Courtesy of Railroad Museum of Pennsylvania (PHMC) Collection.)

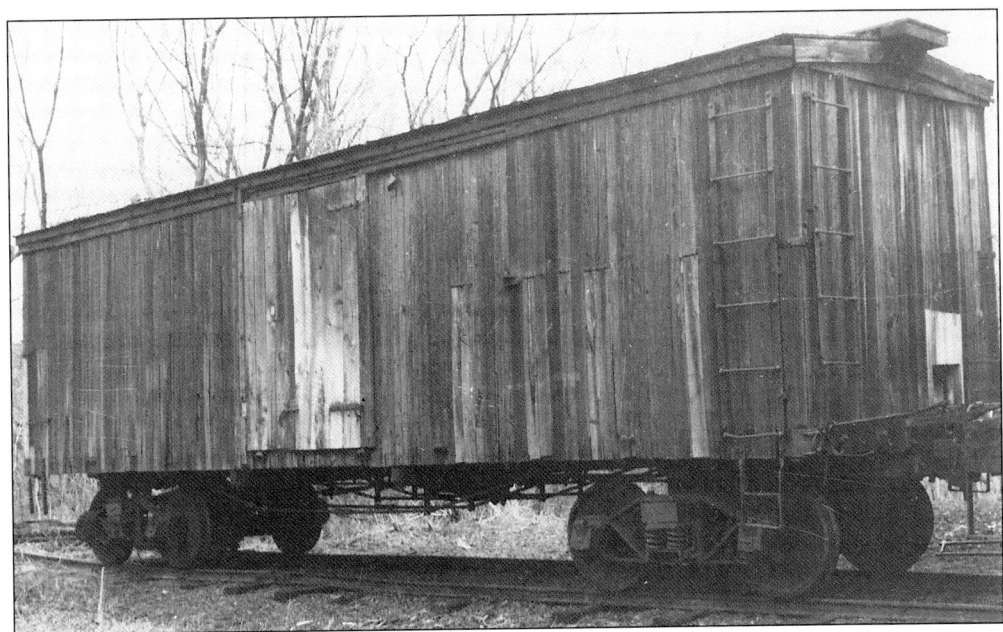

Box car No. 511 was one of the M&E's fleet of 38 wooden cars purchased from the Pittsburgh & Lake Erie in 1916. This car remained on the property until 1950 when it was dismantled due to its deteriorated state. Three of the box cars were converted into storage facilities, and one of them still remains in use at the Morristown engine terminal. This photo was taken at Morristown on March 27, 1943. (Courtesy of Donald Van Court.)

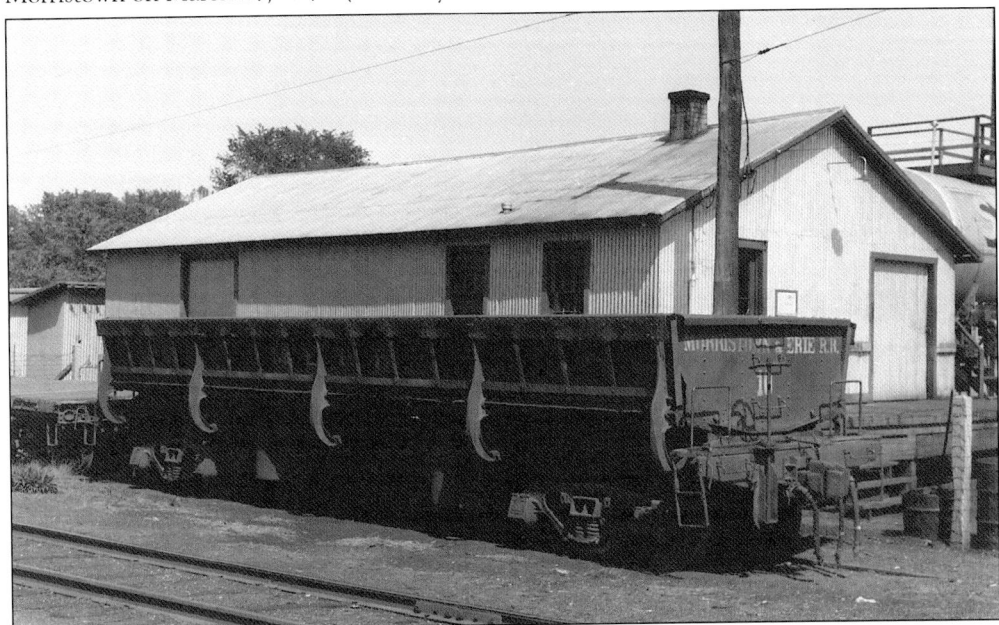

M&E Air Side Dump Car No. 10 at Abbett Avenue in Morristown is seen here c. 1945. The car had a 50-ton capacity and was acquired new from the Magor Car Co. in 1929. It was intended to be used for the disposal of ashes that had been dumped from the fireboxes of the steam locomotives. The ashes would then be used for ballasting the track. (Collection of Steven Hepler.)

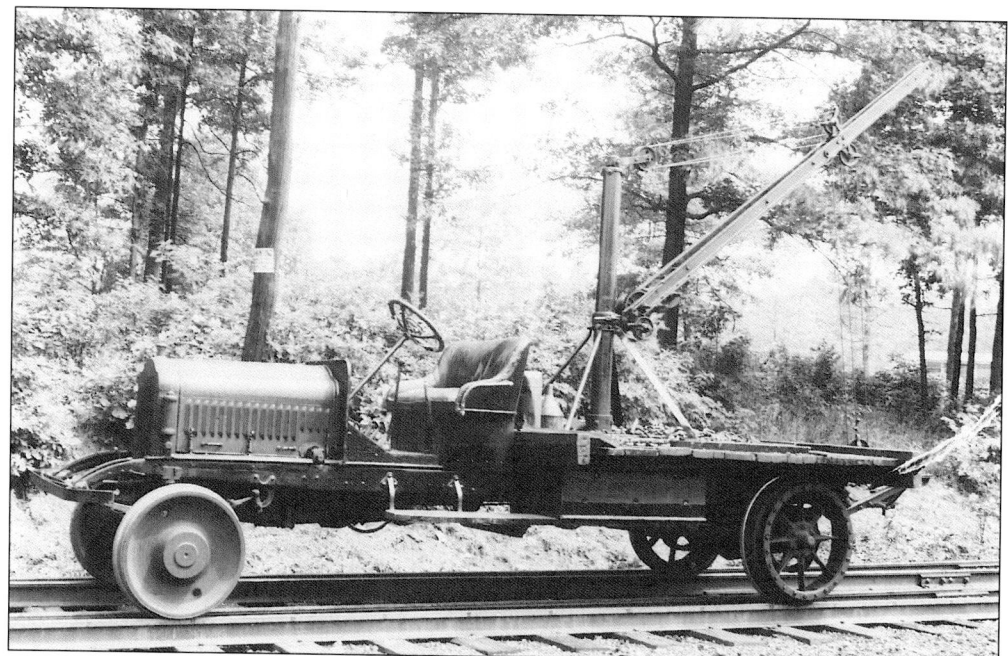

After cessation of passenger service in April 1928, the M&E removed the bus body from No. 10 in late 1929 and converted the vehicle into a self-propelled track maintenance car. Re-numbered "5," it was fitted with a deck-mounted, hand-operated crane for use in lifting rail. It is seen here near Monroe on June 29, 1946. (Photo by Thomas T. Taber III; courtesy of Railroad Museum of Pennsylvania (PHMC) Collection.)

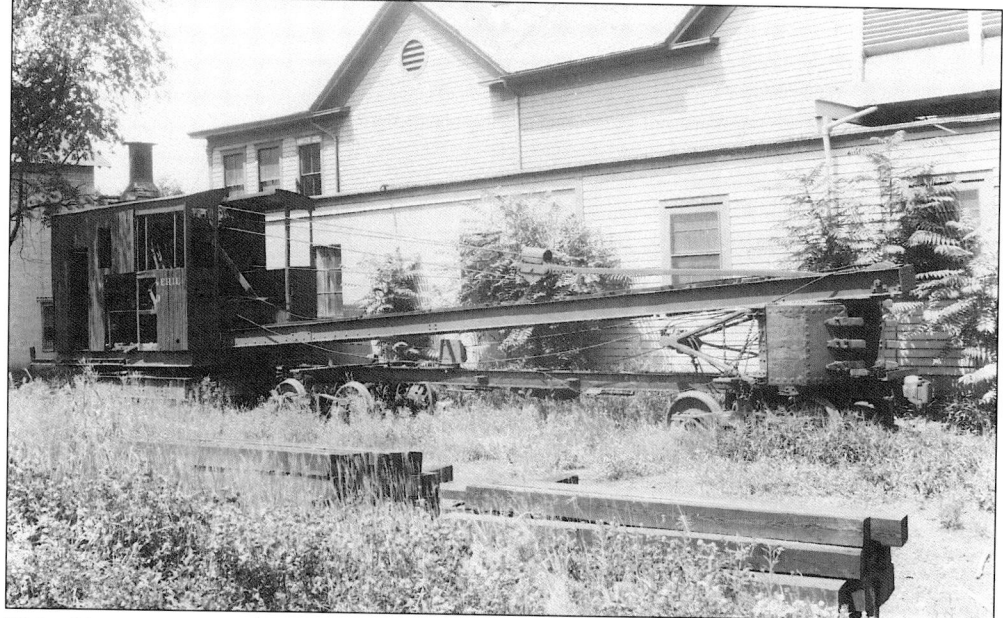

This old, steam-powered Terry Crane, with its clamshell bucket and idler car, is seen in storage on June 24, 1946. Used in maintaining the M&E's right-of-way, it was a very useful piece of equipment when the Passaic River trestle required rebuilding. (Photo by Thomas T. Taber III; courtesy of Railroad Museum of Pennsylvania (PHMC) Collection.)

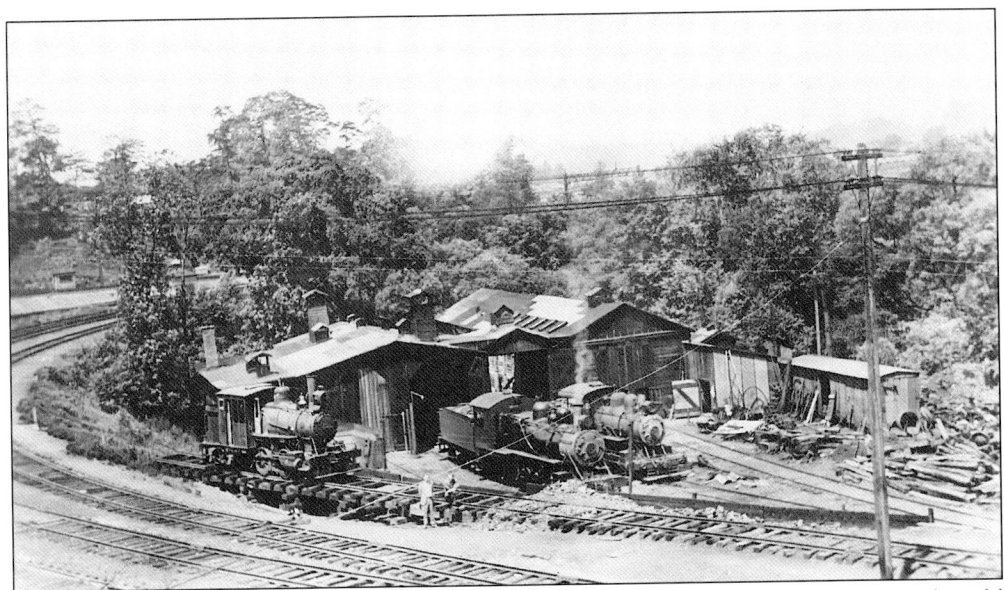

Even by mid-1930s standards, the working conditions at the Morristown engine terminal could be considered fairly archaic. The drafty, wooden sheds with their patched roofs were surrounded by spare parts and assorted castoffs. In the shop building on the right, various machines were driven by leather belts, adding to the 19th-century charm of this cluttered, but unique place. (Photo by Charles B. Chaney; courtesy of Railroad Museum of Pennsylvania (PHMC) Collection.)

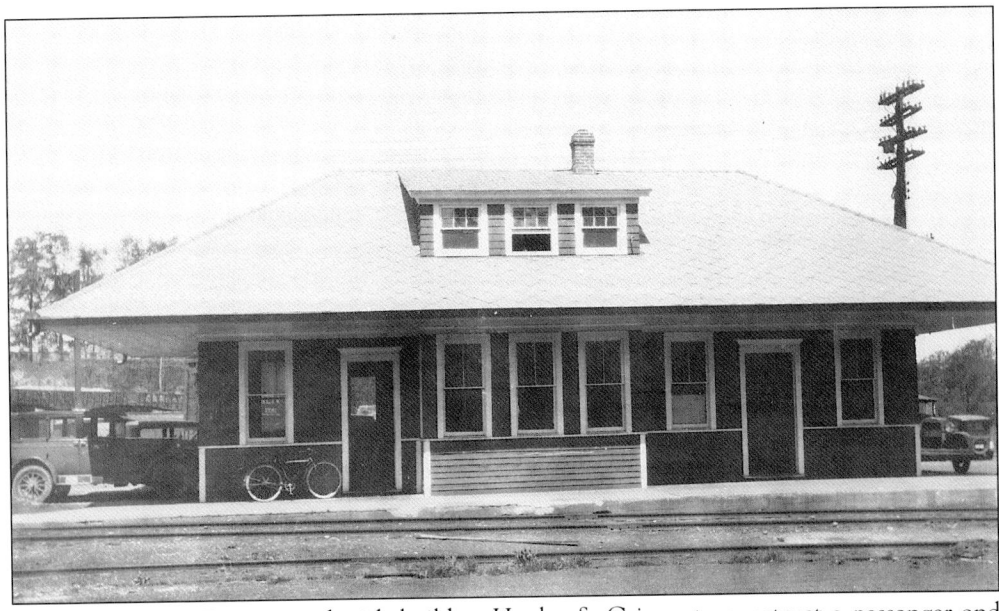

In 1904, the M&E negotiated with builders Hopler & Grimes to construct a passenger and freight station at Morristown, as well as a freight station at Whippany. This view of the 48-by-18-foot Morristown depot dates from 1929, not long after the roof and second floor were replaced following a fire. In the same year, an inferno destroyed the Monroe station, but it was not rebuilt. (Photo: Morristown & Erie RR; collection of Steven Hepler.)

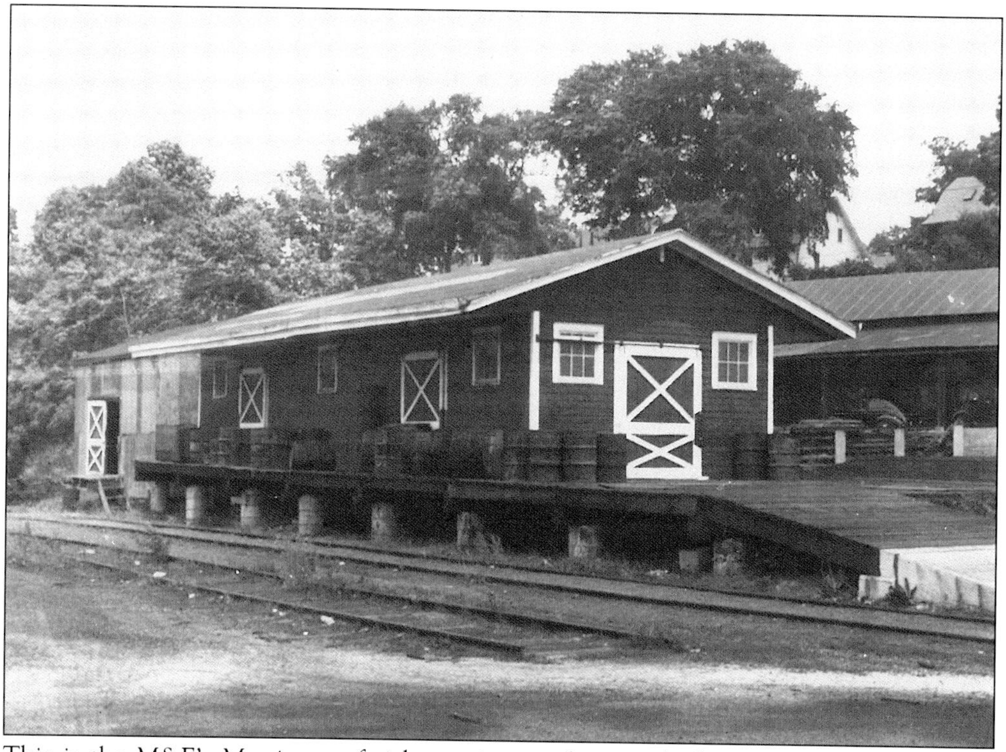

This is the M&E's Morristown freight station as photographed on March 27, 1943. This 18-by-60-foot building was erected by Hopler & Grimes in 1904 and survived until 1976 when it was razed. In the background, one can see the loading dock of Consumer's Coal Company, a dealer of "Old Company's Lehigh" anthracite coal. (Courtesy of Donald Van Court.)

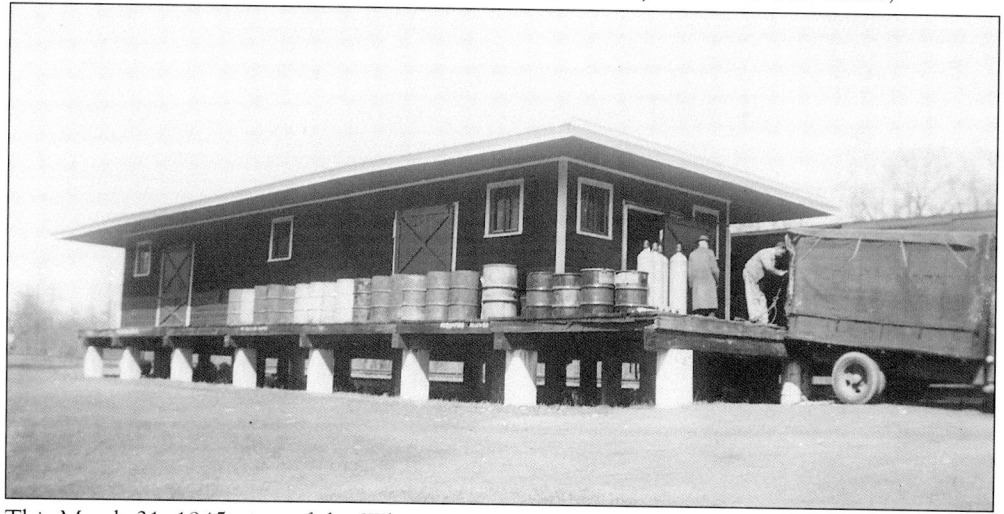

This March 31, 1945 view of the Whippany freight house shows an abundance of steel drums lined up on the platform. A local delivery man appears to be loading bottled gas tanks into his canvas-covered truck. This 18-by-60-foot building is yet another Hopler & Grimes structure built in 1904 and survives today (in altered form) as the home of the Whippany Railway Museum. (Photo by Thomas T. Taber III; courtesy of Railroad Museum of Pennsylvania (PHMC) Collection.)

The water tank at Whippany, from which M&E steam locomotives once quenched their thirst, was erected in 1903 and, incredibly, still stands today as a true historic landmark. It is one of the very few surviving railroad water tanks left in America still in its original location and still capable of performing its intended function. (Collection of Steven Hepler.)

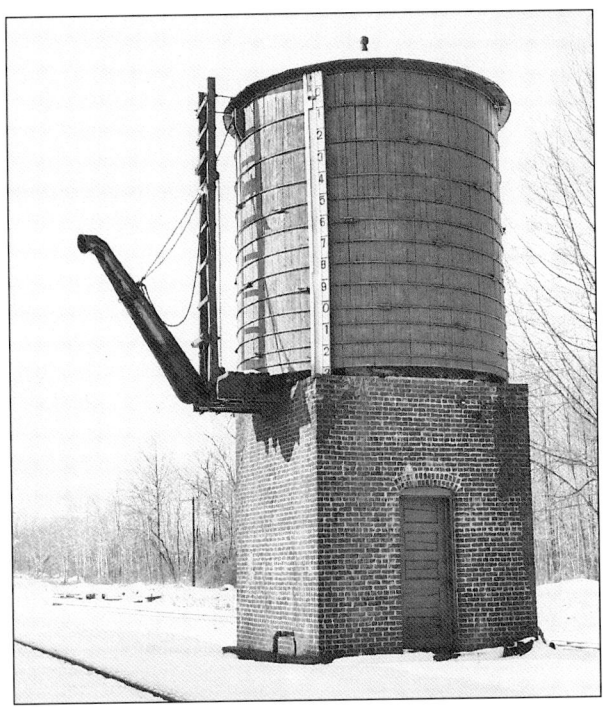

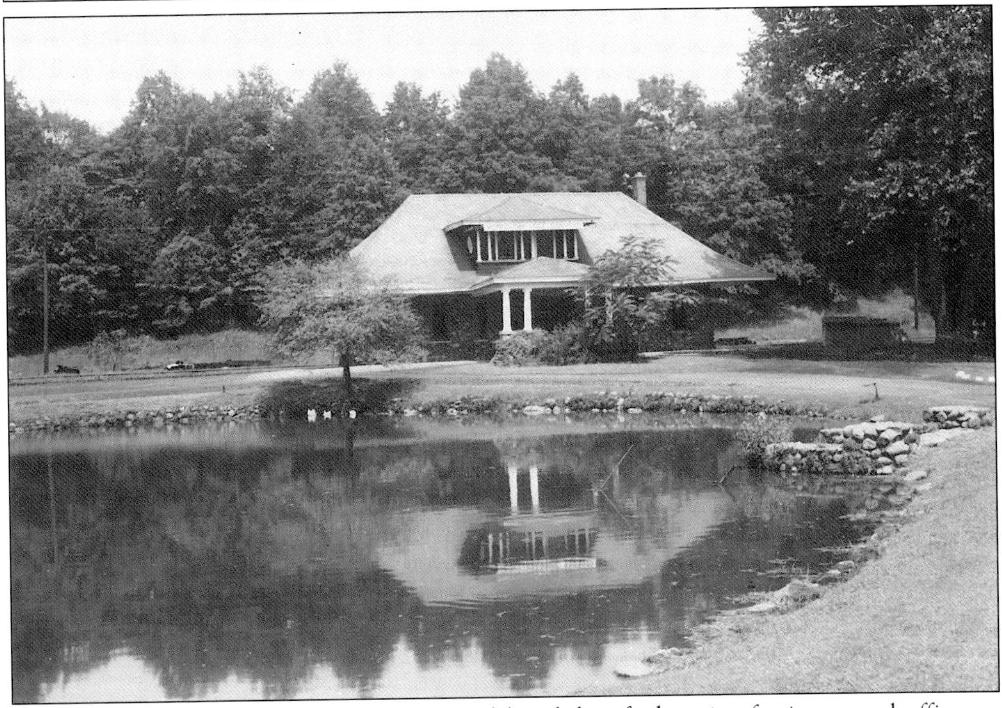

No railroad anywhere ever had such a peaceful and dignified setting for its general offices as did the Morristown & Erie. Constructed in 1904 by D.H. Grimes, the 32-by-60-foot fieldstone station featured a portechochere, baggage rooms, toilets, and a stone fireplace in the passenger waiting room. The second floor housed the company offices. The depot opened for business on January 7, 1905. This photograph is c. late 1950s. (Courtesy of Edward J. Ruland.)

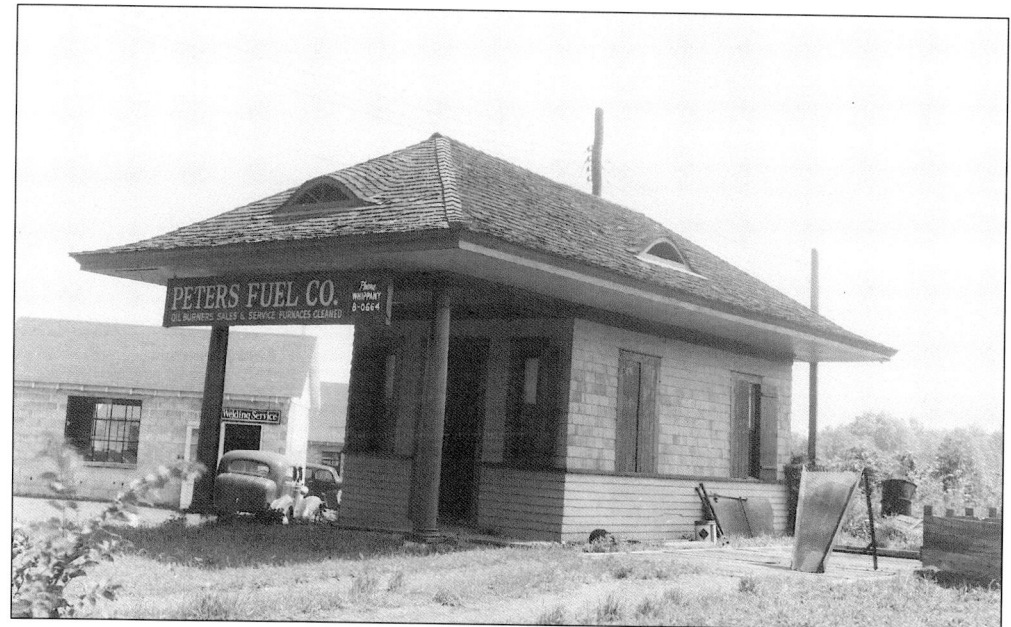

The Hanover station, photographed on July 30, 1947, at DeForrest Avenue in East Hanover, was the original Whippany station of the Whippany River Railroad. When the M&E came into existence, this little depot was moved up the line to the Hanover area. After passenger service was discontinued, it became home to a fuel dealer, but was leveled in the late 1950s. (Photo by Thomas T. Taber III; courtesy of Railroad Museum of Pennsylvania (PHMC) Collection.)

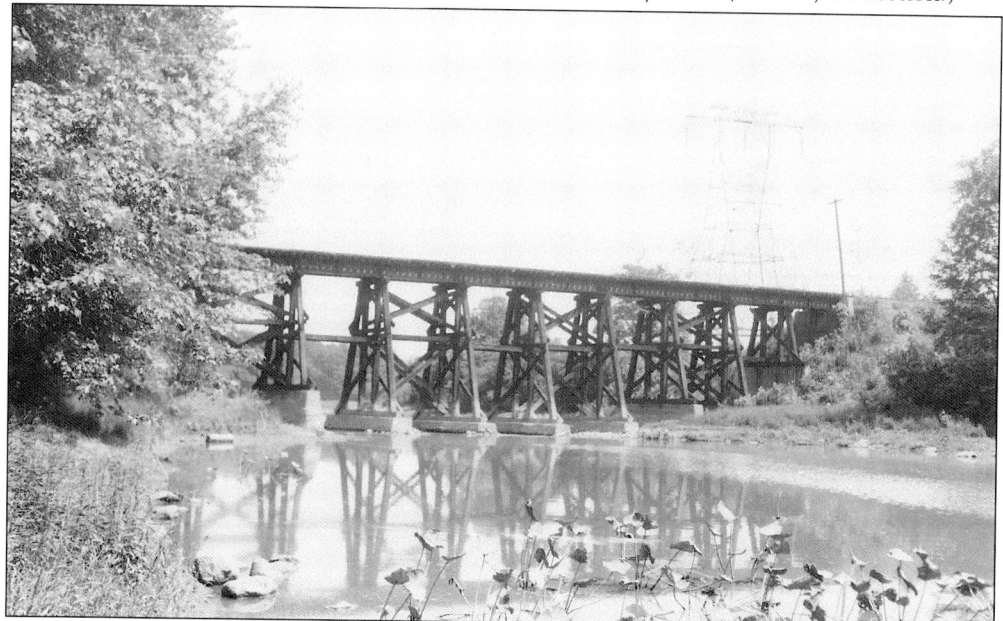

The Passaic River trestle is located just west of present-day Eisenhower Parkway (Beaufort Avenue) in Livingston. The 30-foot-high, 464-foot-long bridge was originally built by D.H. Grimes in 1903. The all-wood trestle was rebuilt in the late 1920s using concrete and steel in addition to the timber bents. (Photo by Thomas T. Taber III; courtesy of Railroad Museum of Pennsylvania (PHMC) Collection.)

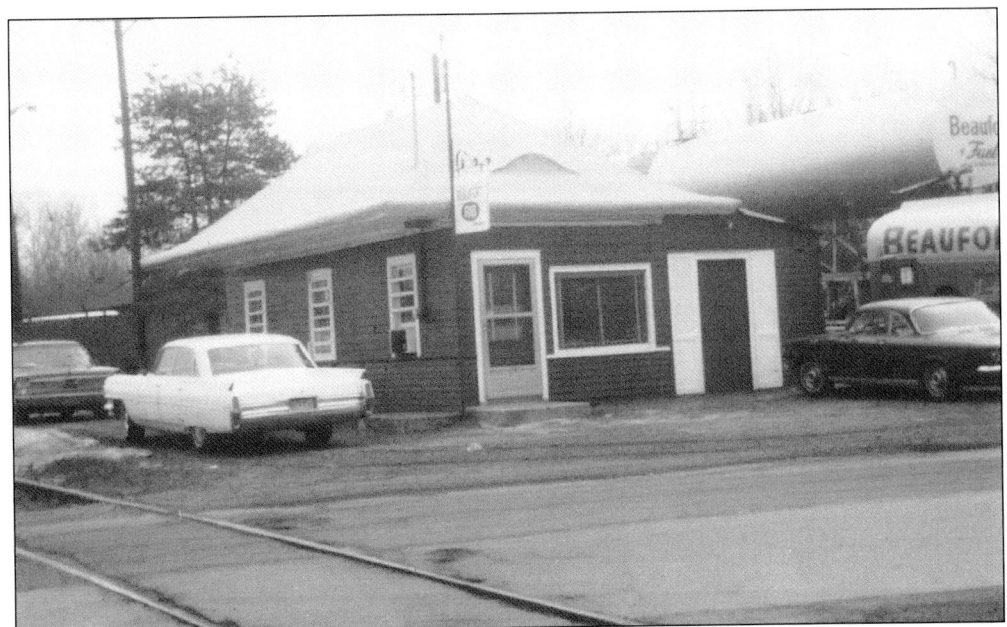

This small depot at Beaufort Avenue (Eisenhower Parkway) came into existence mainly because, in 1903, the M&E had no plans to erect a station here. Angry residents of the Beaufort section put up their own 5-foot-square shelter in 1906 and eventually forced the railroad to build this fine little station. It was photographed in 1968 while serving as the office of the Beaufort Fuel Company. (Photo by Steven Hepler.)

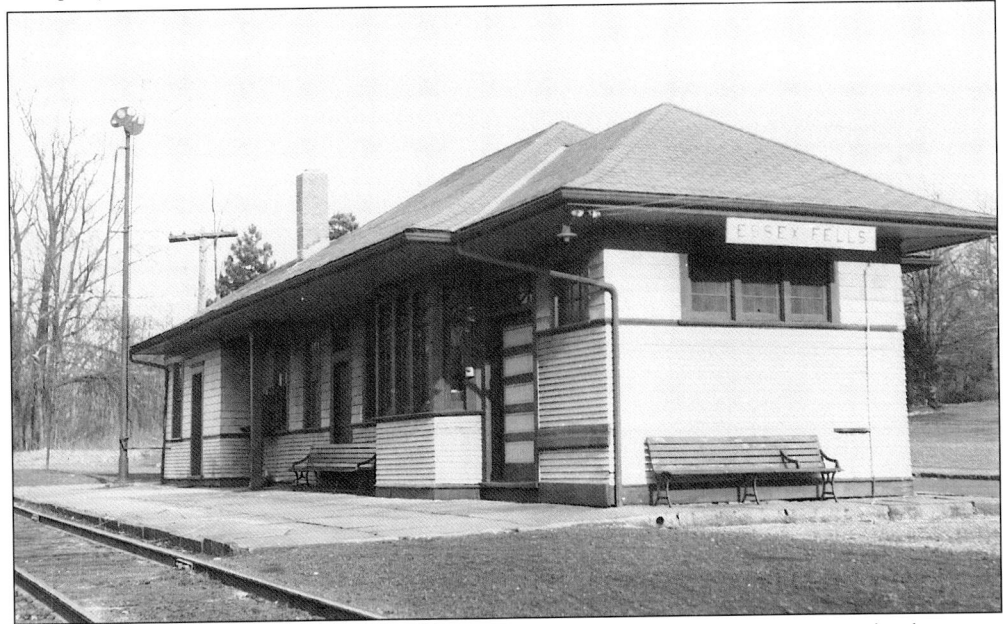

This is a view of the Erie Railroad station at Essex Fells on February 13, 1954. At this location, the Erie's Caldwell Branch terminated, and the M&E exchanged freight and passengers with the larger road. When the Erie Lackawanna discontinued passenger service on the branch in October 1966, the mayor of Essex Fells insisted that this charming and historic depot be demolished. The end came one month later. (Courtesy of Railroad Avenue Enterprises.)

Four
COAL SMOKE ALONG THE WHIPPANONG

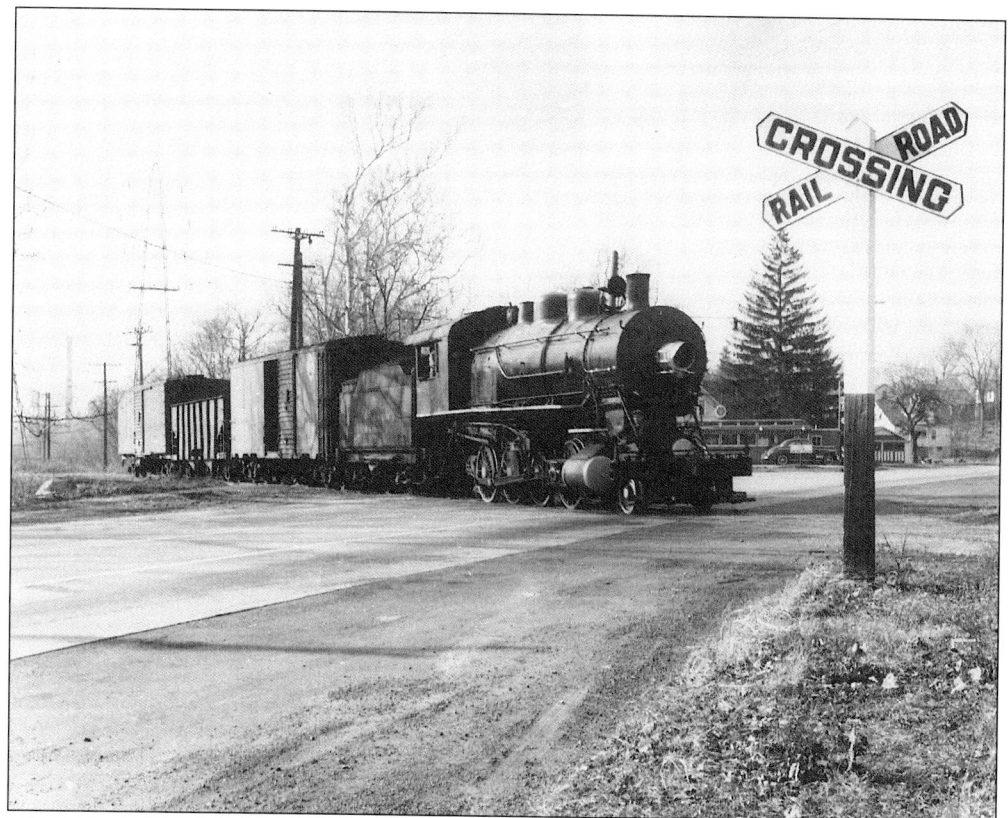

M&E No. 9 is seen backing a short train across the three-lane Newark and Mt. Pleasant Turnpike (present-day Route 10) in Whippany on November 16, 1942. The train is headed back to the McEwan Brothers Paper Box Board plant. The camera looks westbound up the highway and not one automobile or truck can be seen on the road. (Courtesy of Donald Van Court.)

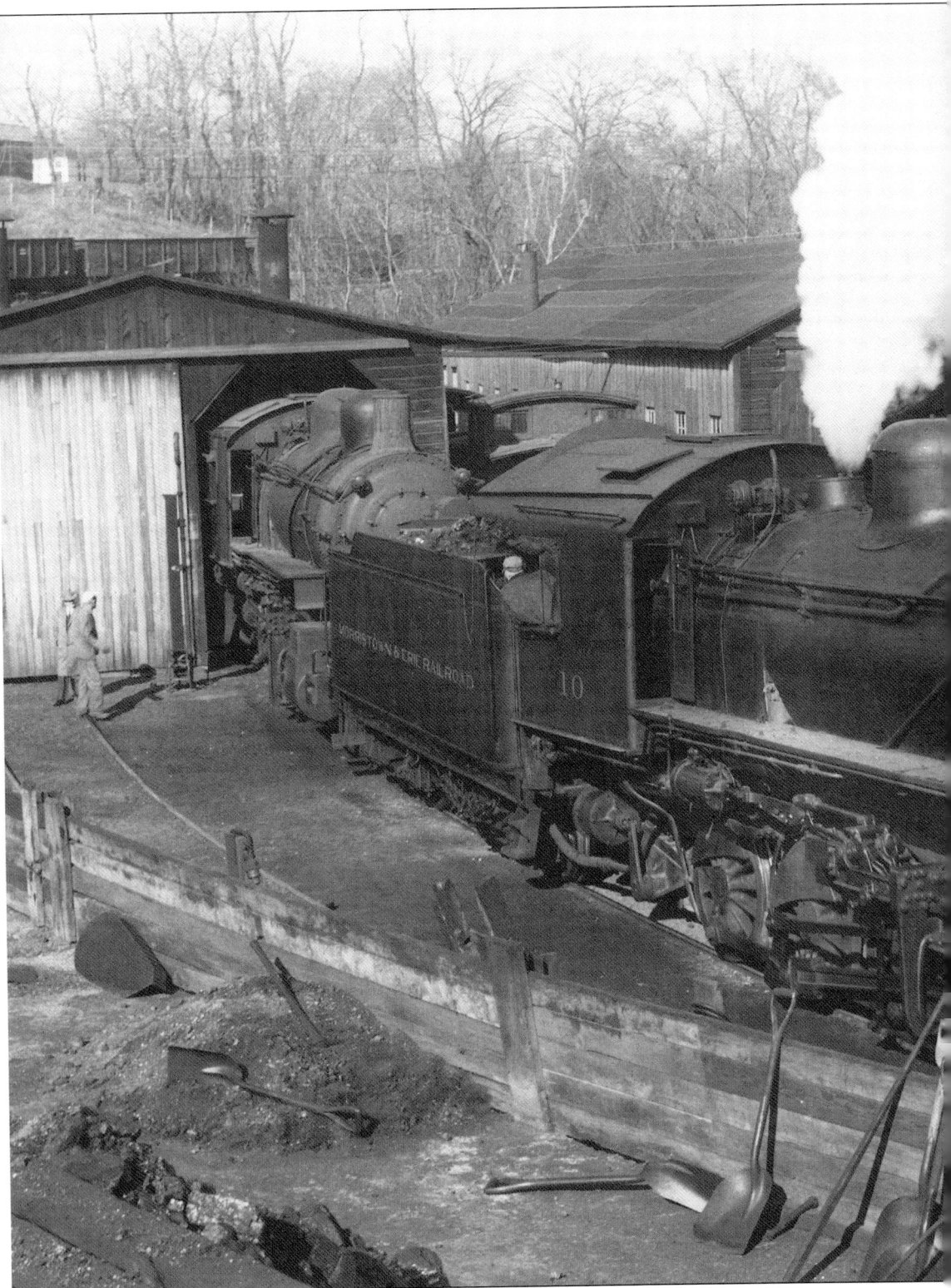

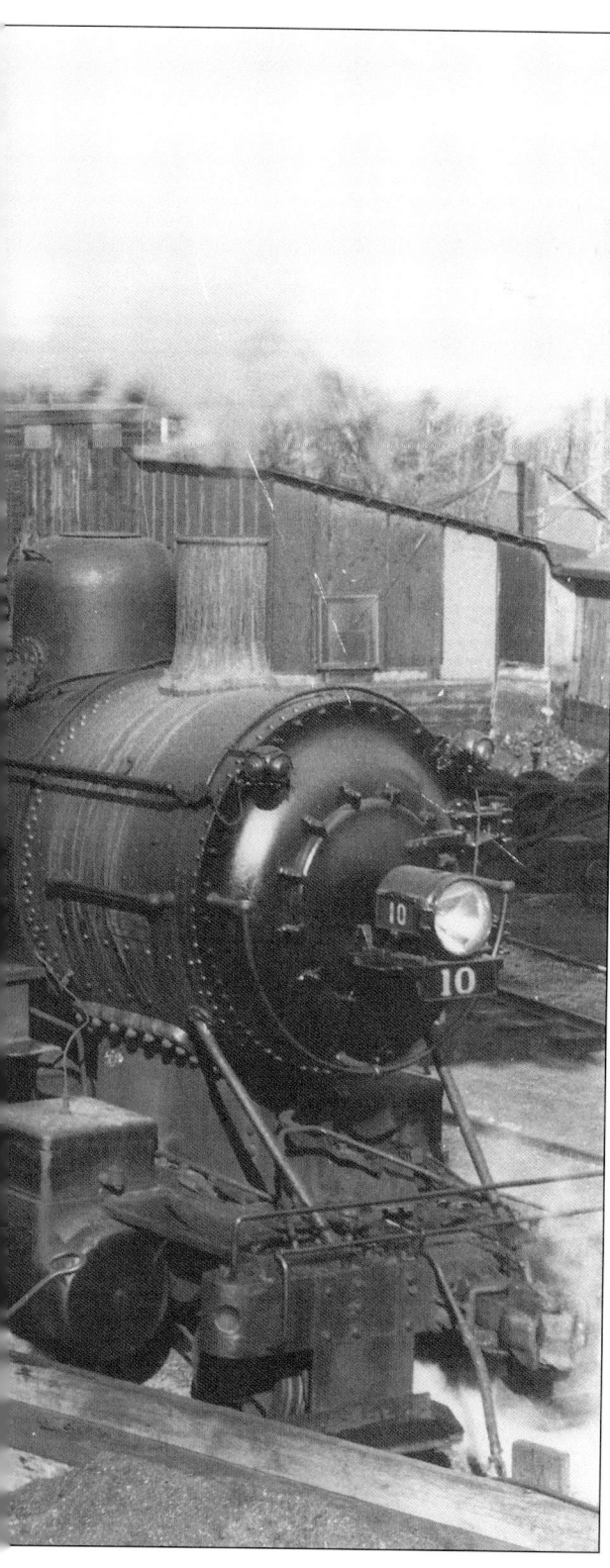

With its polished bell, No. 10 looks great as the center of attention in this finely crafted photograph by Homer Hill. Perhaps more intriguing are some of the other details in this shot, such as the variety of coal scoops, clinker bars, and coal rakes that can be seen lined up along the timber retaining walls of the locomotive coal storage bin. No. 10, with Harold Meslar at the throttle, is placing No. 12 into the enginehouse as Phil Dahill keeps a watchful eye on the proceedings. The man behind Phil wearing the fedora is Superintendent Fletcher Williams. This photo was taken in early April 1952, just before the arrival of a new diesel switcher which would retire the steamers. (Courtesy of Homer R. Hill.)

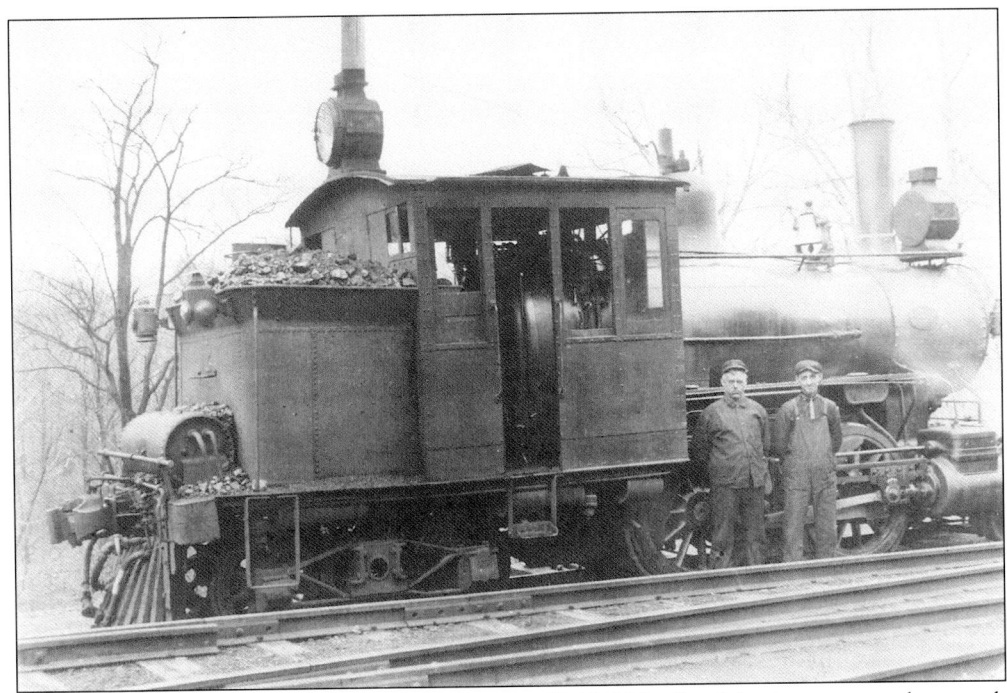

For those who like seldom-seen details, this view of M&E No. 2 at Morristown reveals several, including the cab roof-mounted rear headlight, the rear pilot (or "cowcatcher") for the engine's reverse westbound runs, and the rear endsill-mounted air reservoir. Standing proudly alongside "the Dinky" on January 24, 1913, are from left to right, George Burnet, engineer, and Henry Brown, fireman. (Courtesy of Morristown/Morris Township Library, Curtiss Collection.)

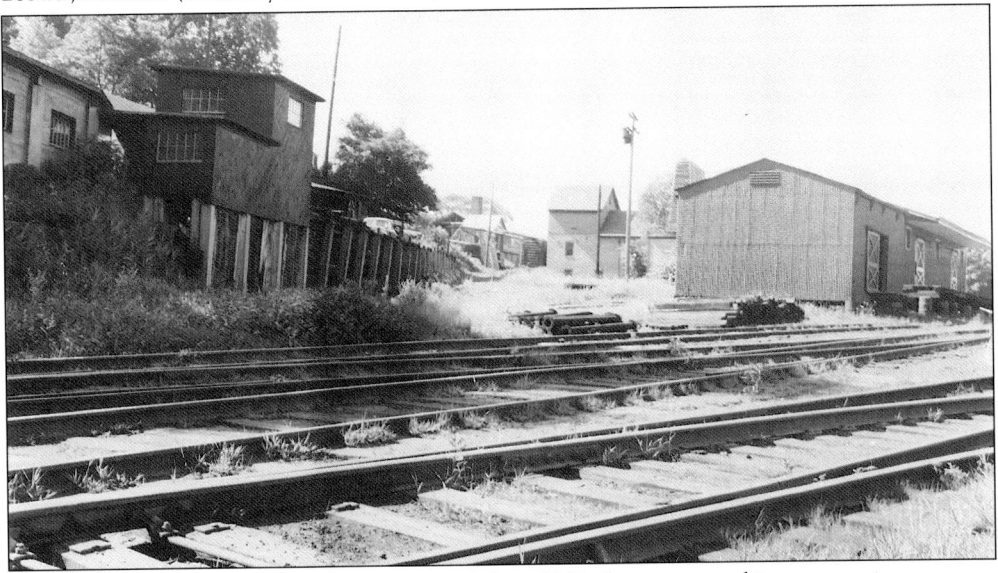

Looking west at the Morristown terminus of the M&E, this scene and its companion on page 47 presented themselves on August 2, 1947. On the left is the Consumer's Coal Company, whose elevated track was accessed by a switchback. Next in line, to the rear is the Swifts Meat Packing plant, and on the right are the freight storage buildings. (Photo by Thomas T. Taber III; courtesy of Railroad Museum of Pennsylvania (PHMC) Collection.)

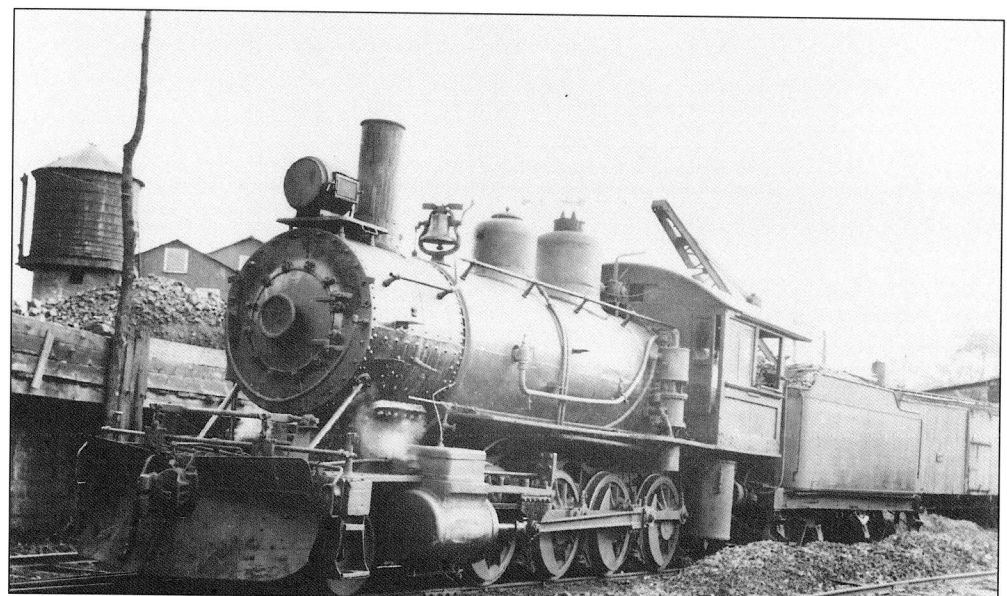

This view of No. 6, simmering alongside the coal dock on March 28, 1936, affords us a relatively good view of the rarely photographed Morristown water tank. After the steam locomotives on the M&E were retired, the wooden tank was pulled down, but the brick base was used for storage until it too was demolished in 1976. (Courtesy of California State Railroad Museum, Railway and Locomotive Historical Society Collection.)

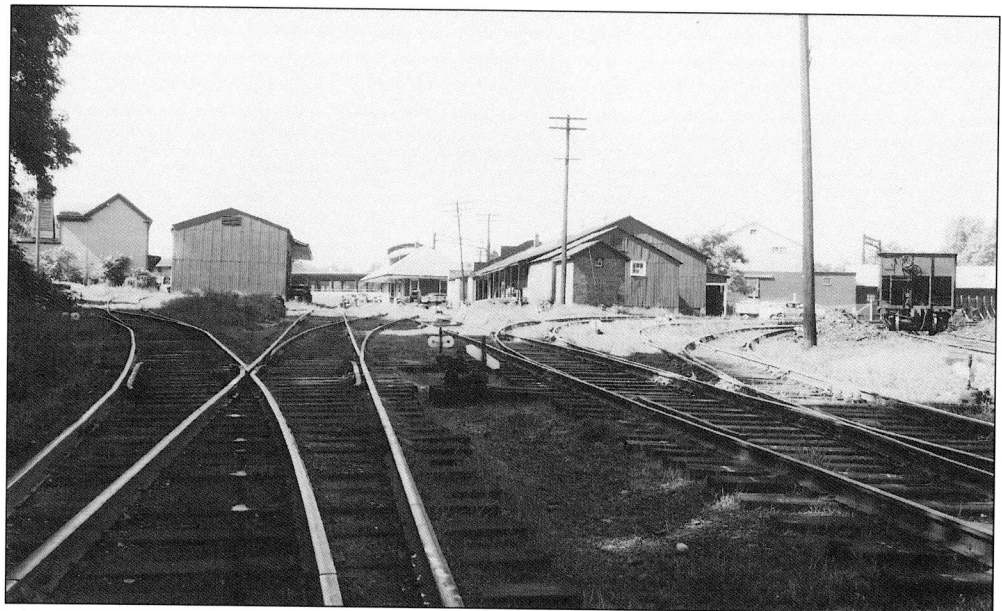

This photo expands the view of the Morristown yard. Still looking west, we see, from left to right, the Swifts plant, the freight station, the passenger depot, and the Farm Service Exchange. The interchange tracks with the Lackawanna curve off to the right. In 1976, the turn-of-the-century atmosphere of this yard disappeared forever when the property was developed into a shopping center. (Photo by Thomas T. Taber III; courtesy of Railroad Museum of Pennsylvania (PHMC) Collection.)

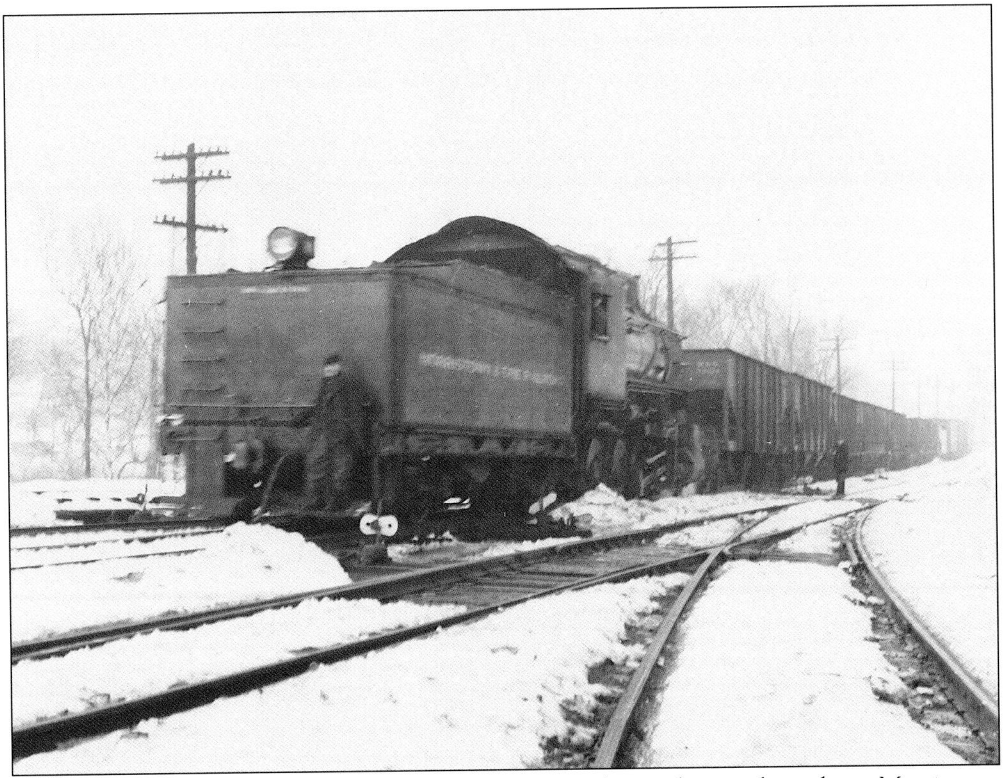

The sharp exhausts of a steam locomotive hard at work reverberate throughout Morristown as M&E No. 10 labors up the steep 4-percent grade to the interchange with the Lackawanna Railroad. Eighteen cars are in tow on this cold winter day in 1945. (Courtesy of Donald Van Court.)

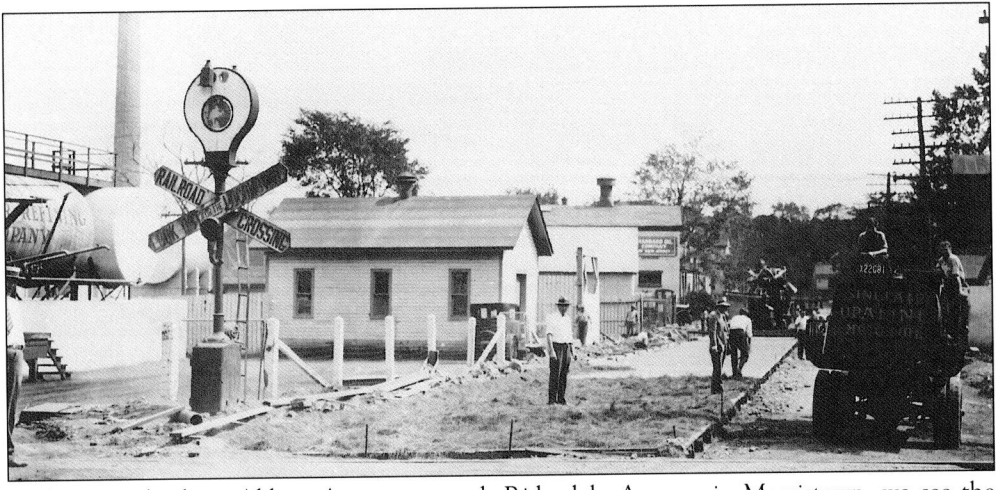

Looking south along Abbett Avenue towards Ridgedale Avenue in Morristown, we see the roadway under construction in this c. 1920s view. The railroad crossing is still protected by an 1890s banjo-style "wig-wag" signal. A large red disk housed within the upper portion of the "banjo" would, at the approach of a train, swing back and forth, ringing a bell and warning motorists. (Courtesy of Railroad Museum of Pennsylvania (PHMC) Collection.)

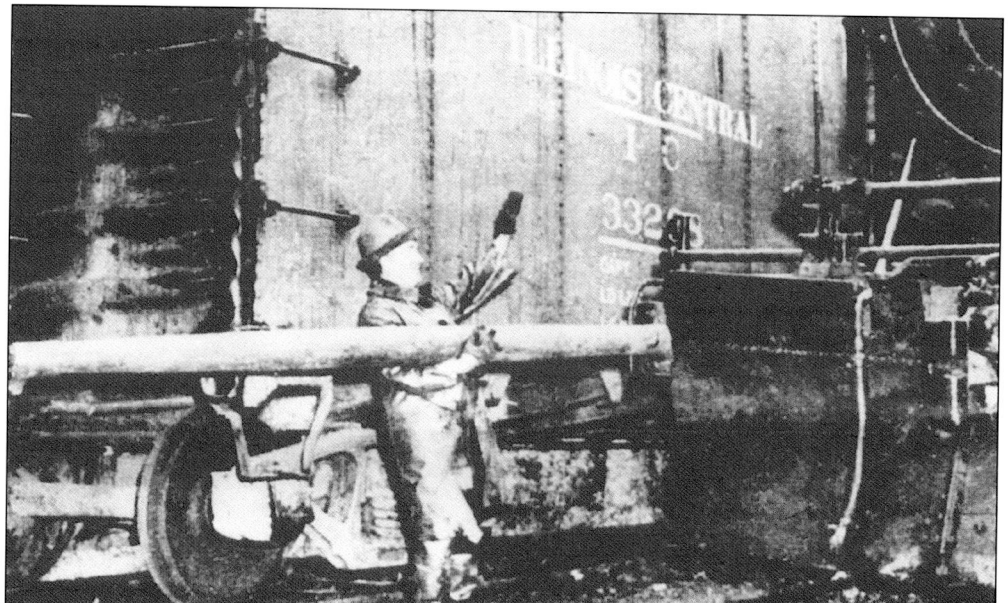

Brakeman Tommy Gee signals to the engineer of No. 6 as he holds up a stout pole placed in the "poling pockets" of both the locomotive and the car on the adjacent track. The engine slowly shoves its weight against the pole and moves the cars. Although outlawed throughout the industry today because of the danger, "poling" was an effective method of moving cars around a cramped yard. (Collection of Steven Hepler.)

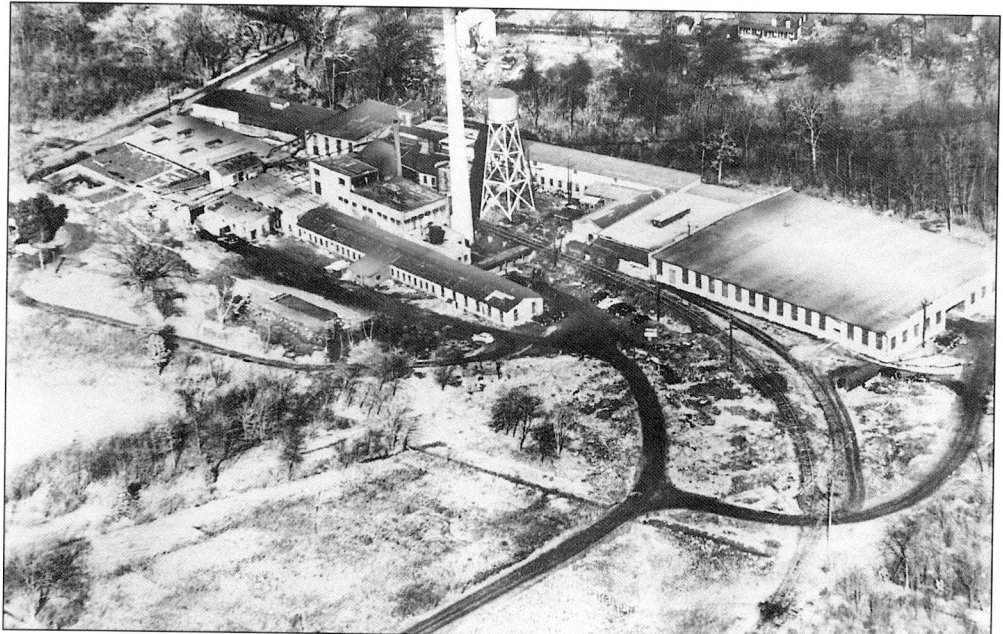

This aerial view shows Whippany Paper Board's Stony Brook Mill, c. 1960, one of the many paper-producing mills in Whippany served by the Morristown & Erie. At one time, Stony Brook produced approximately 150 tons of paperboard product daily. Of that, nearly 60 tons emerged as folding boxboard, while another 90 tons appeared as tube stock, chipboard, and special grades of paper. (Courtesy of Hanover Township Landmark Committee.)

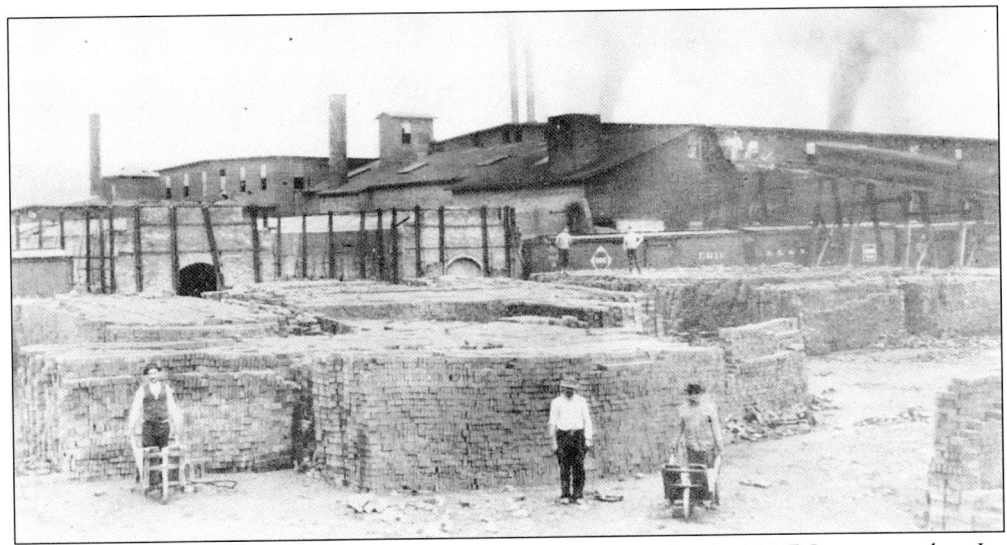

This photograph of the Hanover Brick Works was reportedly taken by M&E Superintendent Ira Meslar sometime in the late 1920s. The plant was at the end of the railroad's 3-mile Malapardis Branch that was built in 1899. The brick works was not a successful venture, however, and it closed in 1931. The branch was removed in 1936. (Courtesy of Railroad Museum of Pennsylvania (PHMC) Collection.)

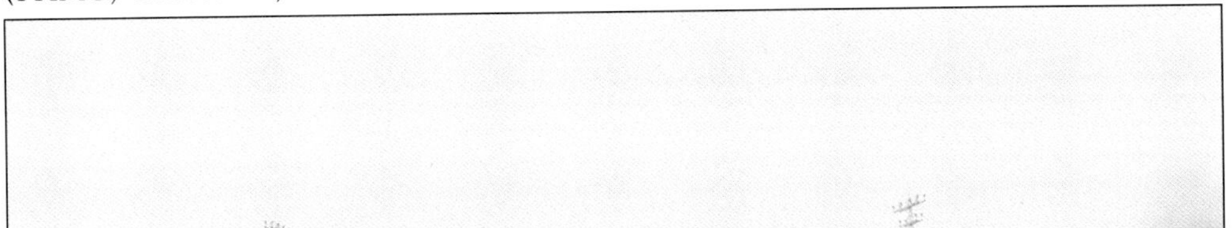

The Hanover Brick Manufacturing Company was once located near Whippany, and this image of their gasoline-powered locomotive coupled to two cars is quite rare. The big steam shovel is loading the cars with clay. The locomotive was purchased by Hanover Brick to replace its own steamer, former M&E No. 2, which they had purchased in 1922 and used for several years. (Courtesy of Morristown/Morris Township Library, Curtiss Collection.)

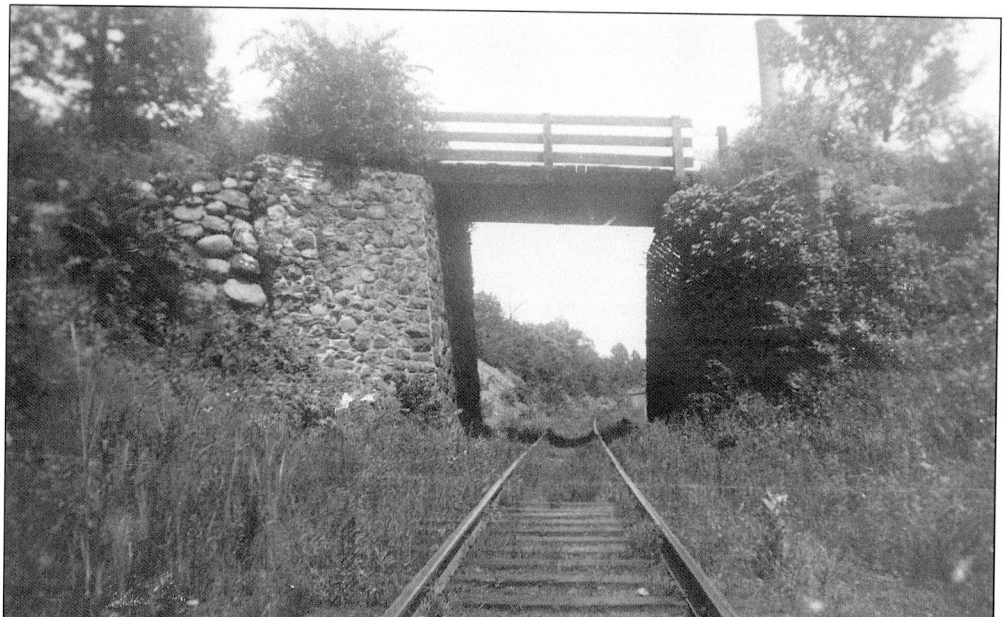

This June 23, 1945 view of Eden Mill Lane bridge at Whippany looks east. The original railbed here had gone up and over a very steep hill with the road crossing the tracks at the crest. In 1900, the hill was cut back, and this overpass was built. When Eden Mill began to expand, the road was closed, and the overpass was removed in 1950. (Photo by Thomas T. Taber III; courtesy of Railroad Museum of Pennsylvania (PHMC) Collection.)

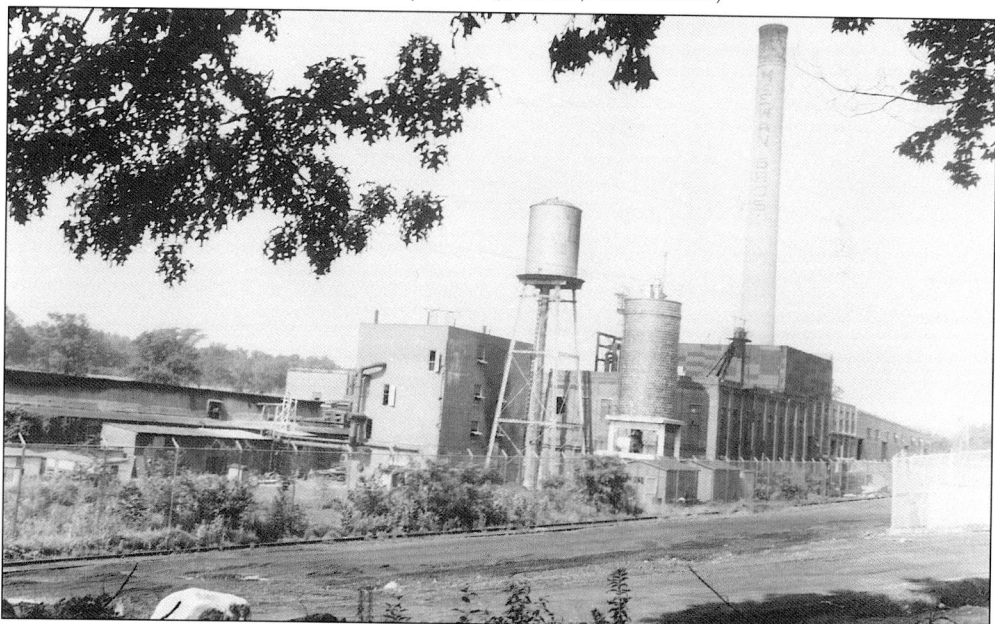

Even though the giant smokestack still says "McEwan Bros.," by the time this photo was snapped on Independence Day 1955, Eden Mill had been under the ownership of the Desiderio Brothers' Whippany Paper Board Co. for ten years. The M&E runs alongside the complex, at one time one of the largest paper-producing mills in the country. (Photo by Thomas T. Taber III; courtesy of Railroad Museum of Pennsylvania (PHMC) Collection.)

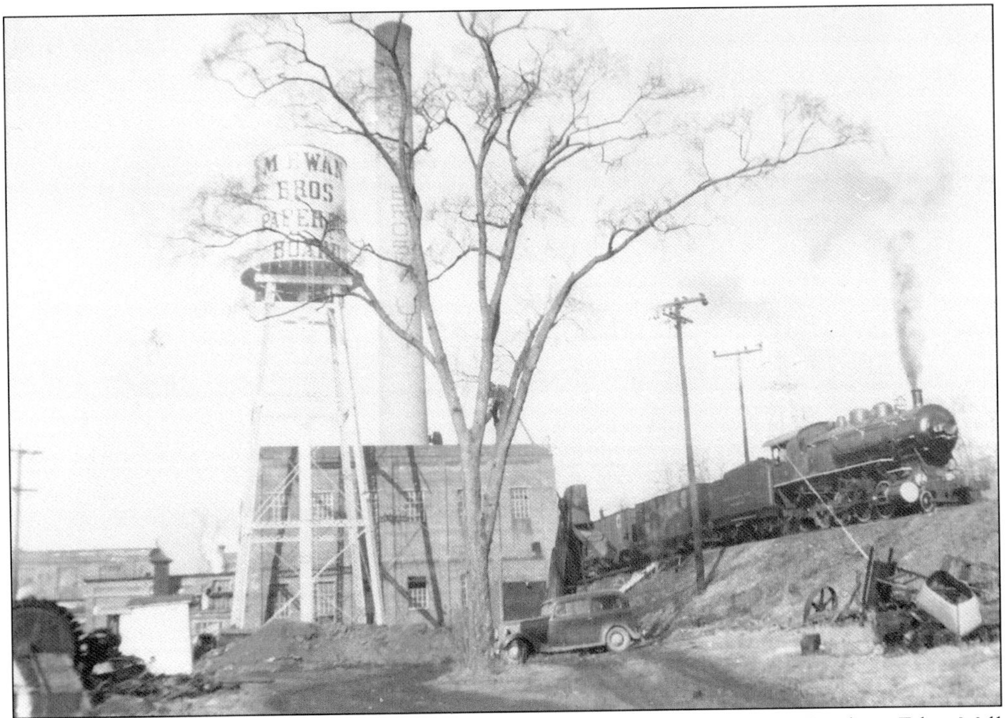

M&E 2-8-0 No. 9 switches a cut of coal-laden hopper cars for the McEwan Brothers Eden Mill power house on Eden Mill Lane in Whippany on Friday, March 8, 1940. This nostalgic scene was recorded by Eden Mill personnel manager John Durkota. Today, only memories remain of the daily activities at this huge paper mill. (Courtesy of John Durkota.)

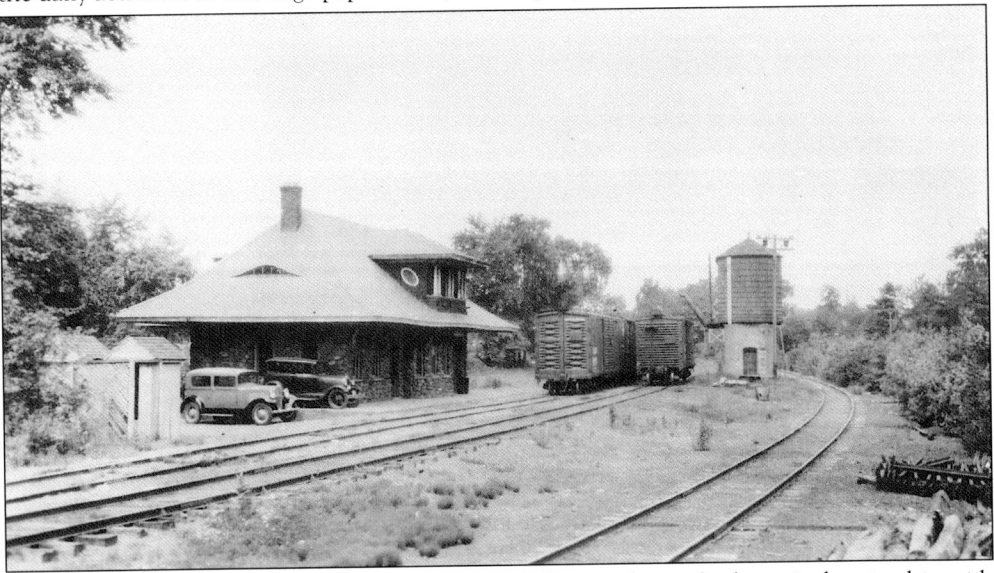

The Whippany station sign swings in the summer breeze above the bay window in this mid-1930s view of the depot. Except for the chirping of birds and the rustle of leaves, the yard is quiet. But soon a locomotive whistle will pierce the stillness, and the sleepy little yard will spring to life again. (Courtesy of California State Railroad Museum, Railway and Locomotive Historical Society Collection.)

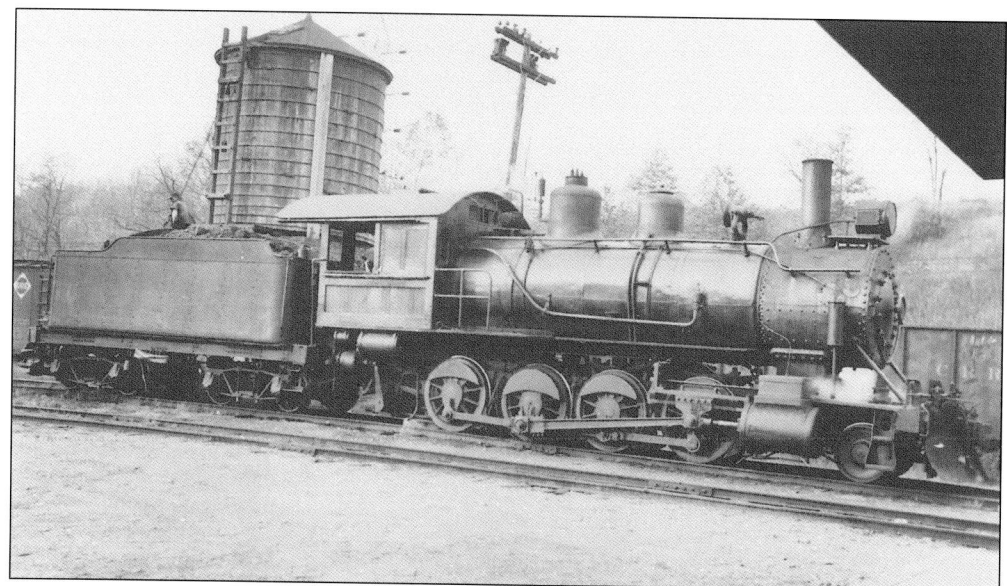

The fireman is busy filling the tender of No. 6 with water from the Whippany tank on an early spring day in the mid-1930s. The engine appears to be clean and well maintained. Indeed, the Morristown & Erie was the only American railroad to rid itself of all debt during the Great Depression and pay dividends at the same time! (Courtesy of California State Railroad Museum, Gerald M. Best Collection.)

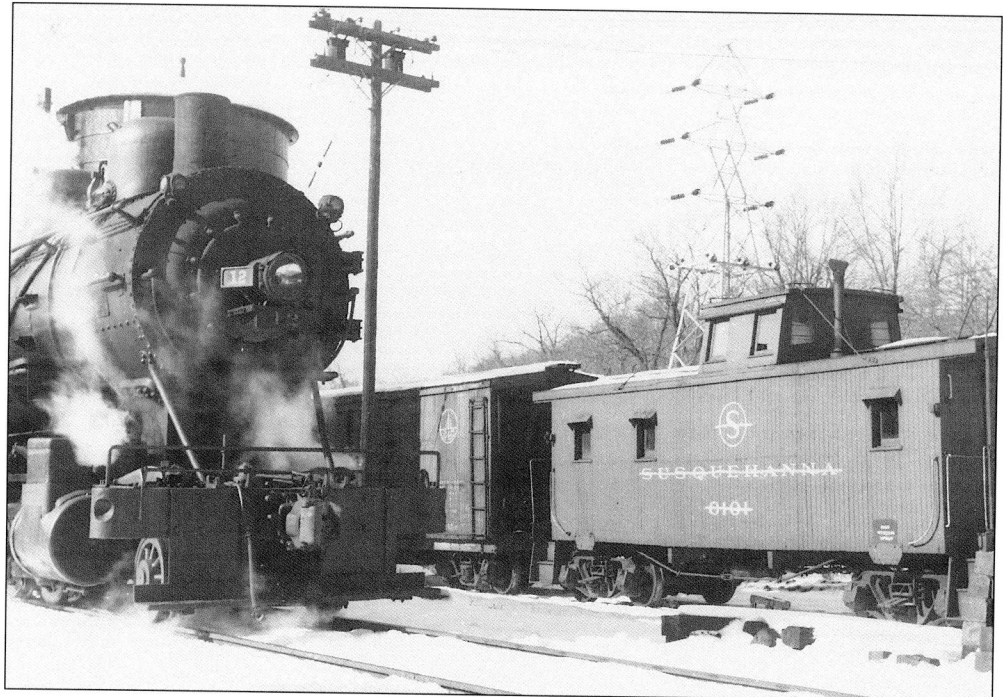

After working her way along the line in the winter of 1952, No. 12 takes a brief respite and pants hard in the frosty air while taking on water at the Whippany tank. On the adjacent track is newly acquired caboose No. 2, which still retains its original Susquehanna Railroad markings. (Courtesy of Donald Van Court.)

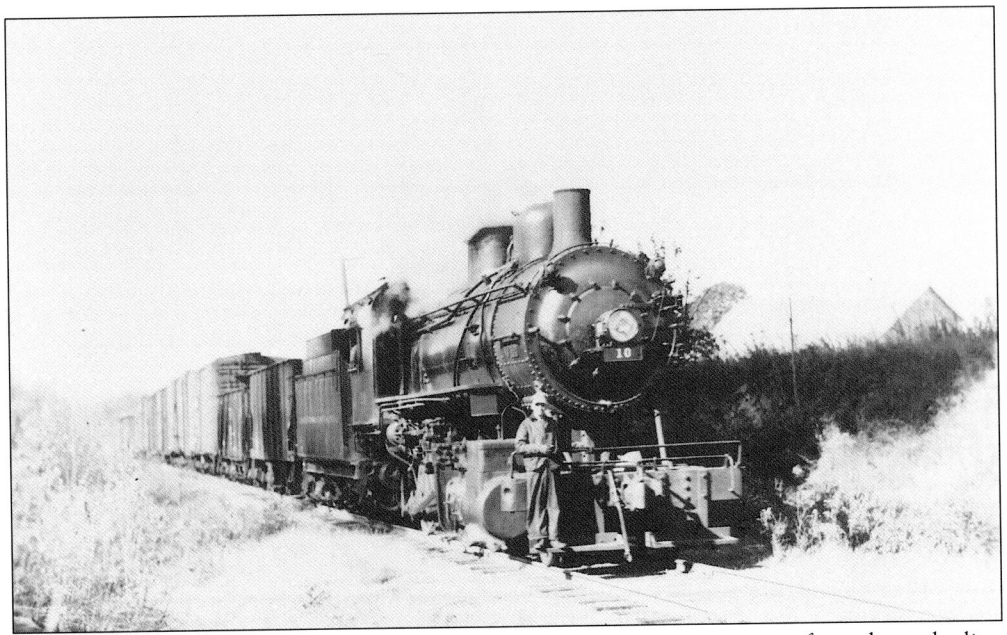

No. 10 will drop only a few cinders over Hanover as she easily moves a string of cars down the line on October 28, 1944. The locomotive has been on the M&E for about three months, and she is already favored by the crew, owing to her ability to move the M&E's sizable daily tonnage with relative ease. (Courtesy of California State Railroad Museum, Gerald M. Best Collection.)

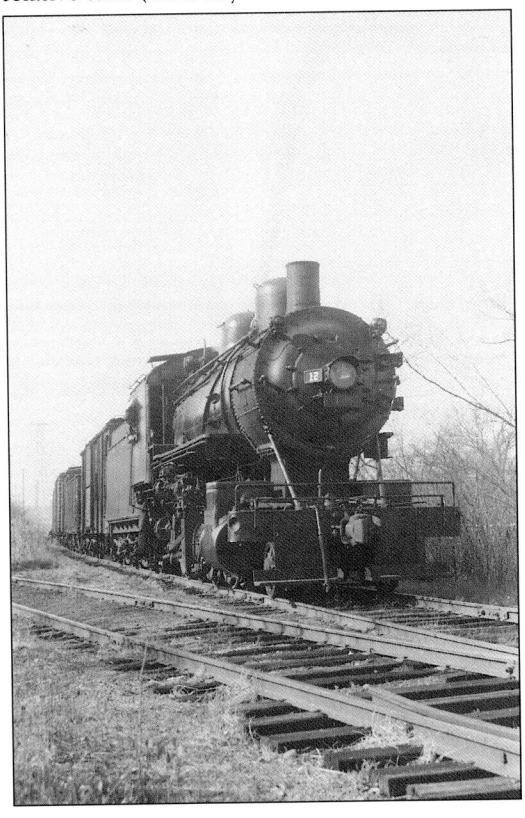

No. 12 drifts down the grade from Troy Hills Road in Whippany and is seen about to trundle over the switch leading to the Minisink Branch. No doubt, several cars in this train are consigned for the Minisink Oil Company, which distributed Sun Oil Products (Sunoco) to area residents and businesses. (Courtesy of Railroad Avenue Enterprises.)

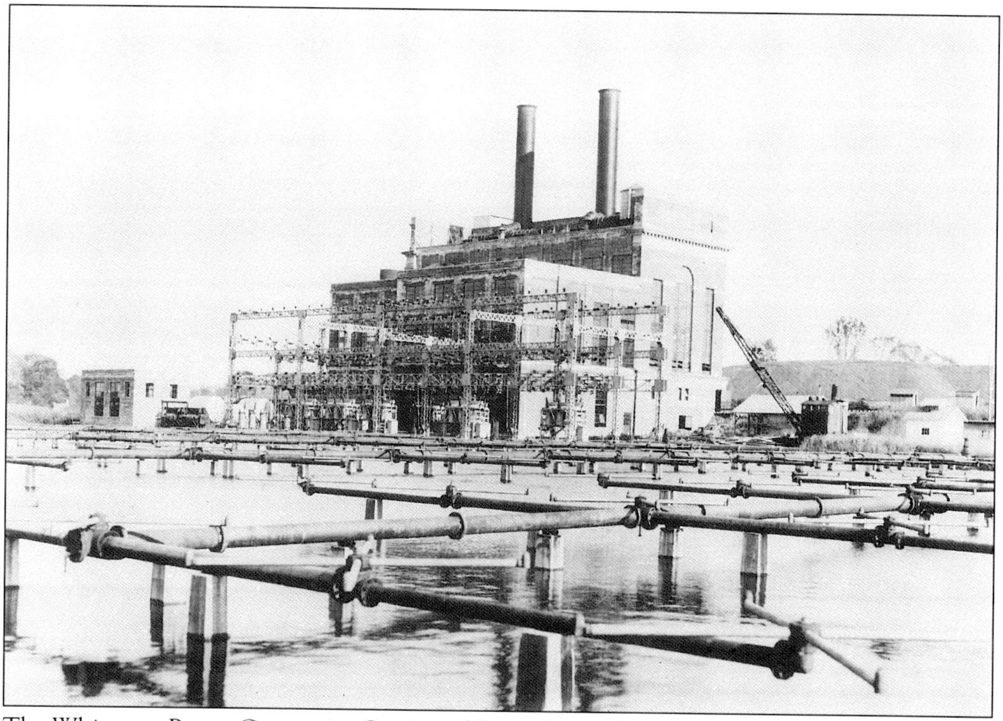

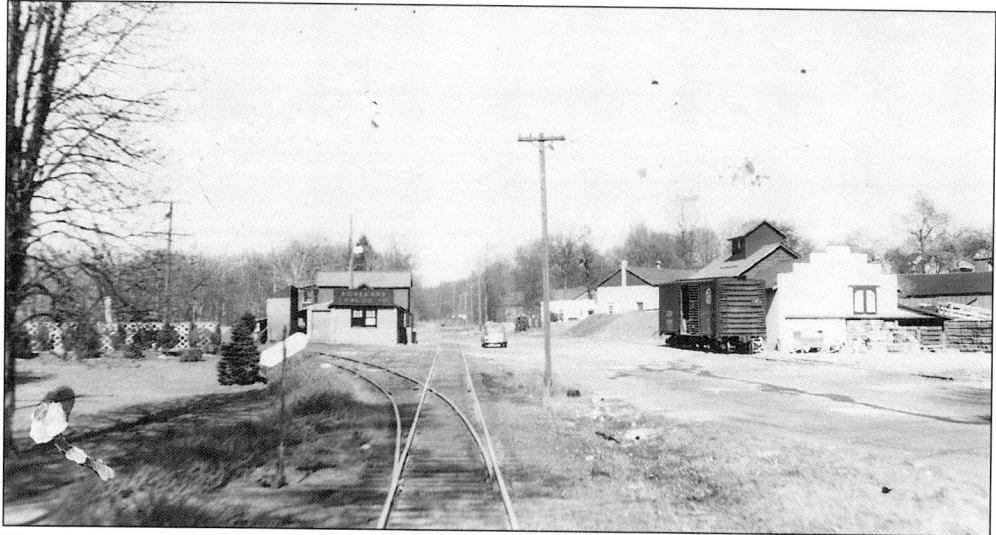

The Whippany Power Generating Station of Jersey Central Power & Light, once located in the meadows east of Whippany, is seen on October 21, 1927. This plant generally burned 150 tons of anthracite coal per day and, for many years, was the largest customer on the M&E, surpassing even the paper mills' daily inbound and outbound shipments. (Courtesy of Morristown/Morris Township Library, Curtiss Collection.)

This April 19, 1946 view at Roseland looks east towards Essex Fells. The track curving off to the left is the spur to the Roseland Coal Company. Today, the area off to the right is occupied by Baer Concrete Co. This stretch of railroad was abandoned by the M&E in the 1980s after Conrail tore up the Caldwell Branch. (Photo by Thomas T. Taber III; courtesy of Railroad Museum of Pennsylvania (PHMC) Collection.)

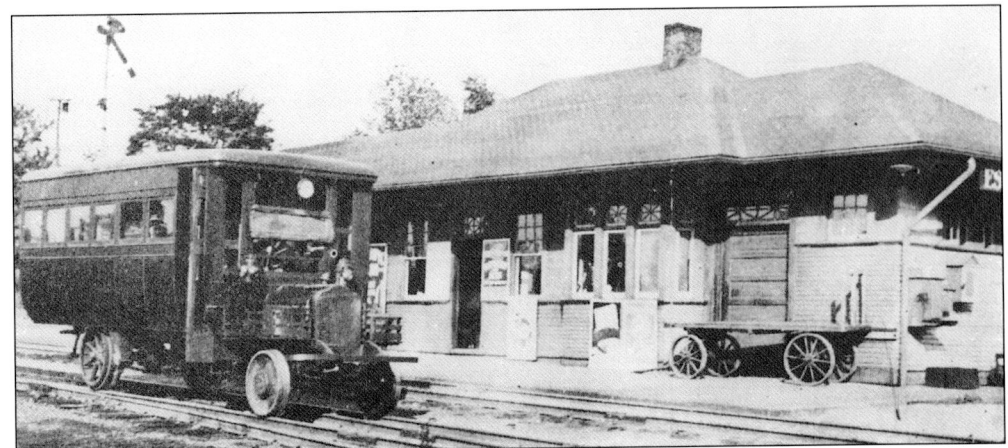

Perhaps because the original light color (see pages 22 and 34) was too hard to keep clean, the M&E repainted Railbus No. 10 in the darker scheme seen here sometime during the mid-1920s. The bus is awaiting passengers at Essex Fells in 1926. (Collection of Steven Hepler.)

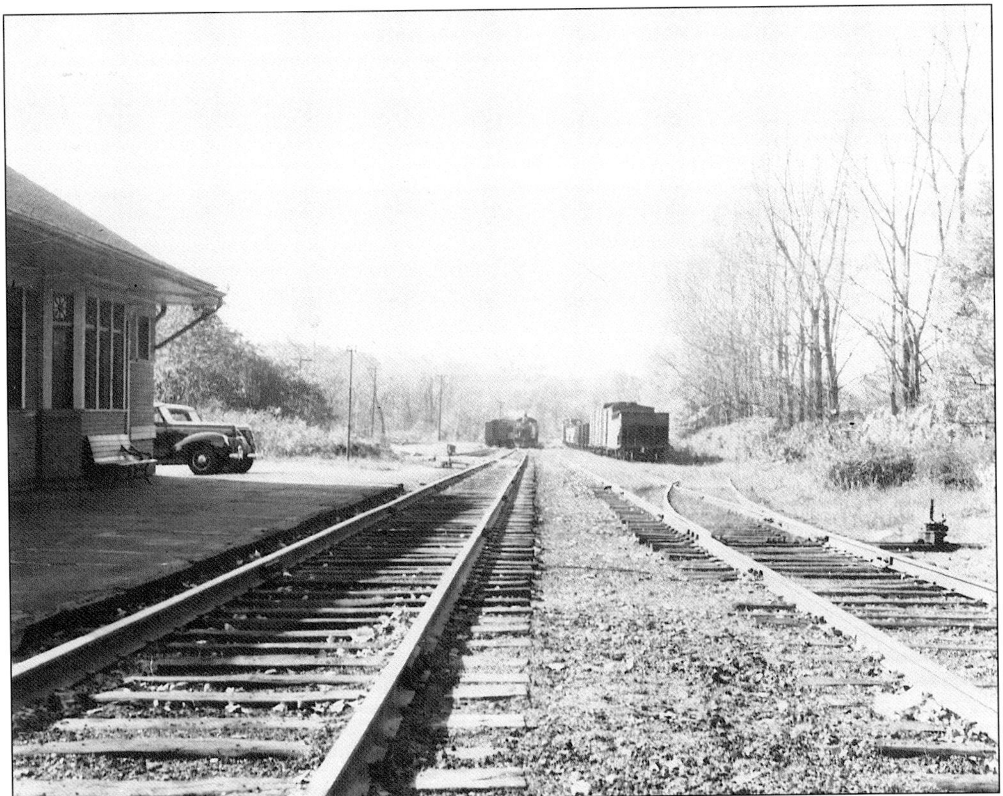

This October 24, 1942 view is of the Essex Fells depot and yard, the end of the Morristown & Erie Railroad, and the terminus of the Erie Railroad's Caldwell Branch. The photo shows M&E No. 6 in the distance switching freight cars destined for interchange with the Erie. (Courtesy of Donald Van Court.)

Five
WORKIN' ON THE RAILROAD

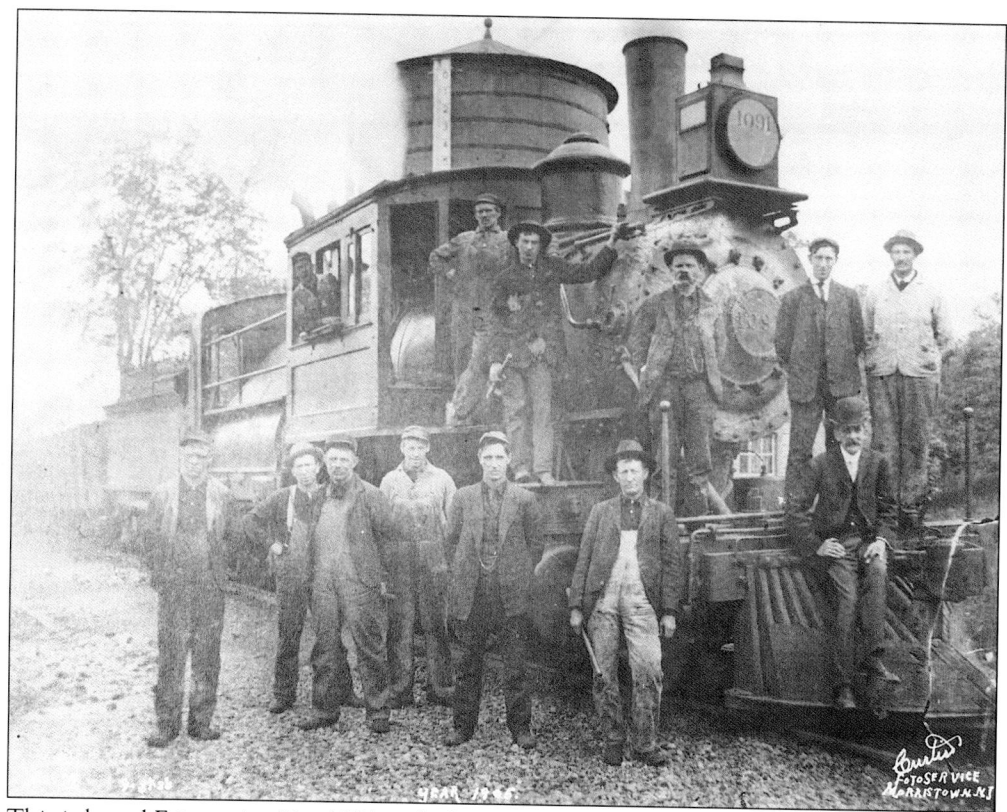

This is leased Erie engine No. 1091 with the M&E crew at Whippany in 1905. On the engine are, from left to right, John Deremer, engineer; Tom Meslar, fireman; Marvin Tyson; Halmagh Ryerson, brakeman; Charlie Tyson; Ira Meslar, conductor; C.E. Pettit (sitting on pilot), auditor; George Burnet, brakeman; Tom Keyes, brakeman; George Young, brakeman; and Rudy Kelch, Jack Batson, and Tom Peer, all brakemen. (Courtesy of Whippany Railway Museum Collection from the estate of Richard W. McEwan Jr.)

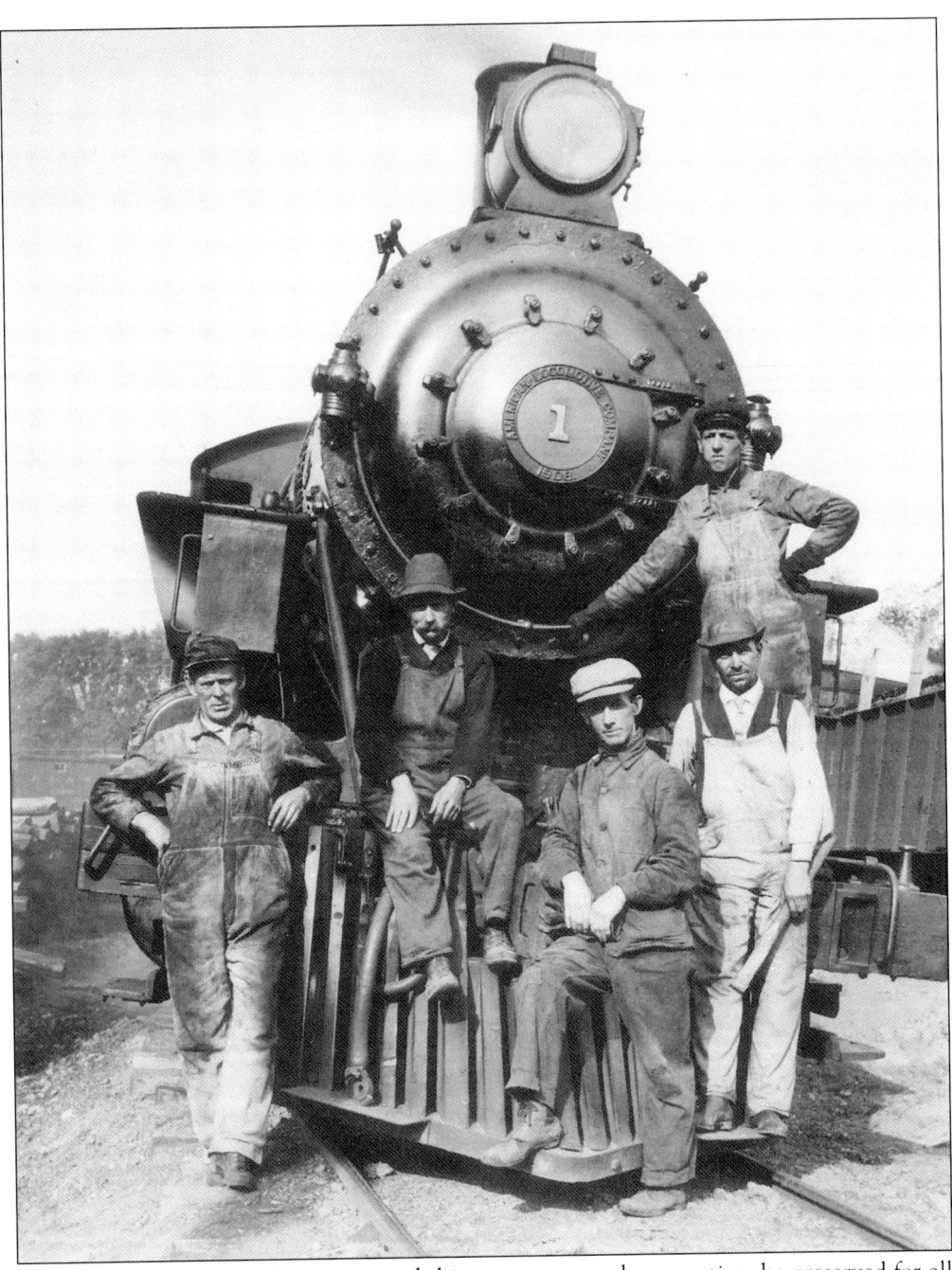

When Frederick Senton Curtiss exposed this scene onto a glass negative, he preserved for all time a classic vignette of the Morristown & Erie train crew at Morristown on May 1, 1913. One look at this photo is all it takes to feel the pride that these men obviously had in their jobs, locomotives, and the company that employed them. The paint on No. 1 gleams in the morning sun, and the men have a full day of road freight work ahead of them. From left to right are Tom Meslar, engineer; Charlie Koelsh, conductor; Barney Higgins, brakeman; Marve Tyson, brakeman; and Fred Rommiehs, fireman. (Courtesy of Morristown/Morris Township Library, Curtiss Collection.)

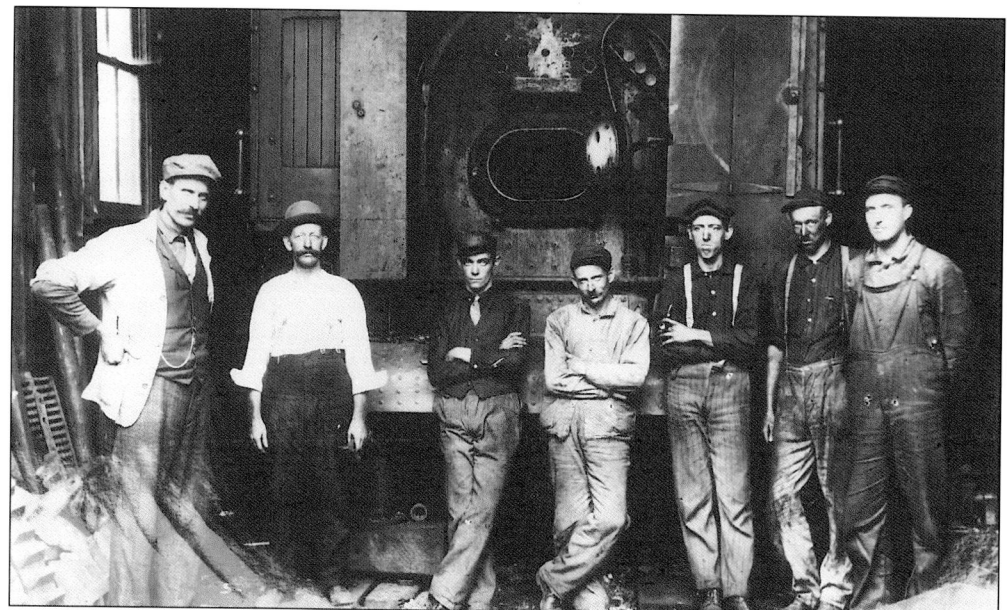

We are inside the shop at Morristown, c. 1915, as the men oblige the photographer by holding still for the powder flash. Ira Meslar stands to the extreme left; Fred Rommiehs is third from right; and Oscar Erickson is on the right. The shopmen are giving a complete overhaul to what appears to be newly acquired 2-8-0 No. 6. (Photo by Hugh Boutell; courtesy of Railroad Museum of Pennsylvania (PHMC) Collection.)

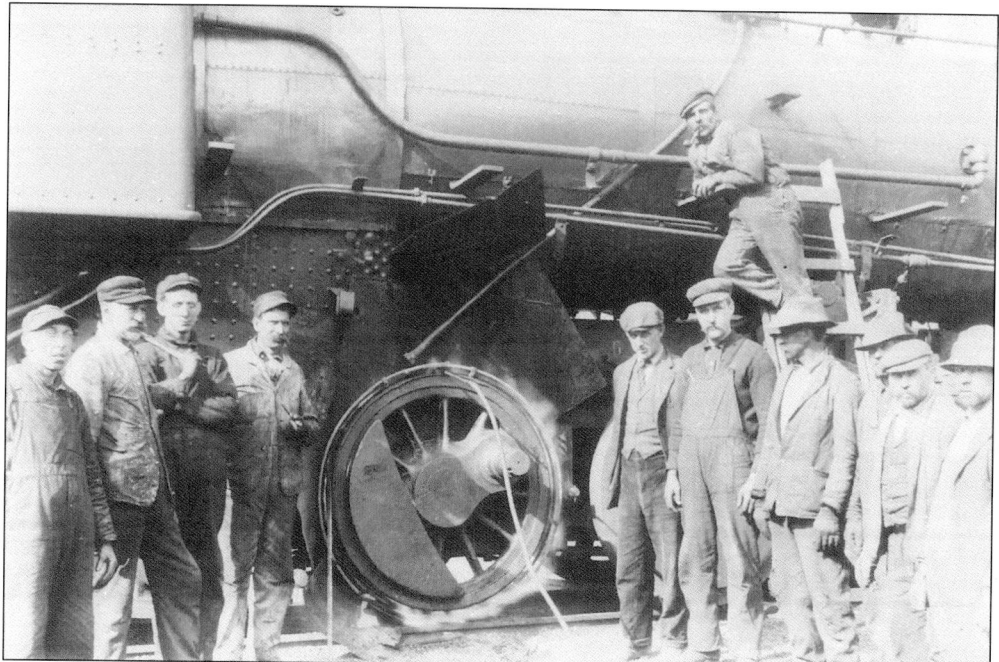

The shop crew stands for their portrait at Morristown on March 29, 1913, after they finished refitting a new steel tire to the rear driving wheel of No. 1. When tires needed to be replaced, the only way to fit a new one on was to expand it with a ring of fire, and then force fit it on with sledge hammers. (Courtesy of Morristown/Morris Township Library, Curtiss Collection.)

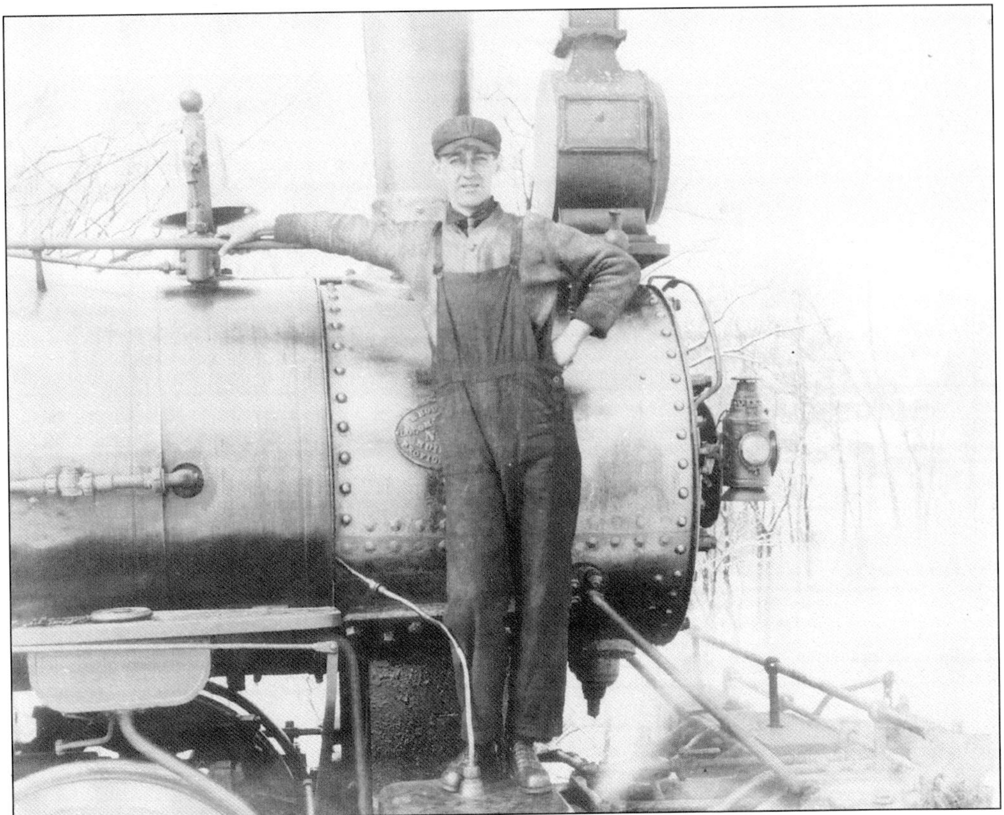

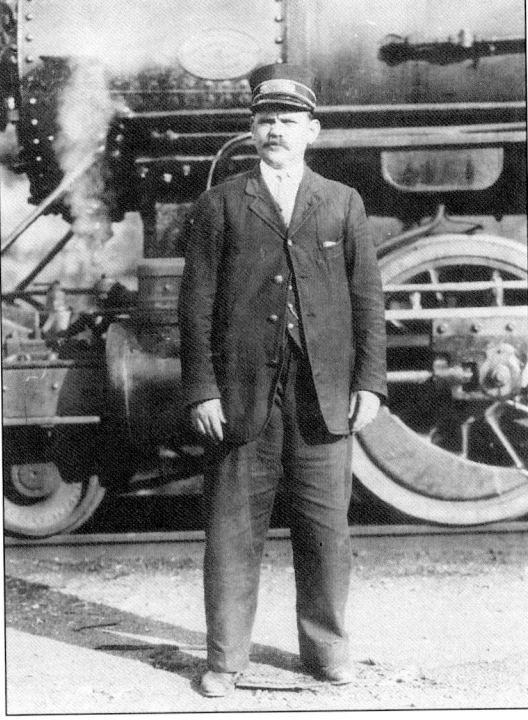

Fireman Henry Brown has "The Dinky" hot and ready for the first run of the day to Essex Fells, so he has a minute or two to stand for his portrait with No. 2 at Morristown on February 4, 1913. According to Henry's account, he was the engineer on the M&E's final passenger run on April 28, 1928. (Courtesy of Morristown/Morris Township Library, Curtiss Collection.)

On August 30, 1913, Conductor Halmagh (Ham) Ryerson took his turn and posed for the camera alongside No. 2 at Morristown. Ham started working for the M&E in 1904 and was well known along the route and very popular with the local children. After passenger service was discontinued, Ham continued his conductor's position on the freight train until he retired in 1942. (Courtesy of Morristown/Morris Township Library, Curtiss Collection.)

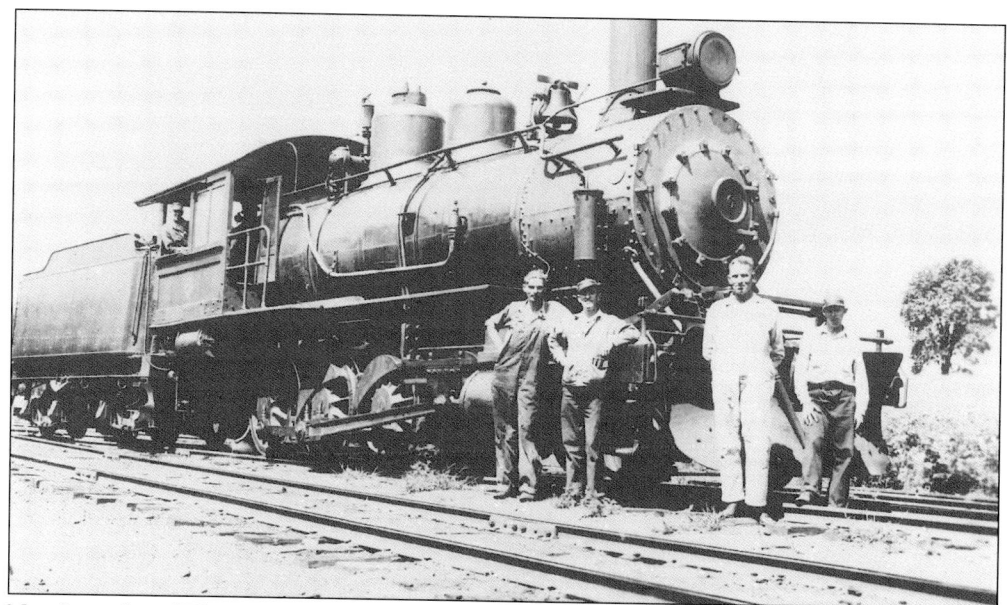

No. 6 stands at Whippany with the freight crew in October 1933. In the cab is engineer Tom Meslar. Standing alongside the locomotive in front of the distinctive snow plow pilot are, from left to right, Jerry Miller, fireman; Ham Ryerson, conductor; Superintendent Ira Meslar, and Howard Roff, brakeman. (Courtesy of California State Railroad Museum, Railway and Locomotive Historical Society Collection.)

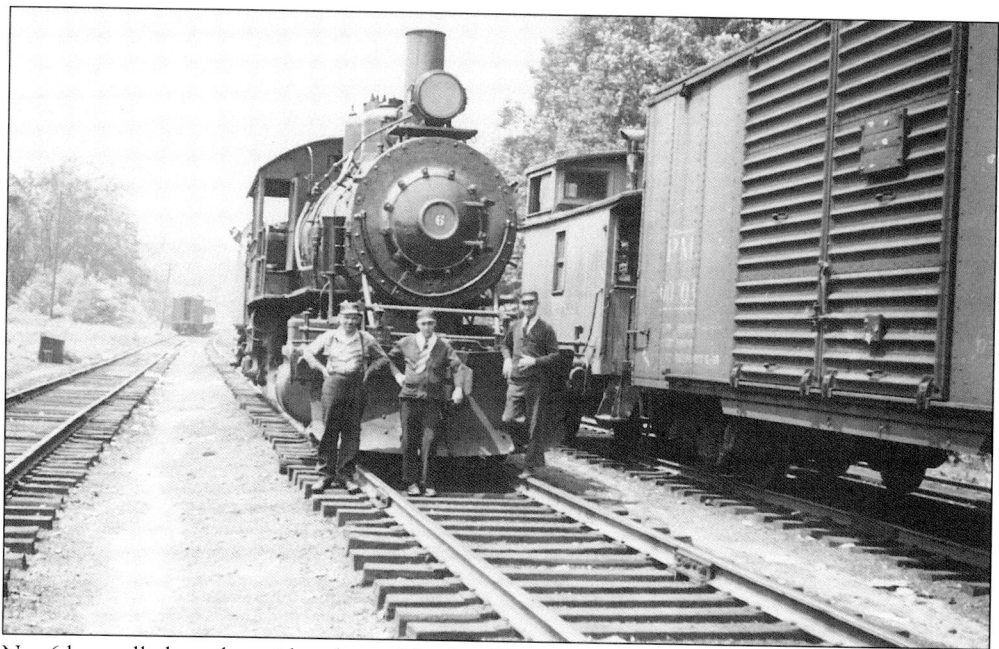

No. 6 has pulled up alongside caboose No. 1 at Essex Fells in May 1936, and Tom Meslar (left), Howard Roff, and Henry Keyes (right) smile for the camera. About this time, Arthur McEwan became president of the railroad, and, although not as familiar with the operation as his late brother Richard, he successfully led the M&E out of the Depression and into the Second World War. (Collection of Steven Hepler.)

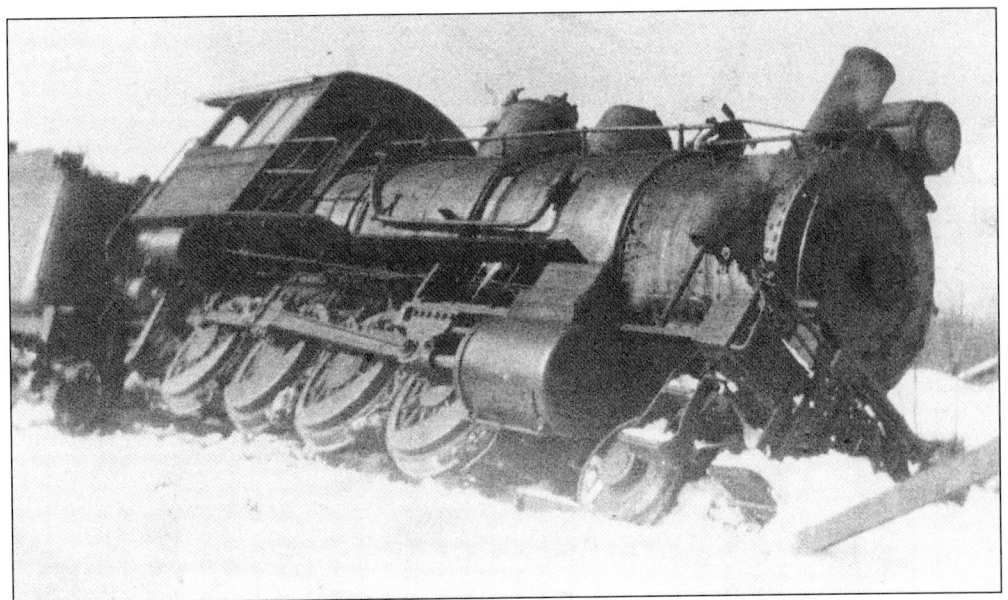

Railroads have an excellent ability to deal with unfavorable weather conditions, but this derailment involving No. 6 at Morristown was caused by frozen snow piled up in the flangeways at a road crossing. Even though 6 was equipped with steam jets used to melt snow and ice, as well as a plow, she still came to grief as witnessed in this 1940 winter scene. (Courtesy of Whippany Railway Museum Collection.)

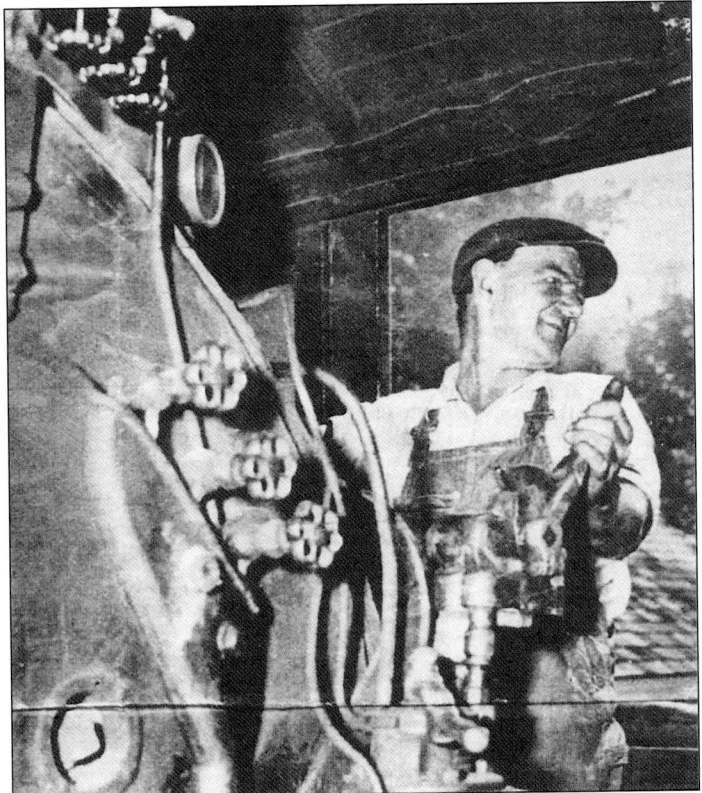

Jerry Miller, who started his career on the M&E in 1912, usually held down the locomotive fireman's position, but, on this day in September 1940, he is seen at the throttle of No. 6 switching cars at Whippany. One year later, Miller would suffer a fatal heart attack after filling his locomotive's tender with water from the Whippany tank. (Collection of Steven Hepler.)

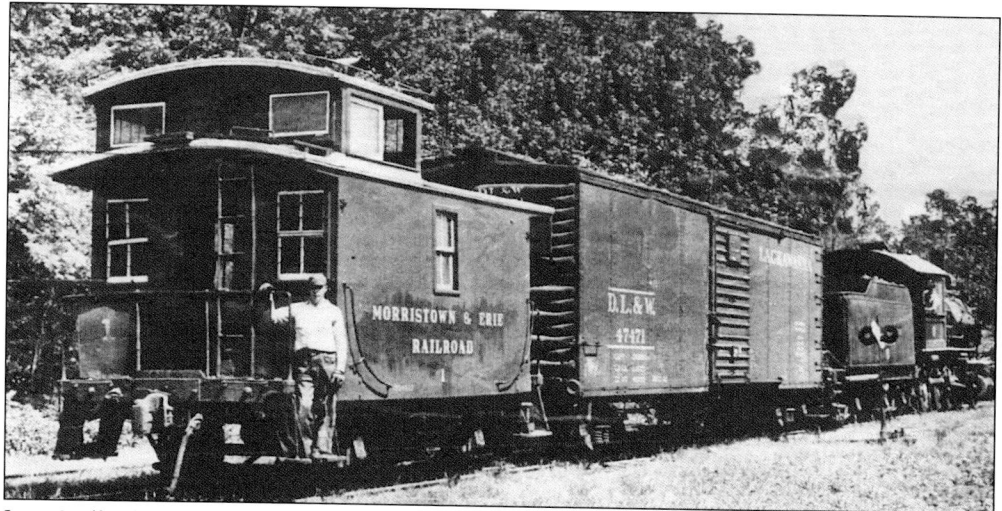

Jerry Miller has brought this short little train to a halt at Whippany so the camera can record the scene on this day in September 1940. On the steps of the caboose is brakeman Howard Roff, who began his career with the M&E in 1926. In the late 1950s, Howard became the regular engineer until he passed away in the mid-1960s. (Collection of Steven Hepler.)

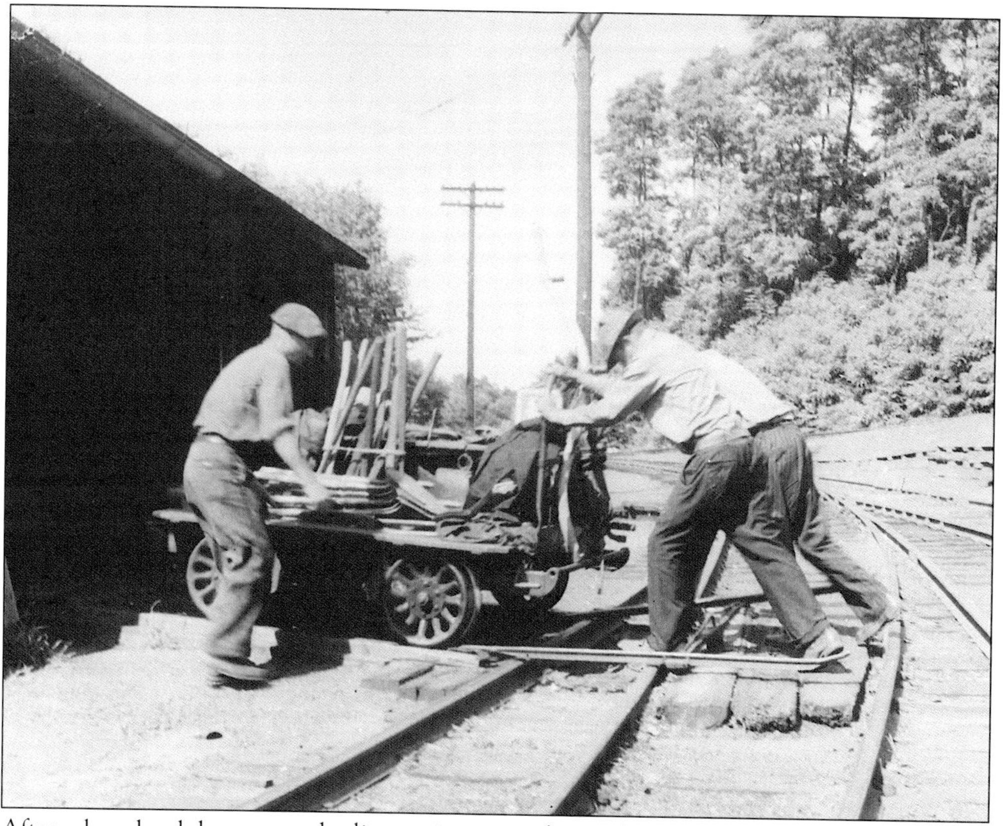

After a long hard day out on the line maintaining the track and right-of-way, the M&E track crew returns Motor Car No. 3 to its shed at Morristown on April 8, 1942. (Courtesy of Donald Van Court.)

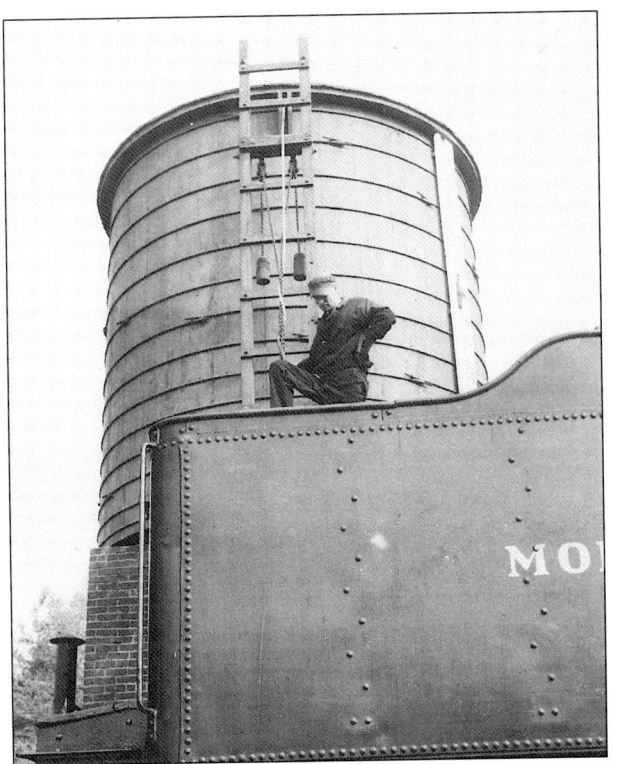

Harold Meslar started working for the M&E in 1917. During the Depression, he was hostler and night watchman at Morristown. He is seen here watering a locomotive at the Whippany tank on July 1, 1942. Harold had taken the fireman's position after Jerry Miller collapsed and died at this same location in the summer of 1941. Harold later became engineer in August 1945 when his uncle, Tom Meslar, retired. (Courtesy of Donald Van Court.)

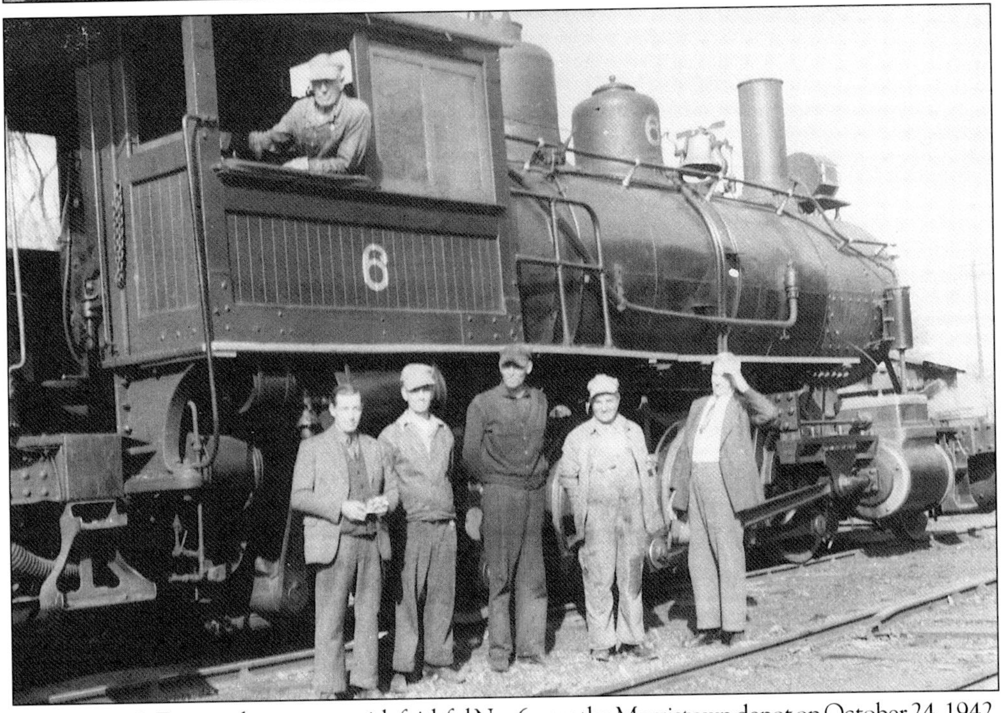

Morristown & Erie employees pose with faithful No. 6 near the Morristown depot on October 24, 1942. In the cab is engineer Tom Meslar, and on the ground, from left to right, are Howard Roff, Henry Keyes, Harold Meslar, Tom Gee, and Ira Meslar. (Courtesy of Donald Van Court.)

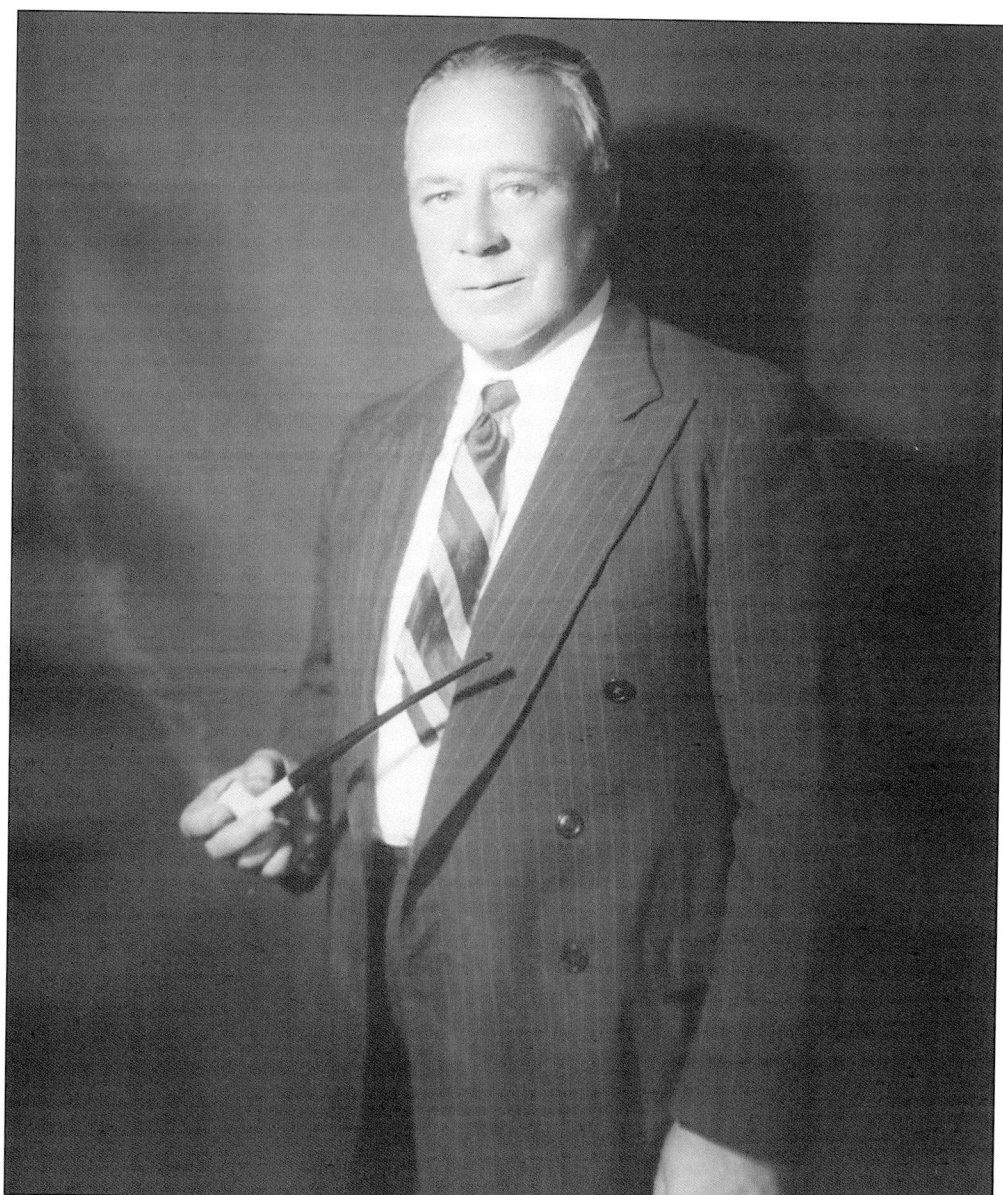

Richard W. McEwan Jr., son of the Morristown & Erie's late president, Richard Sr., became president of the railroad in 1943 after his uncle Arthur passed away. Under Richard Jr.'s leadership, the M&E enjoyed increases in traffic following World War II when an extraordinary housing and construction boom was undertaken throughout the region. Following the building period and the postwar years, the M&E continued to move ahead with Richard at the head of the company. Steam power was retired when a new diesel locomotive arrived on the property, and new industry continued to settle in along the M&E's rails. In September 1961, Richard became chairman of the railroad; however, in 1963, he resumed the presidency until the end of 1963. In later years, he would remain quite active as a stockholder. A colorful era in Morris County industry ended when Richard W. McEwan Jr. passed away in November 1983. (Courtesy of Whippany Railway Museum Collection from the estate of Richard W. McEwan Jr.)

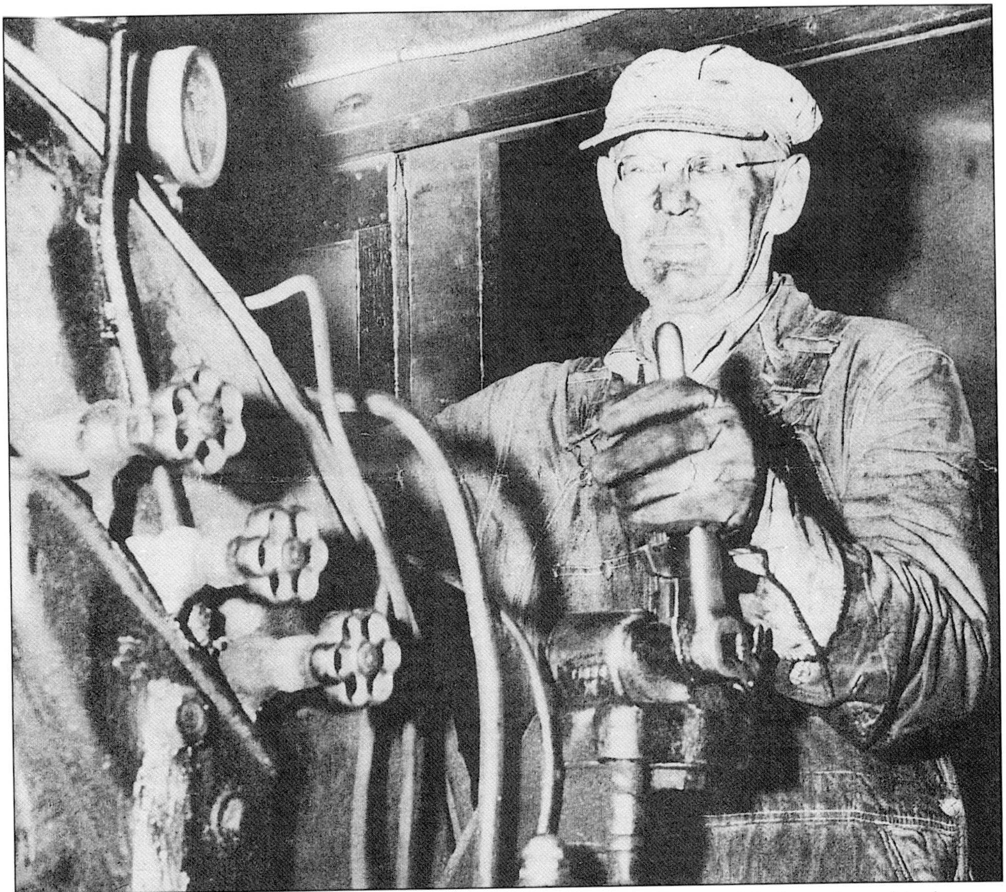

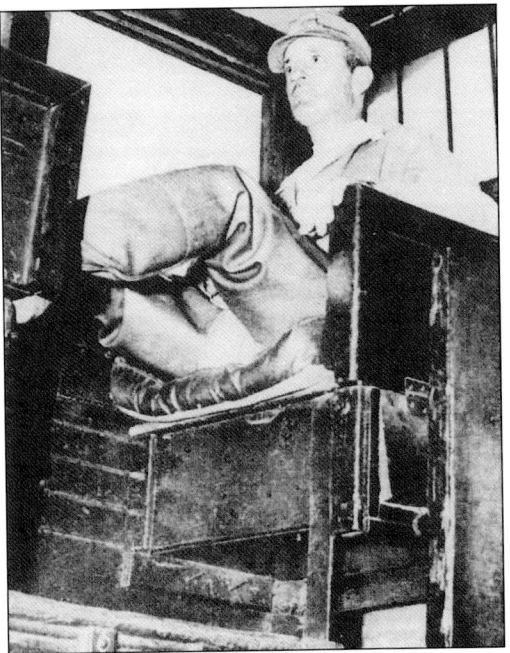

Engineer Thomas Meslar, whose kind disposition was such that he would stop his train to allow automobiles to cross the tracks, started working for the Whippany River Railroad as a watchman in July 1895. He later became a locomotive fireman, and, when he retired as engineer on August 15, 1945, he had 50 years of service with the railroad. (Collection of Steven Hepler.)

One of the pleasant sides of life on a caboose is to sit in the cupola and watch the world roll by. Conductor Henry (Heinie) F. Keyes, who started with the M&E in 1925, checks his consist for any indication of trouble from his perch in caboose No. 1 in May 1943. (Collection of Steven Hepler.)

The caboose was the last car on every freight train. It was the crew's living quarters, office, kitchen, bedroom, and toilet. Here, M&E brakeman Tom Gee is seen warming his lunch over the stove of caboose No. 1. Although the photo is dated May 1943, the weather must have been unusually inclement judging by Tom's outfit and the need for a fire in the stove. (Collection of Steven Hepler.)

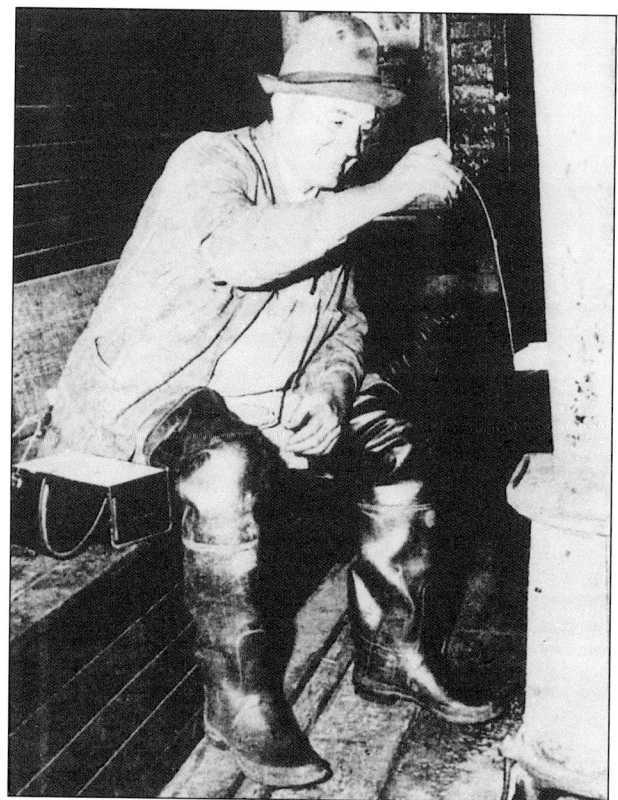

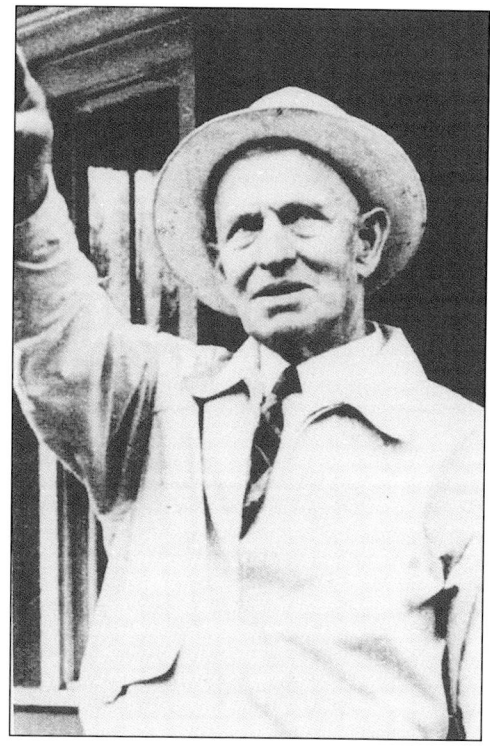

Ira V. Meslar was the M&E's beloved superintendent who hired out on the Whippany River Railroad in 1895 as a brakeman, and he later worked as conductor. Ira enjoyed telling a story about how, in the early days, whenever his train arrived at a bridge near Monroe, he had to go ahead and hold up a tie on end under the bridge to better support the structure while the engine passed over. (Collection of Steven Hepler.)

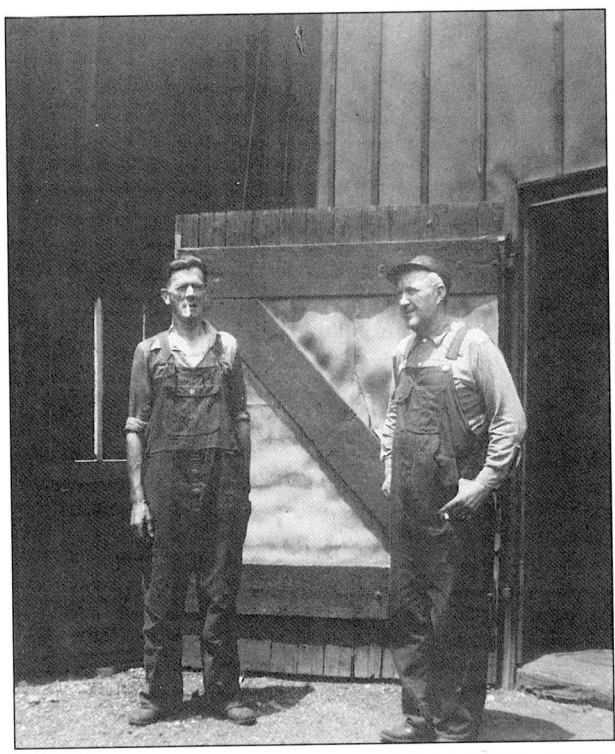

Phil Dahill, machinist (left), and Oscar Erickson, master mechanic (right), take a cigarette break at the Morristown shop on June 16, 1945. These two men were responsible for keeping the M&E's steam engines in top condition for many years. Oscar started as a machinist in 1913 and retired with the arrival of diesel No. 14 in 1952. (Photo by Thomas T. Taber III; courtesy of Railroad Museum of Pennsylvania (PHMC) Collection.)

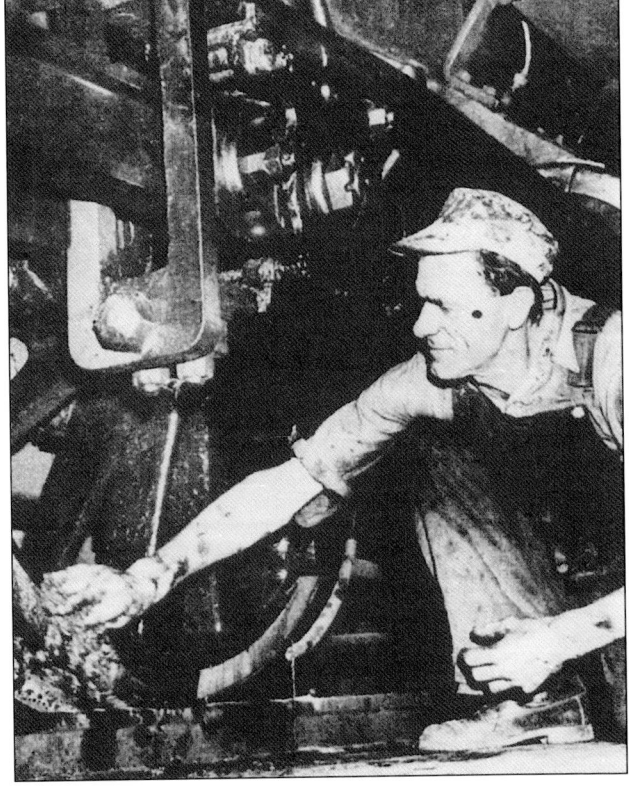

Using cotton waste material soaked in kerosene, machinist Phil Dahill cleans the rims of the driving wheels on one of the M&E's steam locomotives in this May 1943 photo. It was customary for the engines to be thoroughly cleaned and lubricated at the Morristown enginehouse after a long day out on the road. (Collection of Steven Hepler.)

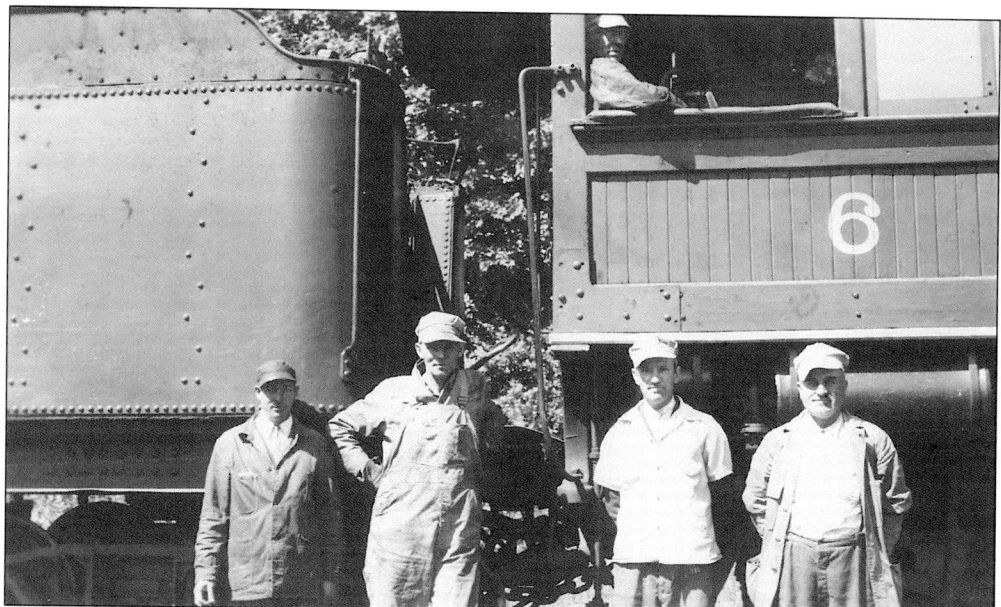

Tom Meslar peers down from the cab of No. 6 on September 18, 1943 as, from left to right, Howard Roff, brakeman; Harold Meslar, fireman; Henry Keyes, conductor; and Tom Gee, brakeman line up alongside the engine at Essex Fells. (Collection of Steven Hepler.)

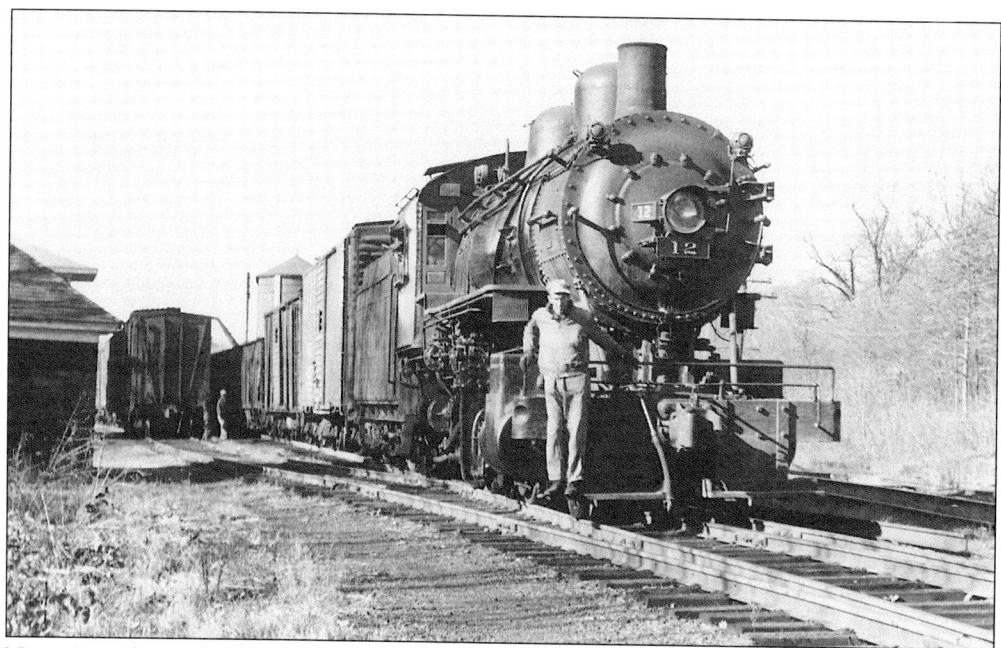

No. 12 works the Whippany yard on November 27, 1946. Brakeman Ken Jones rides the footboards as the train makes its way past the maintenance shanty. "Jonesie" worked on the track gang and was a locomotive hostler and night watchman before he was promoted to brakeman in August 1945. In later years, Ken would be the engineer of the M&E's diesels in the 1960s and 1970s. (Courtesy of Donald Van Court.)

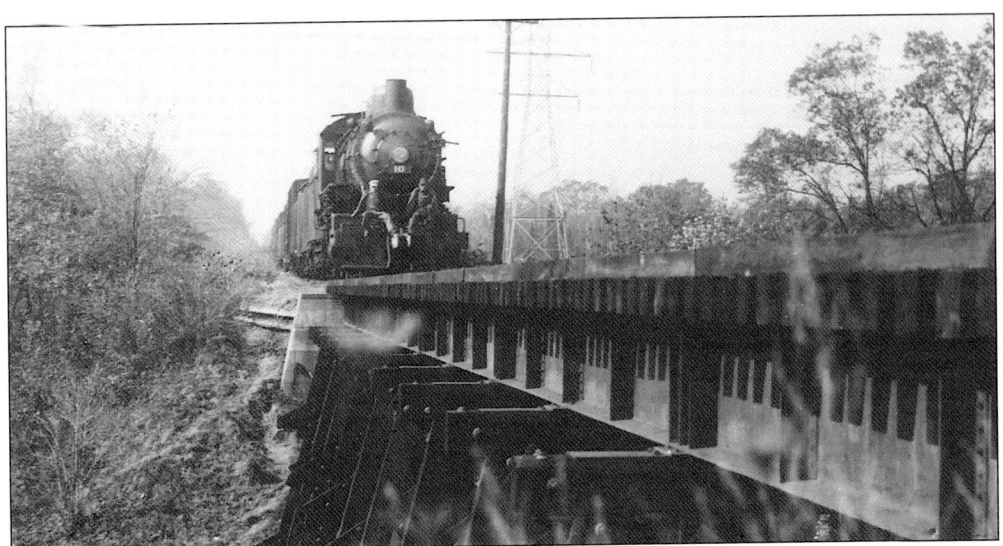

It appears to be a pleasant spring day as No. 10 makes its way across the Passaic River trestle near Livingston, New Jersey, in this c. 1948 photograph. The conductor and brakeman are no doubt enjoying a refreshing breeze as they ride the pilot beam of the locomotive, but this practice would be frowned upon today by inspectors of the Federal Railroad Administration. (Courtesy of Railroad Avenue Enterprises.)

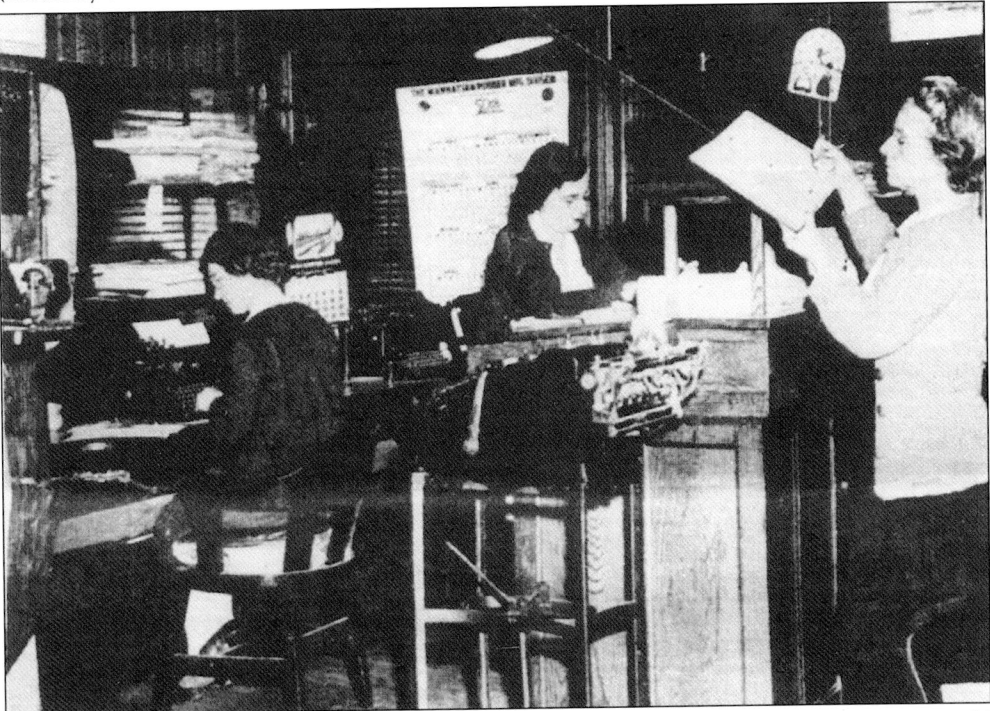

On the second floor of the M&E's Whippany station and general office, three women could be found working on accounts in May 1943. From left to right are Ethel Anderson, Jeanette Anderson (a car accountant who started in 1916), and Margaret Dooling (a bookkeeper who was hired in 1918). Their office decor consisted of rolltop desks, wood flooring, and no air conditioning. (Collection of Steven Hepler.)

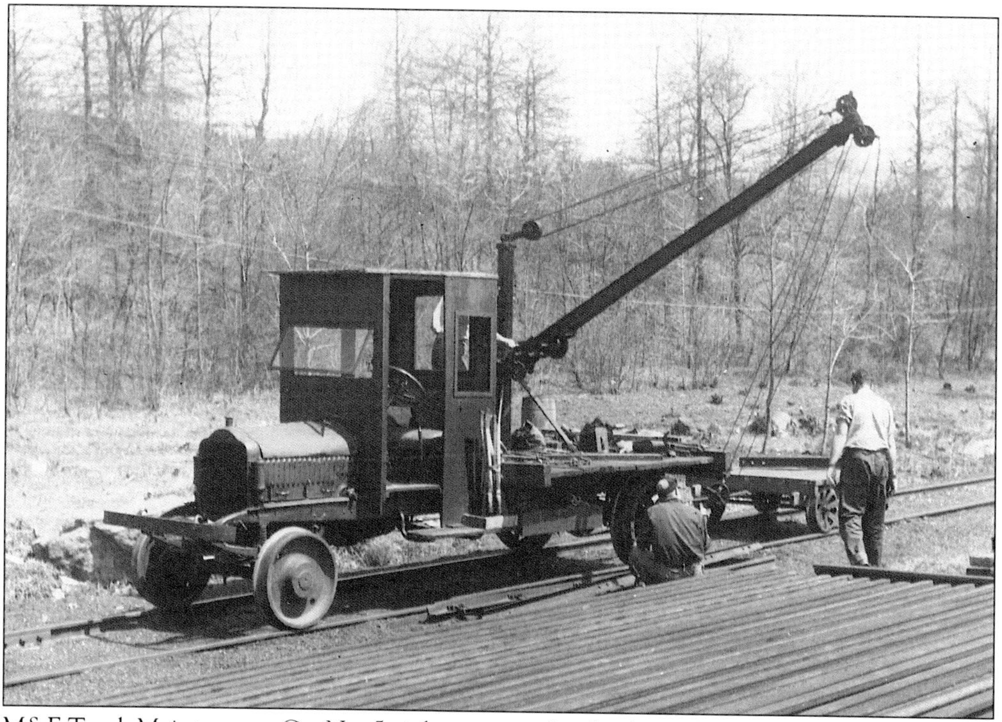

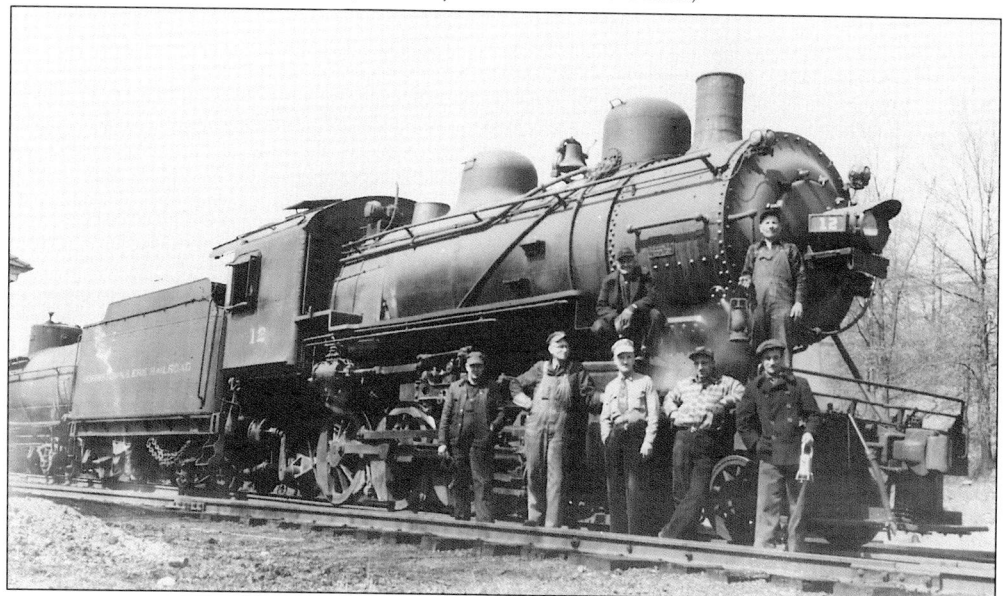

M&E Track Maintenance Car No. 5 picks up a supply of rail at Whippany for construction of a new switch. The vehicle, fashioned from former Railbus No. 10, features a stylish new wooden cab in this April 15, 1949 view. (Courtesy of Donald Van Court.)

The crew gathers around No. 12 for this snapshot at Whippany on March 23, 1951. From left to right are Howard Roff, fireman; Harold Meslar, engineer; Tom Gee, brakeman (above); Henry Keyes, conductor (below); Frank Studley, brakeman; Alex Hominick, Whippany groundskeeper (above), and Joe Dandino, brakeman (below). (Photo by Thomas T. Taber III; courtesy of Railroad Museum of Pennsylvania (PHMC) Collection.)

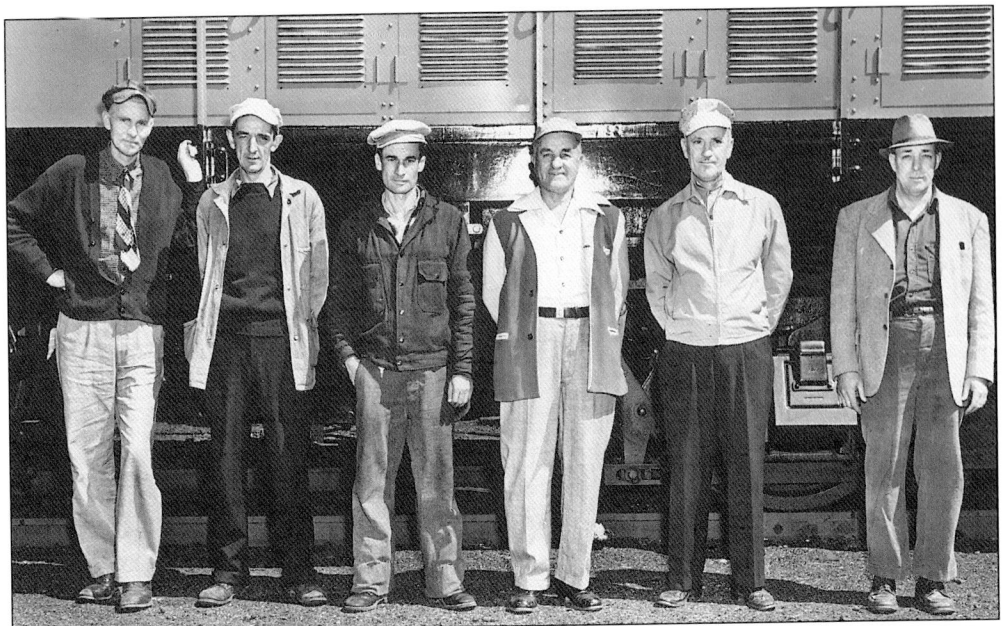

It is April 29, 1952, and the Morristown & Erie's new diesel locomotive No. 14 has arrived at Whippany. The proud crew is asked to pose for the news cameras and this is the result. From left to right are Harold Meslar, engineer; Ken Jones, brakeman; Joe Dandino, brakeman; Tommy Gee, brakeman; Henry (Heinie) Keyes, conductor; and Howard Roff, fireman. (Courtesy of Whippany Railway Museum Collection.)

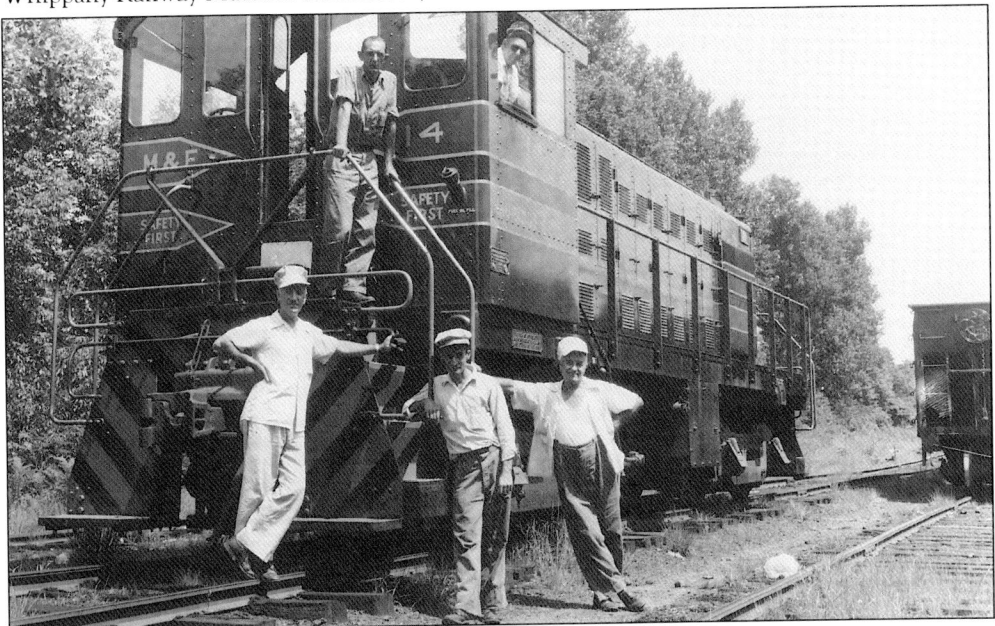

Still shiny and new, No. 14 is seen at Essex Fells on August 11, 1952. Note how the steam-era denim overalls have been replaced. The diesel was cleaner; that's for sure. From left to right are Henry Keyes, conductor; Ken Jones, fireman (on steps); Howard Roff, engineer; Joe Dandino, brakeman; and Tommy Gee, brakeman. (Photo by Thomas T. Taber III; courtesy of Railroad Museum of Pennsylvania (PHMC) Collection.)

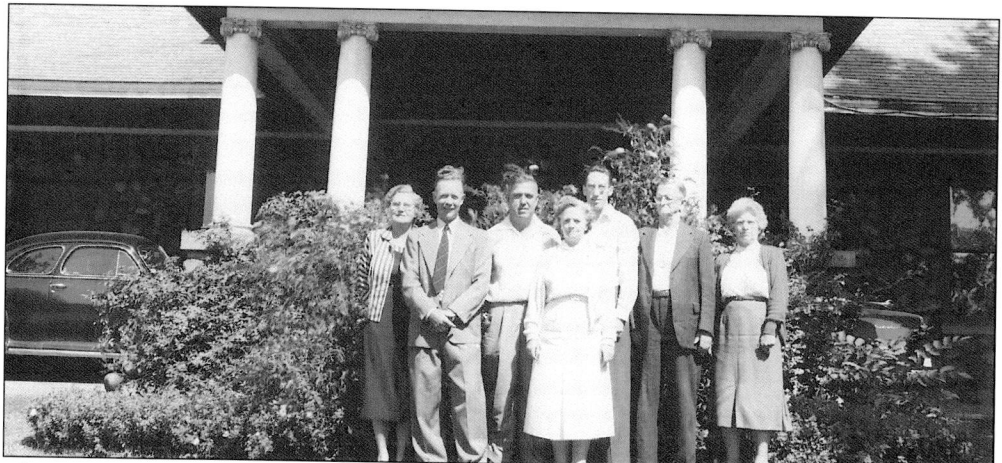

The M&E's general office staff stand in front of the Whippany station portecochere on September 13, 1955. From left to right are Jeanette Anderson, car accountant; Arthur Vreeland, auditor; Bob Griffith, freight agent; Theresa Price, clerk; Tom Peterson, assistant agent; Fletcher Williams, superintendent; and Margaret Dooling, bookkeeper. (Photo by Thomas T. Taber III; courtesy of Railroad Museum of Pennsylvania (PHMC) Collection.)

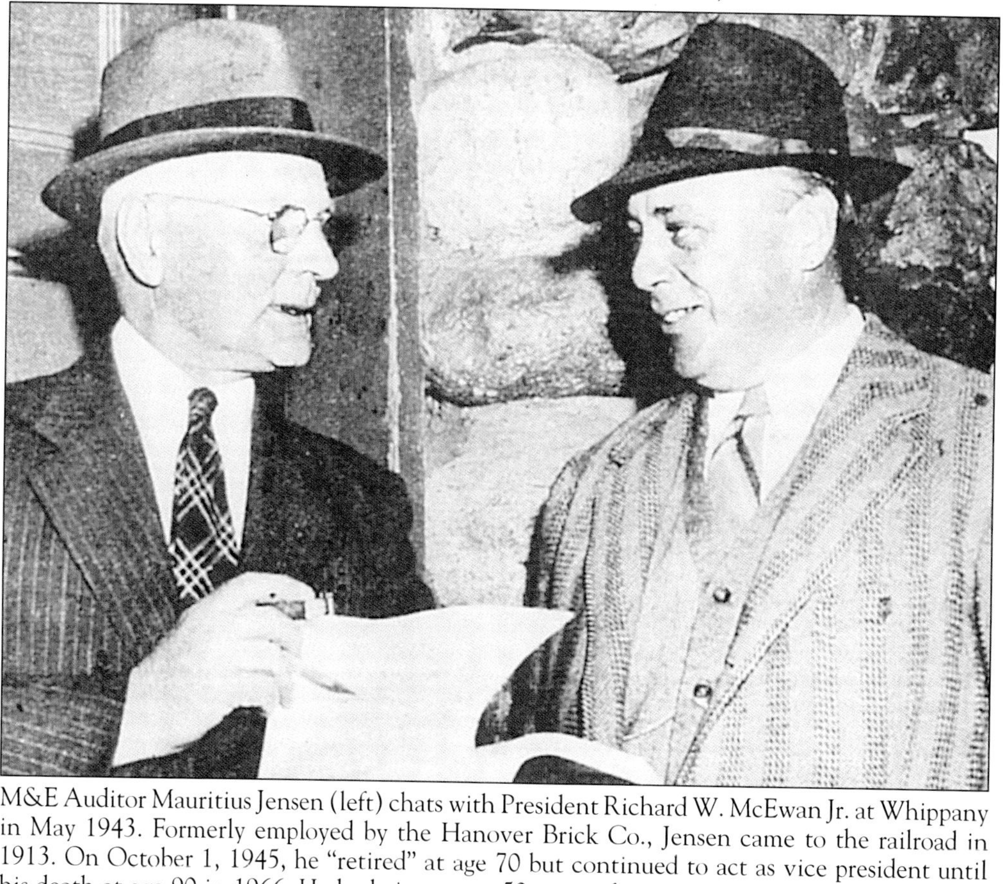

M&E Auditor Mauritius Jensen (left) chats with President Richard W. McEwan Jr. at Whippany in May 1943. Formerly employed by the Hanover Brick Co., Jensen came to the railroad in 1913. On October 1, 1945, he "retired" at age 70 but continued to act as vice president until his death at age 90 in 1966. He had given over 50 years of service to the railroad. (Collection of Steven Hepler.)

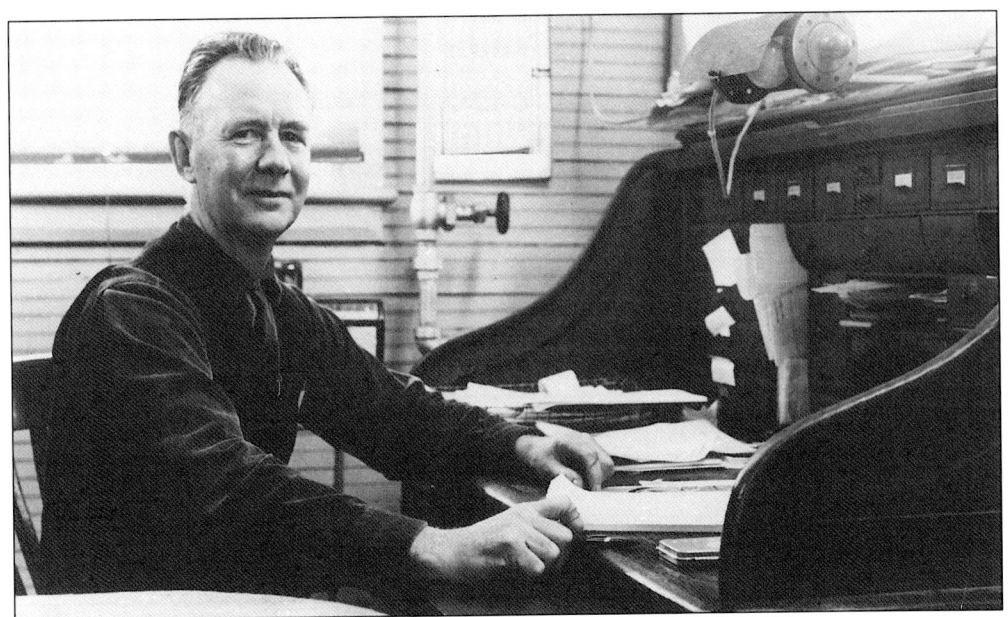

Arthur B. Vreeland, M&E general manager, is seated at his rolltop desk at Whippany in September 1962. Starting as a clerk in 1927, he rose through the ranks of the railroad and, after his return from WW II service, he became auditor when Mauritius Jensen retired. One of the last of the old-time employees, Art was admired for his devotion, loyalty, and diligence. (Courtesy of Railroad Museum of Pennsylvania (PHMC) Collection.)

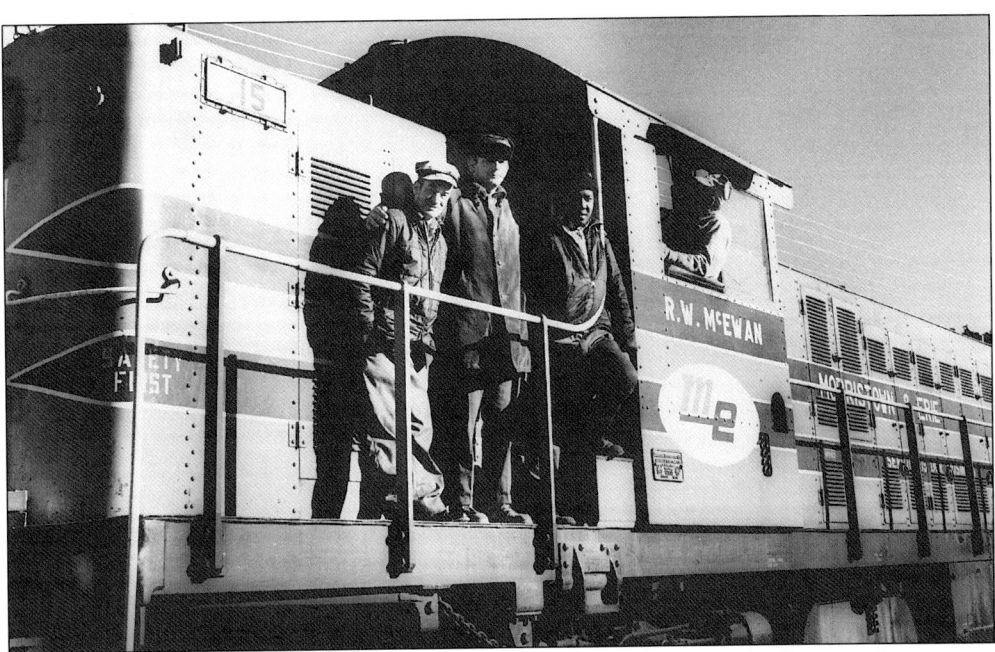

This photo of the M&E freight crew was taken sometime in 1970. Standing on the running boards of No. 15 are, from left to right, Joe Dandino, conductor; Frank McKenna, brakeman; and Roger Cozart, brakeman. In the cab is engineer Ken Jones, who was notoriously camera shy but always a friendly gentleman. (Courtesy of Morristown & Erie Railway.)

Six
THE STEAM ERA PASSES

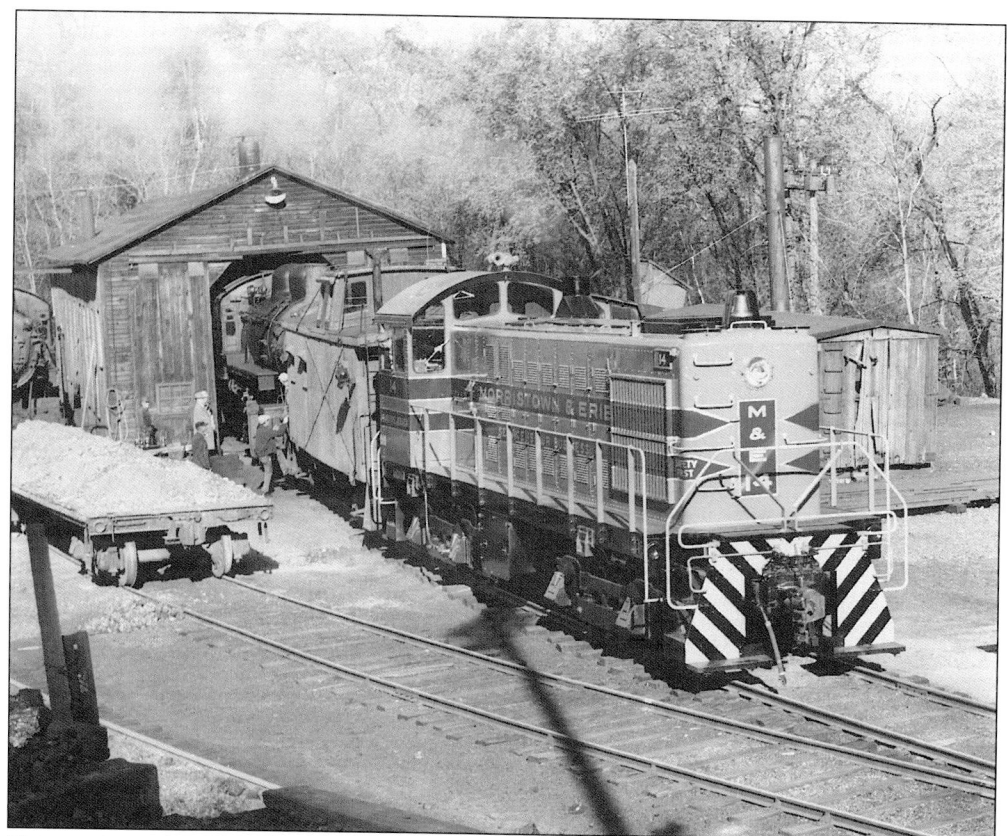

Using caboose No. 2 as an idler car, engineer Harold Meslar guides the Morristown & Erie's new diesel locomotive No. 14 slowly backward as one of the now-retired steam engines is placed into the darkness of the enginehouse on the diesel's second day of service, April 29, 1952. For the veteran steamers, their active days were finally over. (Courtesy of Homer R. Hill.)

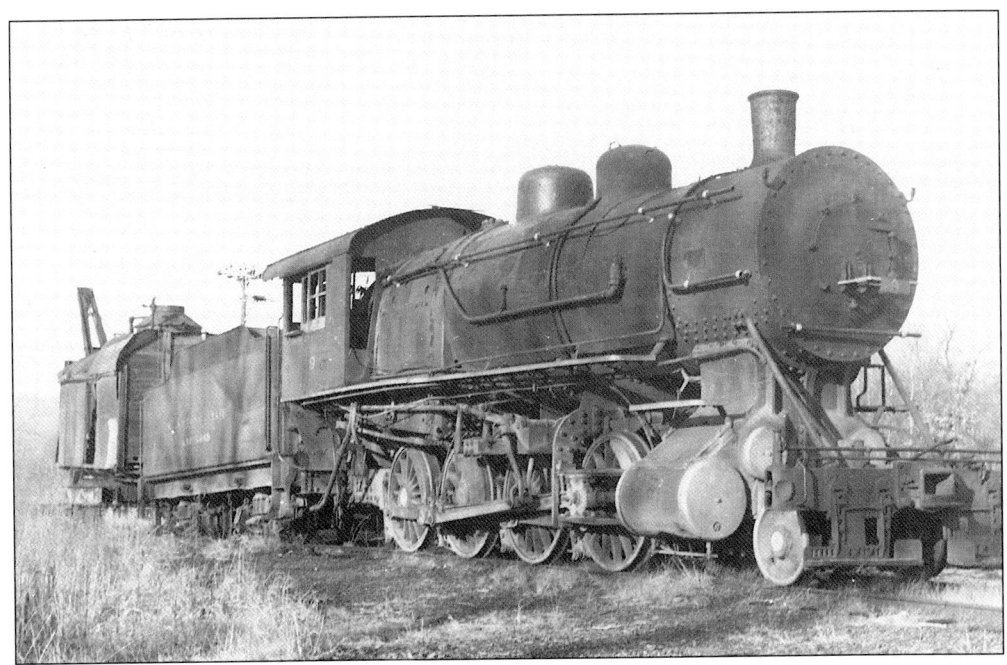

A forlorn No. 9 is stored dead near Cedar Knolls. Keeping the lonesome locomotive company is the Hanover Brick Company's old clamshell crane. On this 1946 Christmas Eve, perhaps the two old-timers were thinking of happier times. In January 1947, No. 9 was cut up for scrap, but the crane managed to survive until 1950 when it too was scrapped. (Courtesy of Donald Van Court.)

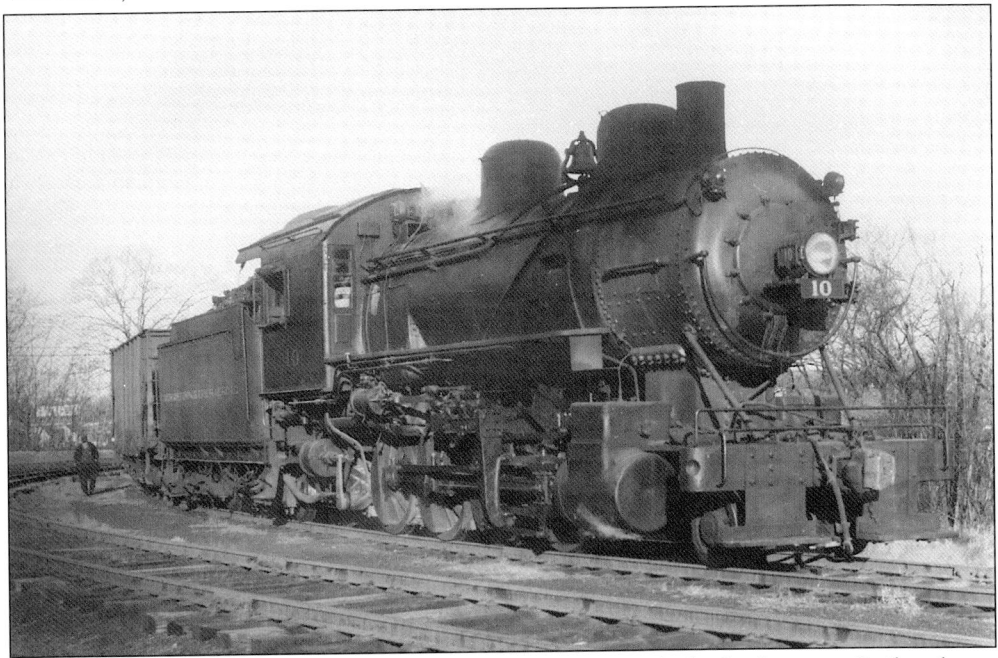

M&E No. 10 is seen switching the Morristown interchange with the Lackawanna Railroad, one week before being replaced by newly purchased diesel-electric switcher No. 14. This photo was taken in late April 1952. (Courtesy of Homer R. Hill.)

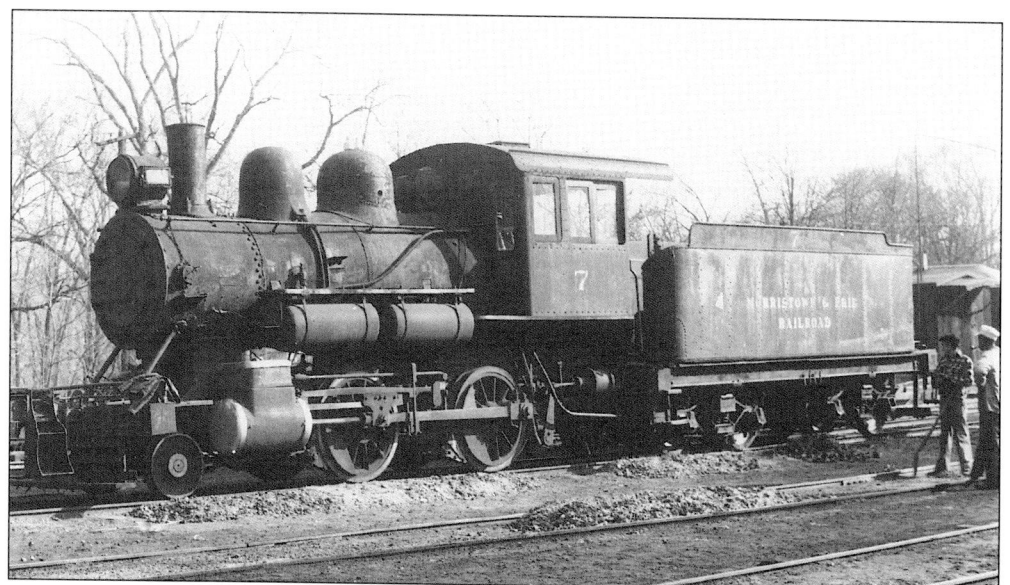

On April 8, 1952, having been declared surplus and obsolete by the M&E, engine No. 7 met its unfortunate fate. Here and in the next six photos are the wretched last hours of this classic little locomotive. At the time of scrapping, No. 7 had not been steamed up in over 14 years. This photo was taken at Morristown, one day before the engine was cut up. (Courtesy of Homer R. Hill.)

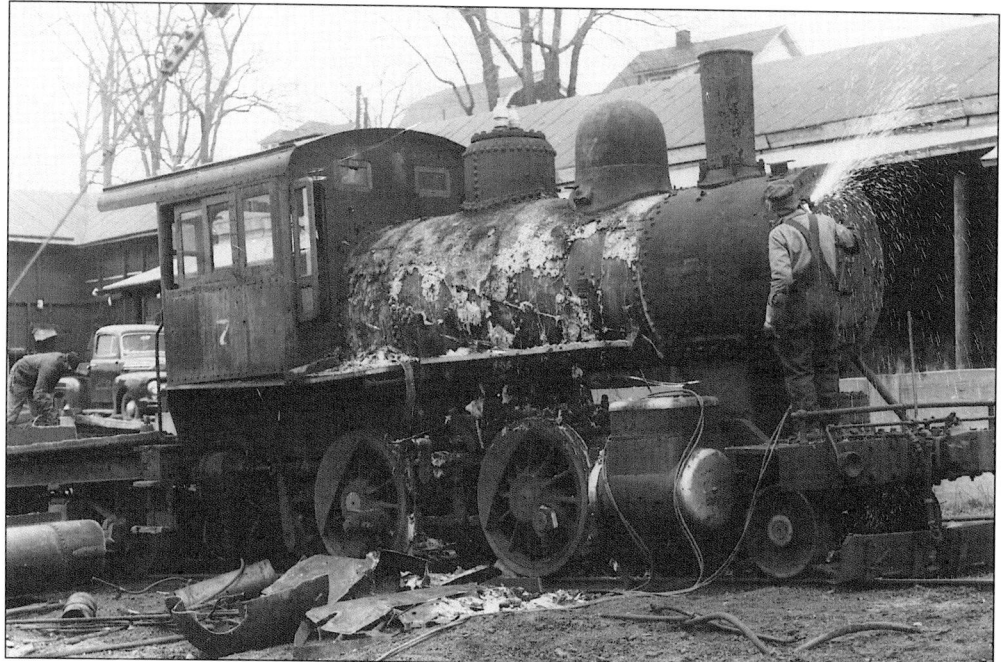

Before she was towed to the site where she would be destroyed, No. 7's bell, headlight, and whistle were removed from the engine and were kept as mementos by M&E president Richard W. McEwan Jr. Having been stripped of her boiler jacket and asbestos lagging, a workman is busy cutting apart No. 7's smokebox front, and another burner is dismantling the tender. (Courtesy of Homer R. Hill.)

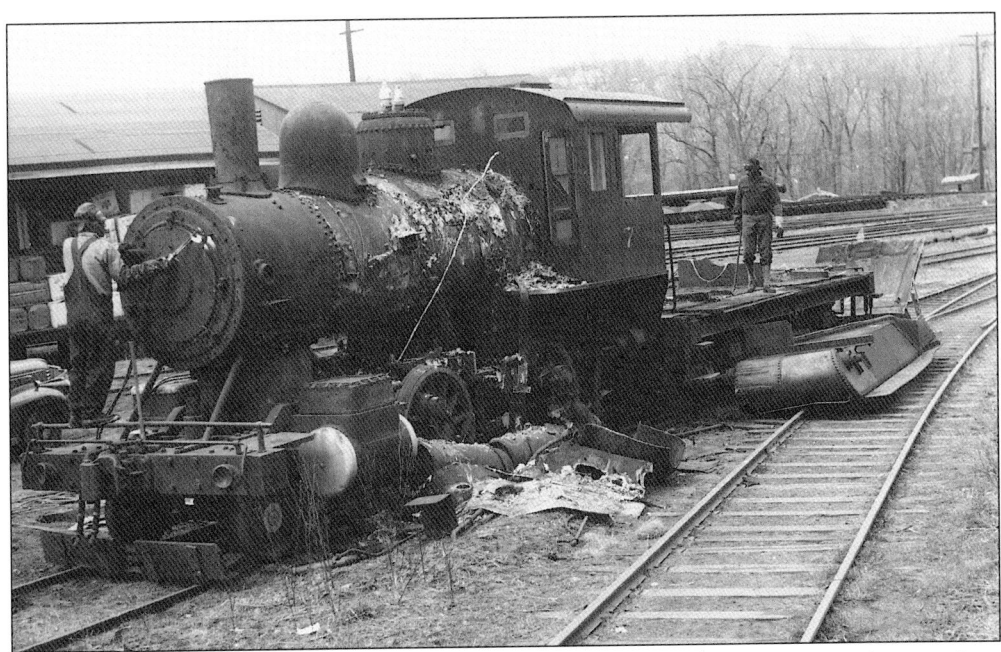

During scrapping, no concern is paid to riveted or welded joints. The engine is cut into sections suitable for transport to the scrapyard where it will once again be cut into pieces small enough to fit into the melting pots. (Courtesy of Homer R. Hill.)

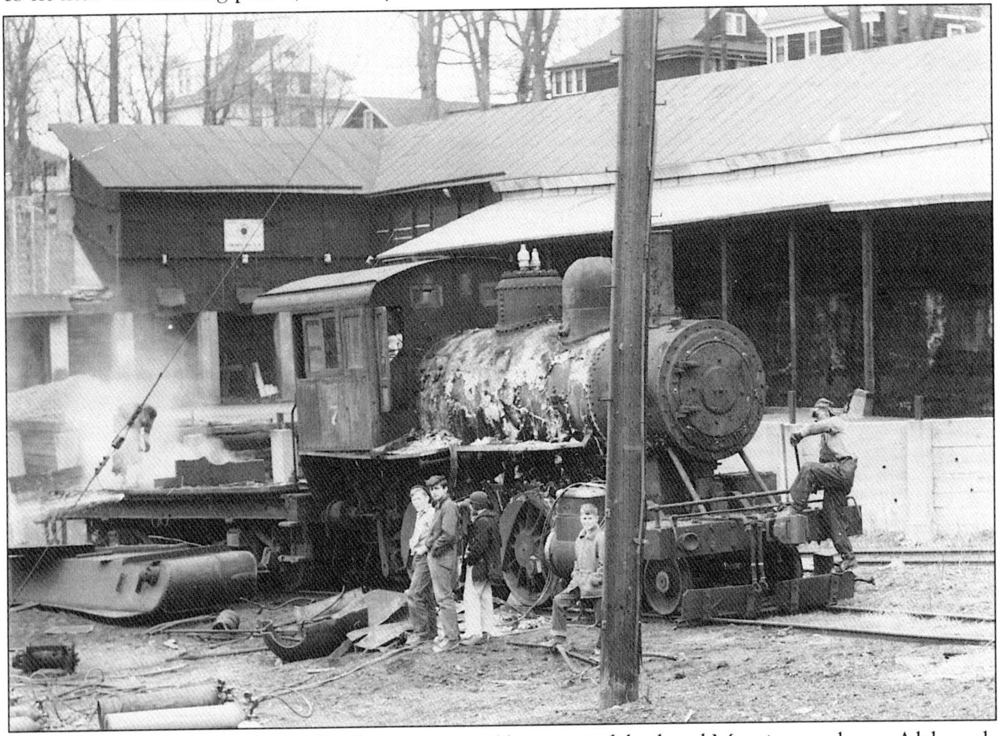

On the first day of scrapping, No. 7 was mourned by some of the local Morristown boys. Although only a machine of cast-iron and steel, in her last tortured hours, No. 7 seems to convey an image of intense suffering and pain. (Courtesy of Homer R. Hill.)

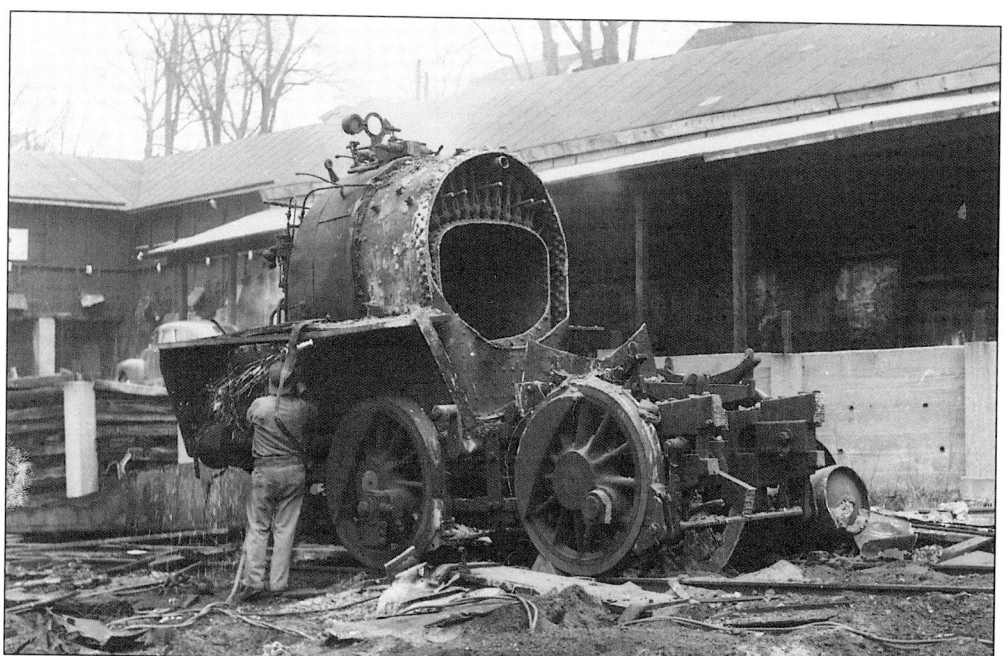

April 9, 1952, was the second day of scrapping. A burner goes to work on the cab floor supports. The major portion of No. 7's boiler, frame, and cab have already been butchered. The ground is littered with the remains of her valve gear and piping. (Courtesy of Homer R. Hill.)

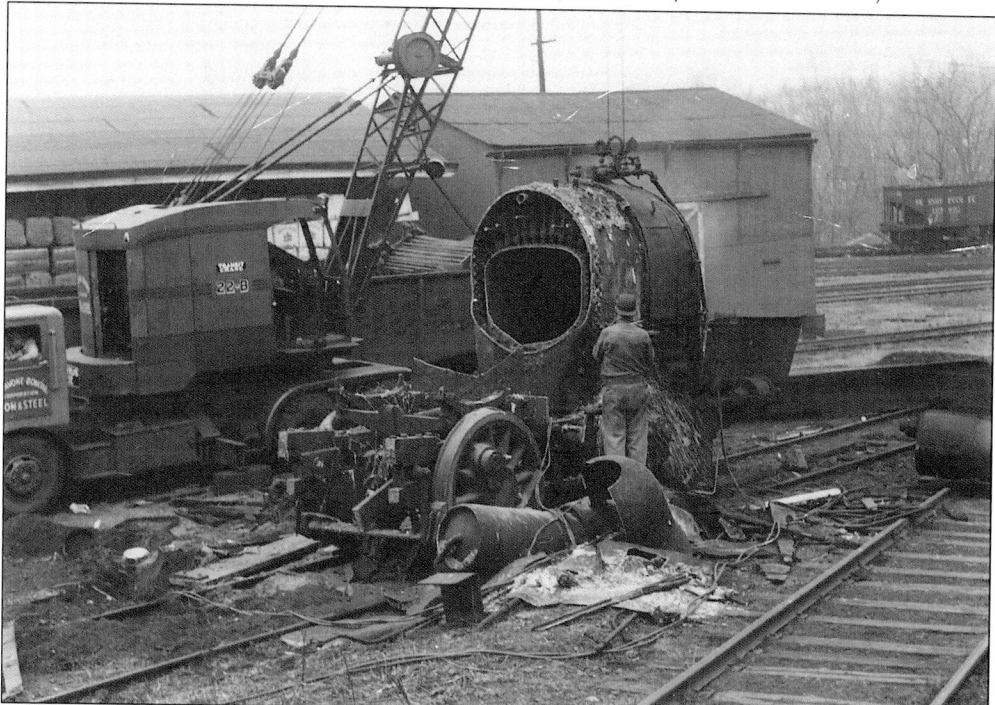

A crane loads the remains of No. 7 into a waiting gondola car. Here, the final section of boiler and firebox is about to be ripped from the frame and ready for its final trip to the steel mill. (Courtesy of Homer R. Hill.)

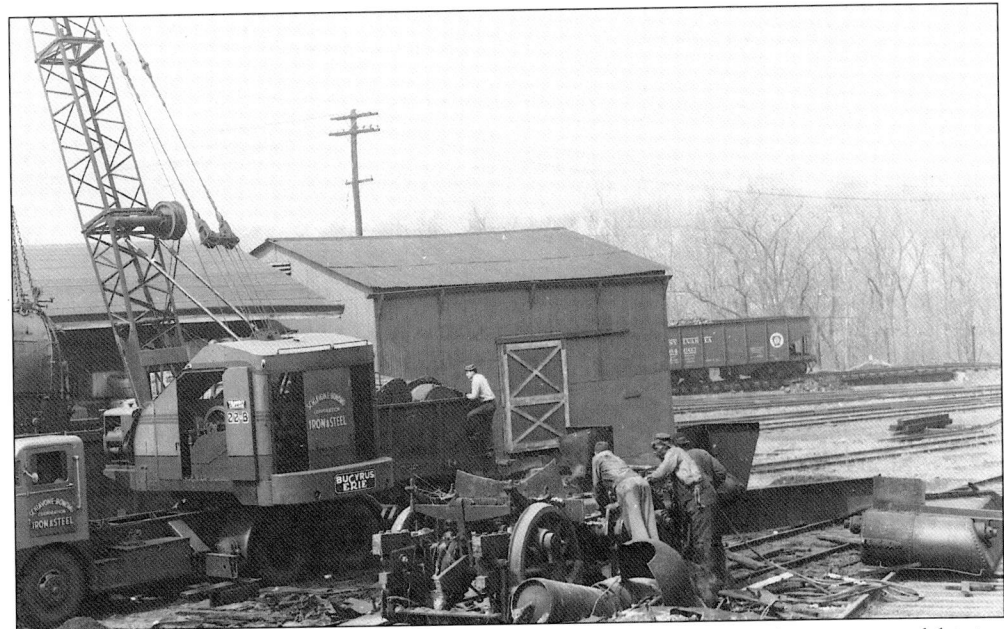

On April 9, 1952, after two days of work, the only pieces left of No. 7 are her two sets of driving wheels and part of the frame. Early in 1952 there was talk of preserving No. 7 along with bobber caboose No. 1 at Whippany, but it was not to be. The engine was consigned to the steel mill and was lost forever in endless bales of wire. (Courtesy of Homer R. Hill.)

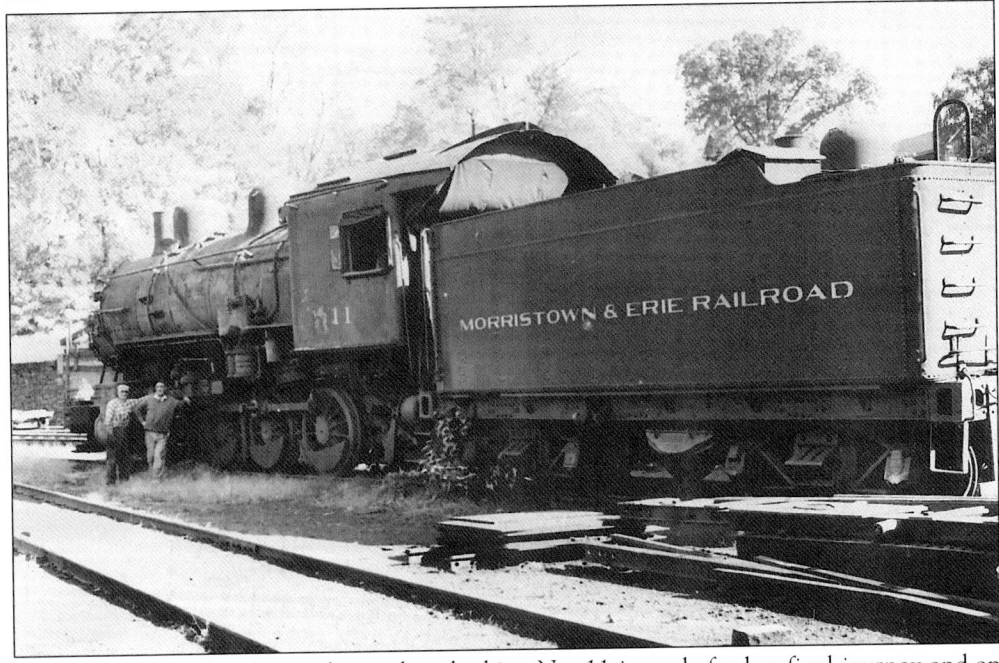

Seeming to know her fate, a despondent-looking No. 11 is ready for her final journey and an ominous meeting with the scrapper's torch. Standing alongside the locomotive, from left to right, are Henry Keyes and Frank Studley. Behind No. 11, Nos. 10 and 12 sleep out their final hours at Morristown in October 1955. No longer will cinders rain down along the route of the M&E. (Photo by Tony Russomanno; collection of Steven Hepler.)

Seven
THE DIESEL ERA . . . 1950s–60s

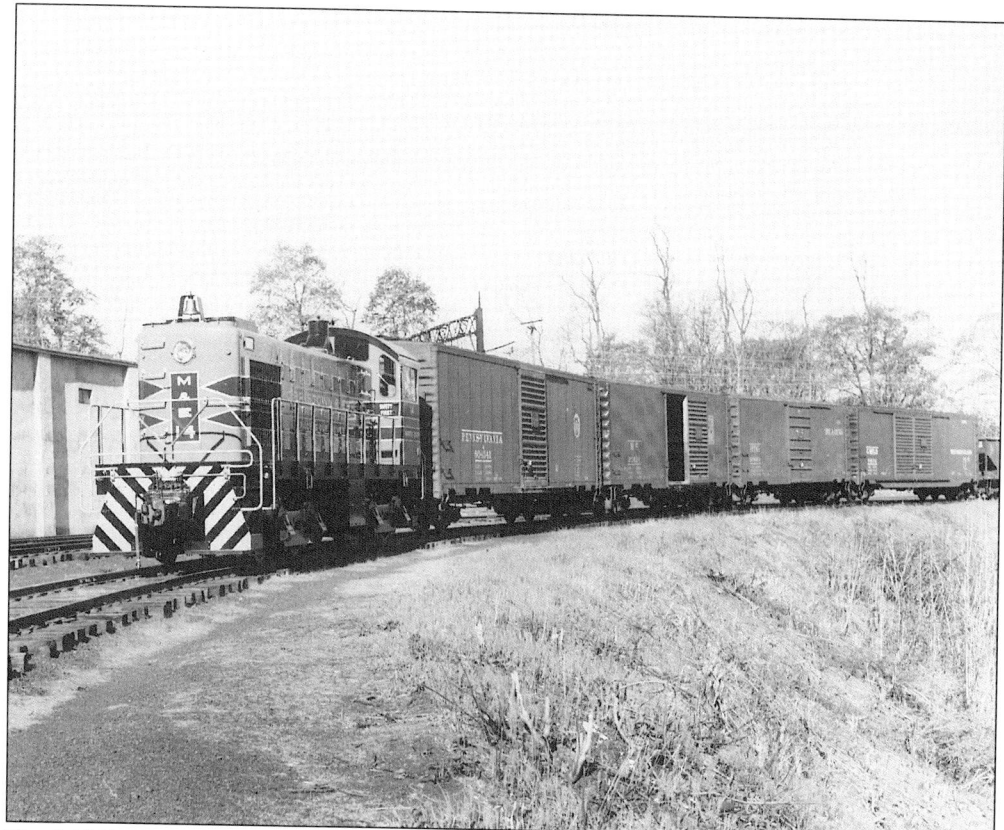

The M&E entered the diesel era on April 28, 1952. This photo shows No. 14 on her second day of service working the interchange with the Delaware, Lackawanna & Western RR in Morristown. The M&E's last three steam locomotives, Nos. 10, 11, and 12 were stored in the enginehouse where they sadly gathered dust until they were finally scrapped in October 1955. (Courtesy Homer R. Hill.)

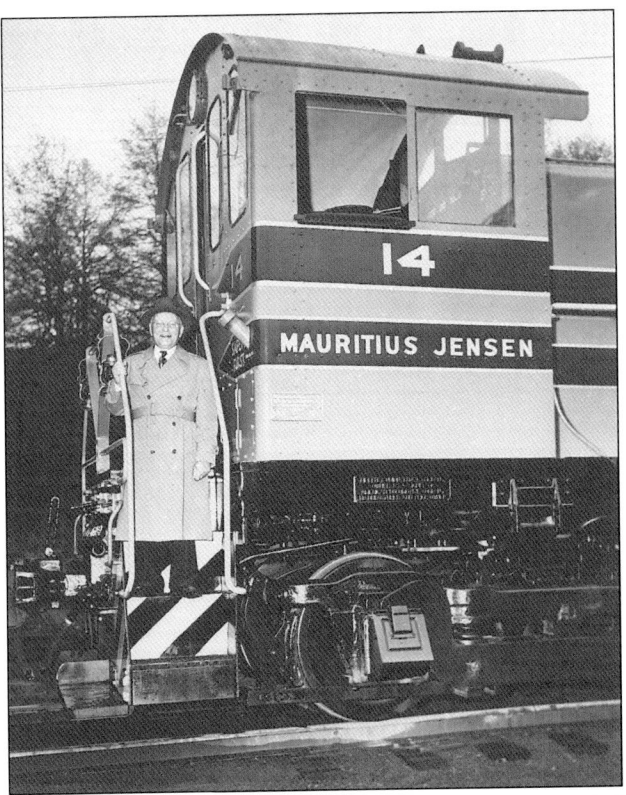

One day after diesel No. 14 made its inaugural trip over the M&E, Mauritius Jensen took part in a ceremony at Whippany on April 29, 1952, in which the new locomotive was named in his honor. On that day, President McEwan paid tribute to Jensen's faithful service as auditor, vice president, and secretary. (Courtesy of Whippany Railway Museum Collection.)

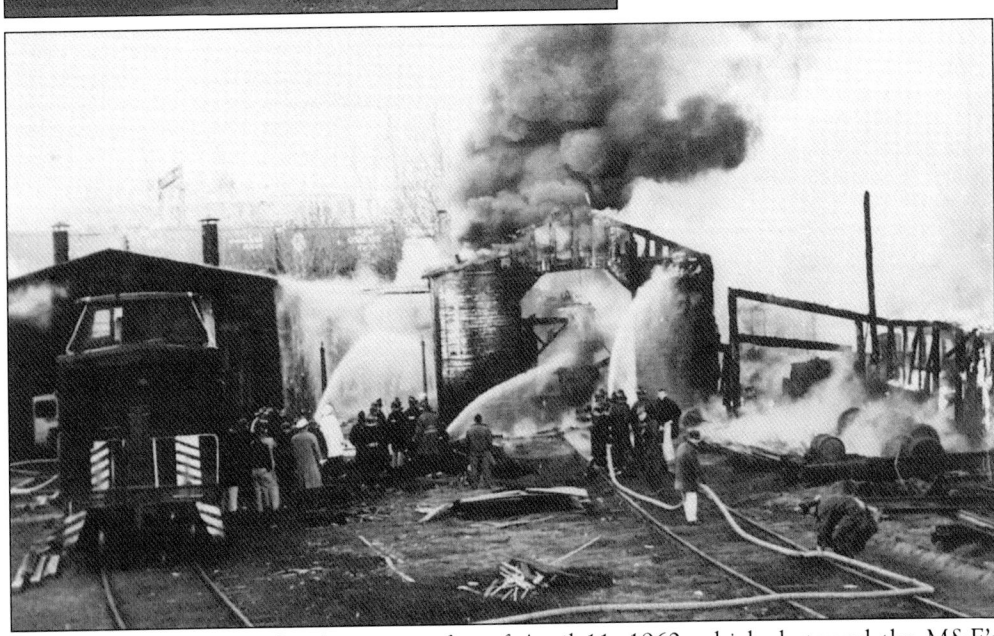

This photograph shows the devastating fire of April 11, 1960, which destroyed the M&E's ancient wooden enginehouse at Morristown. No. 14 is trapped inside the inferno, but, luckily, damage to the locomotive was light. No. 14 was shipped back to ALCO for repairs and a new paint job. While awaiting her return, leased Erie switcher No. 413 handled the freight runs. (Photo by Morristown & Erie Railroad; collection of Steven Hepler.)

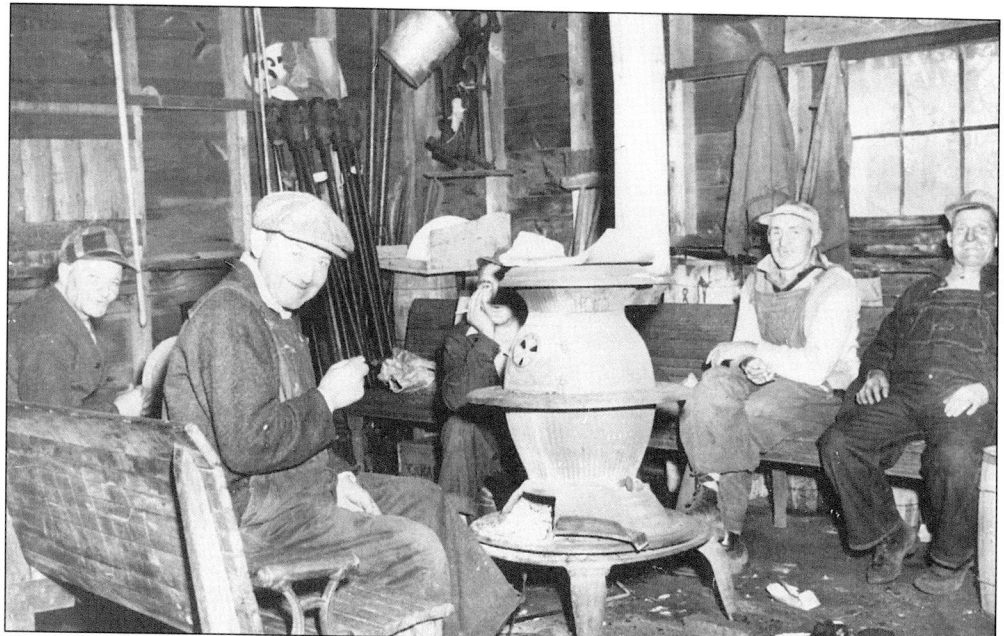

The M&E's track gang appears to be enjoying their lunch break in the old section shanty at Whippany in the early 1950s. The cherry-red glow from the coal stove provides plenty of warmth for the crew on this winter's day. Unfortunately, not everyone here could be identified, but, from left to right, are unidentified; "Bombach"; unidentified; Tom Daven Sr.; and Al Zega, foreman. (Courtesy of Tony Russomanno.)

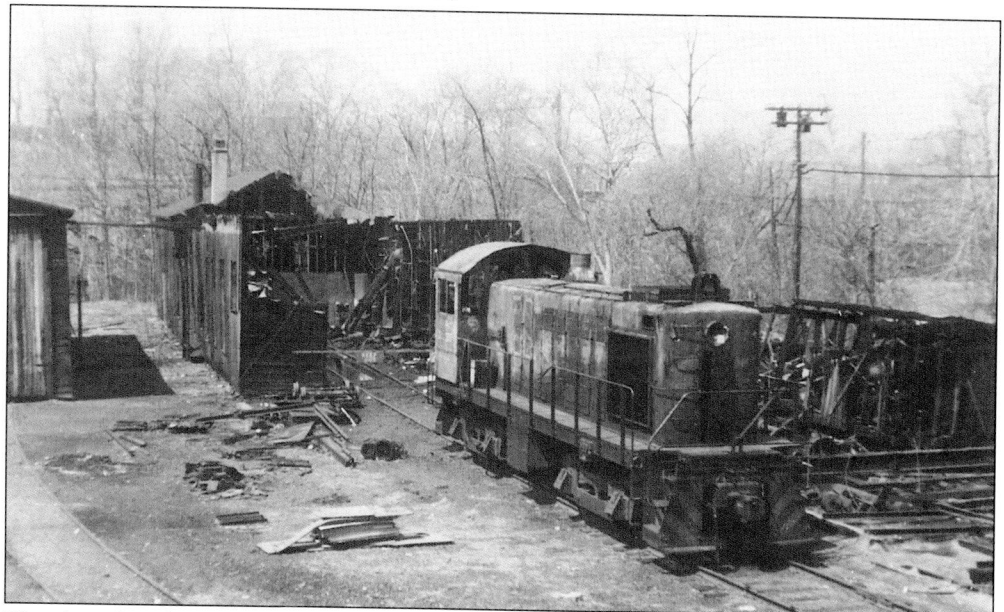

The day after the enginehouse fire, a sad-looking No. 14 sits outside the charred remains of what had been her home. The railroad eventually tore down the entire building and replaced it with a modern, two-track metal structure at the same location (see page 108). Today, it still houses the M&E's current stable of power, as well as the general offices of the company. (Collection of Steven Hepler.)

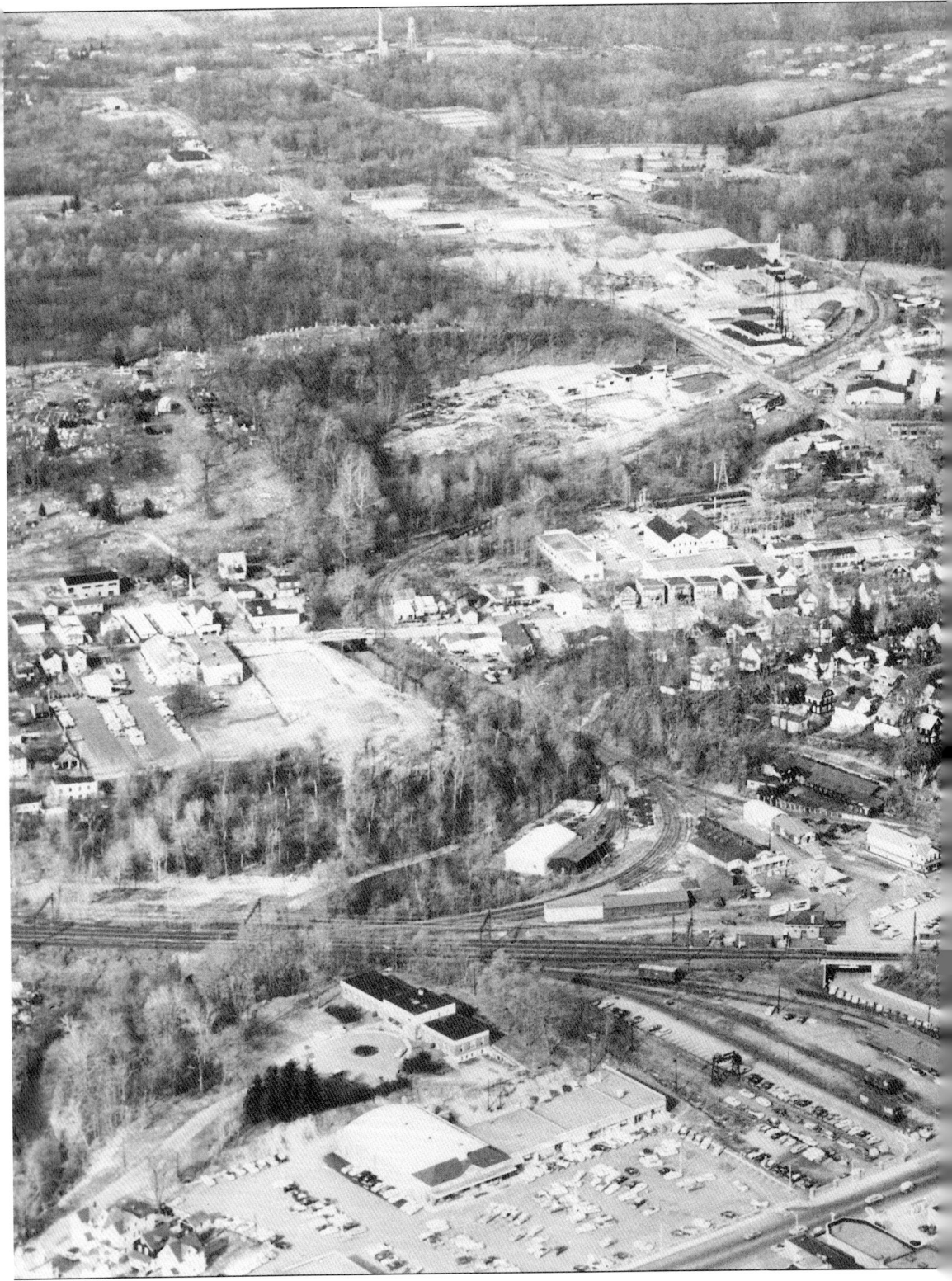

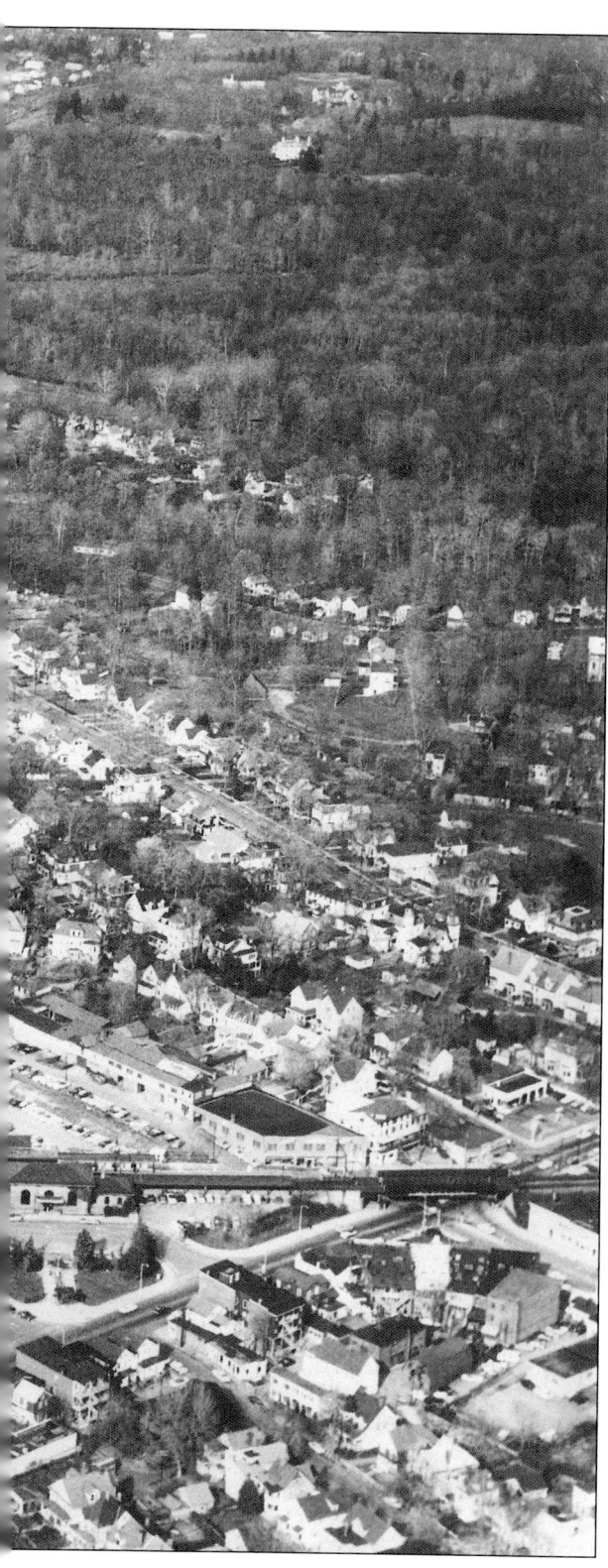

This c. late 1960 aerial view of Morristown looks toward the north. In the lower center of the photo, the mainline of the Lackawanna Railroad travels from left to right (west to east). The Lackawanna's station can be seen beyond the triangular plaza. To the left of center and branching off the Lackawanna is the Morristown & Erie Railroad; its small station and yard are tucked in behind and to the left of the Lackawanna's. One can also make out the M&E's new enginehouse, which is the white building encircled by the interchange tracks. The route of the M&E makes a large "S" curve through town as it winds its way along and across the Whippany River, Abbett Avenue, and Ridgedale Avenue. Curving to the left once more, the railroad begins its long descent into Hanover Township. (Courtesy of Morristown & Erie Railway.)

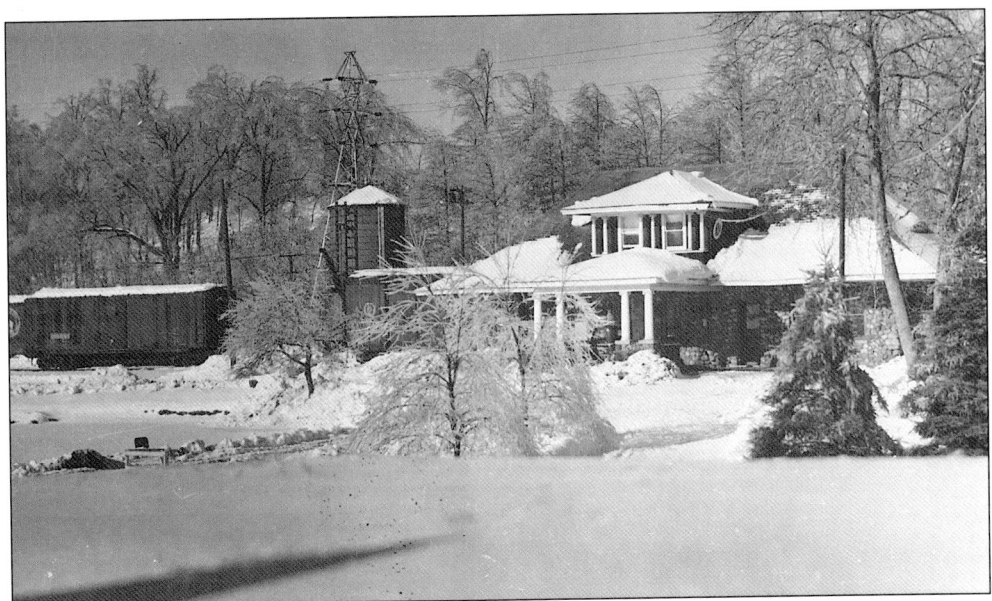

This Christmas card scene of the Whippany station was taken in February 1962 after a particularly heavy snowfall. In warmer seasons, the beautiful landscaped grounds, tranquil duck pond, and depot were lovingly tended to by M&E groundskeeper Alex Hominick. In 1967, most of the land was developed for commercial interests, but Alex did not live to see this come to pass. (Courtesy of Tony Russomanno.)

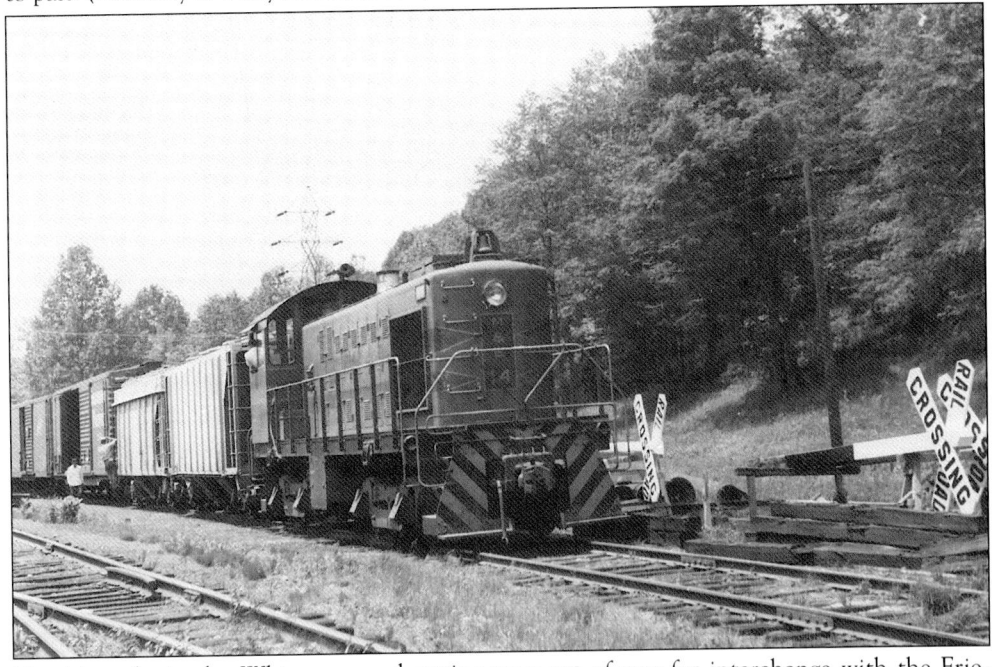

No. 14 works in the Whippany yard setting up a cut of cars for interchange with the Erie-Lackawanna, 7 miles distant at Essex Fells on June 2, 1962. The M&E section crew maintained a small tool shanty here where they also did light carpentry work. Some of their handiwork, in the form of freshly painted, spare crossbucks can be seen in the background. (Courtesy of Bob Pennisi.)

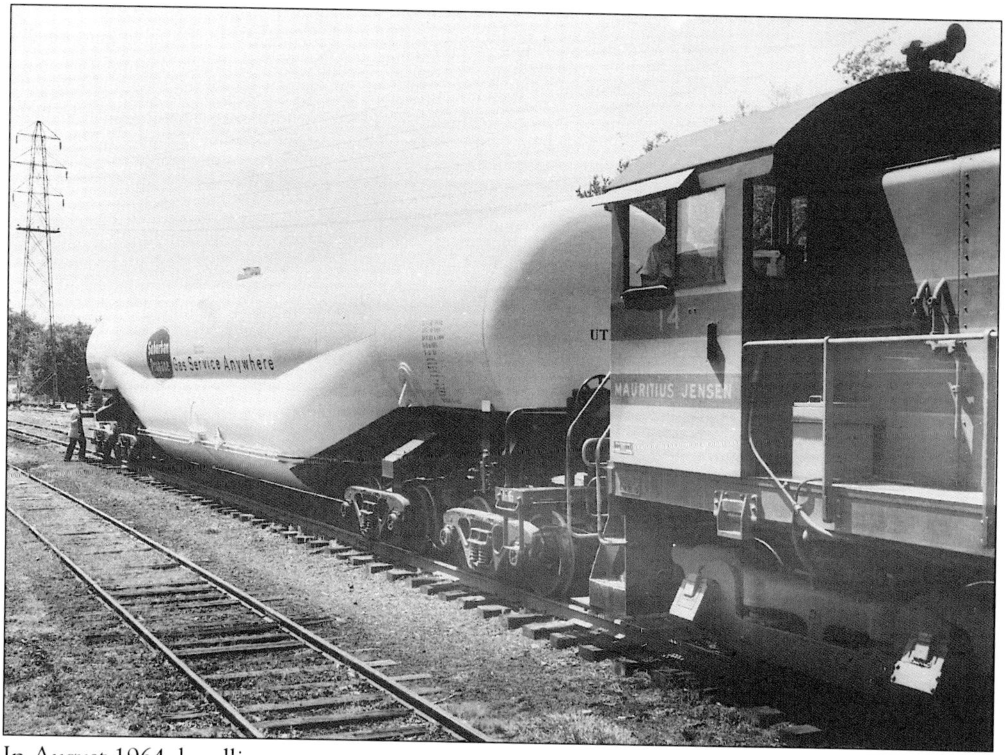

In August 1964, headlines were made when the M&E towed the world's largest tank car into Whippany. The liquid propane carrier, consigned to Suburban Propane on Route 10, was 87 1/2 feet long and weighed 220 tons. The car was built by the Union Tank Car Co. in St. Louis, and this trip was a test to see if the curves on the M&E could be negotiated. (Courtesy of Morristown & Erie Railway.)

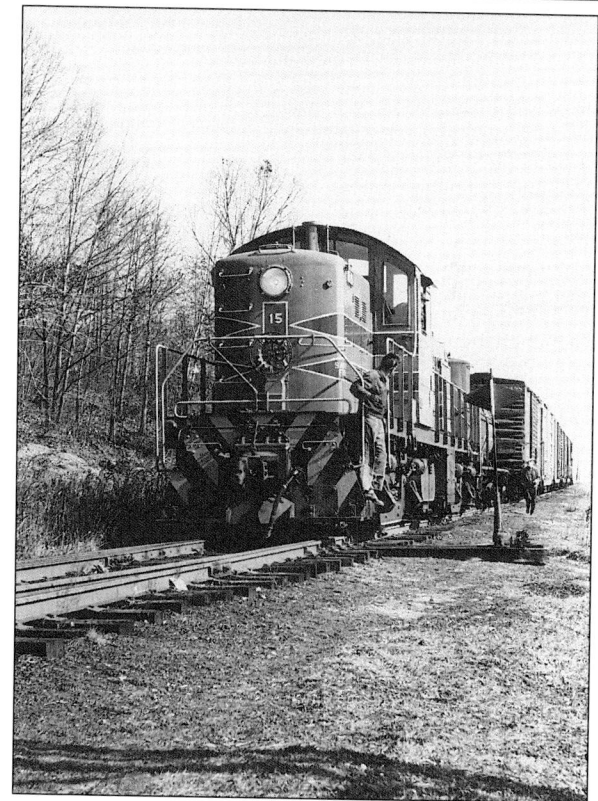

No. 15, the *R.W. McEwan*, with engineer Ken Jones in the cab and brakeman Frank McKenna on the steps is stopped at Whippany on February 18, 1965. Knowing they are pressed for time, conductor Henry Keyes sprints down the track. There is still plenty of switching to do here before the crew gets their train back to Morristown and heads home for the day. (Courtesy of Bob Pennisi.)

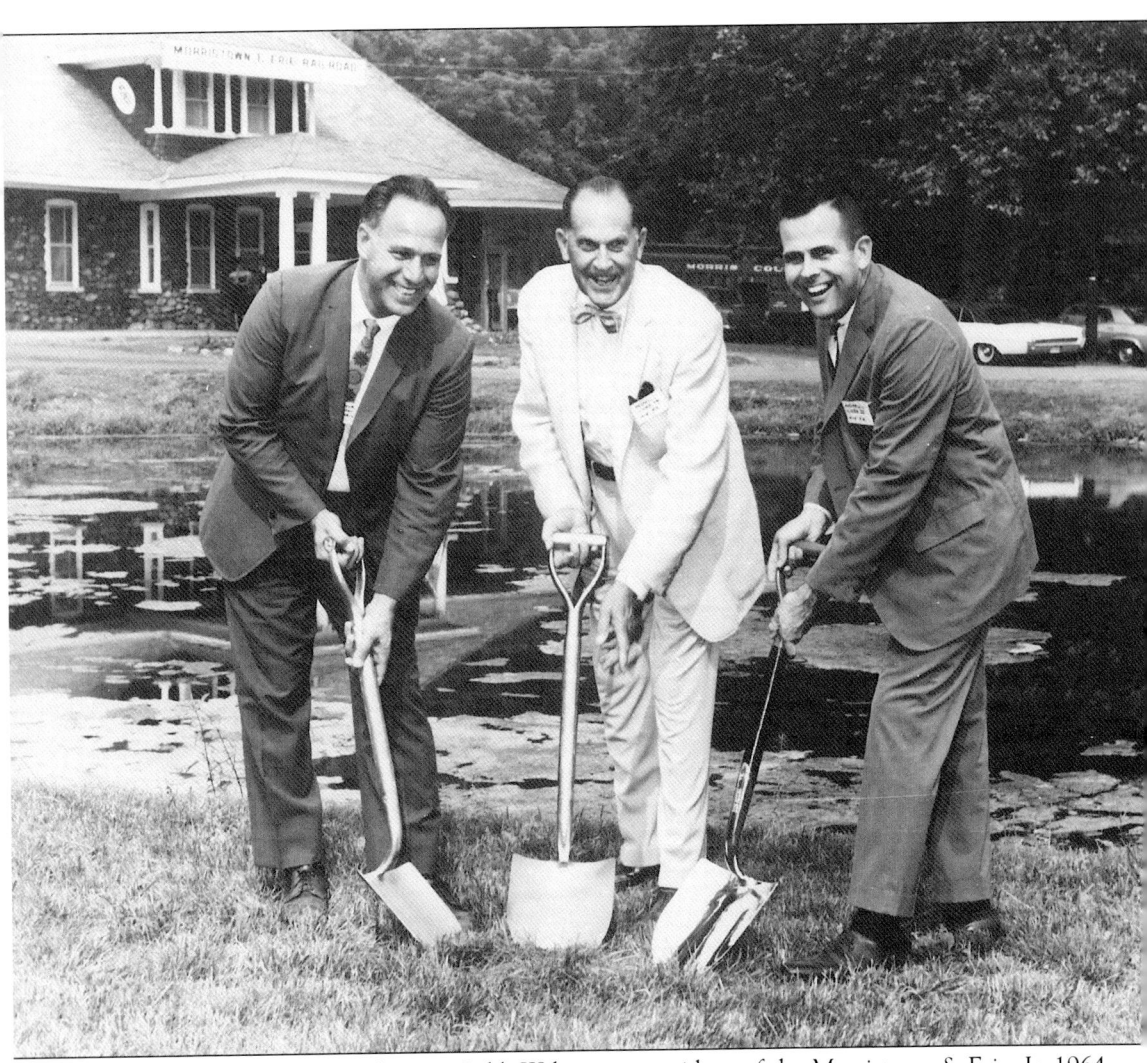

In September 1961, Andrew L. Cobb III became president of the Morristown & Erie. In 1964, for the first time, most of the directors and officers of the company were not members of the McEwan family. Ever so slowly, the operation of the railroad was to become secondary to the needs of the Whippany Development Company, a subsidiary of the M&E created in 1965. In the spring of 1966, the new regime began an ambitious plan to develop the bucolic station-front property in Whippany for commercial purposes, culminating in an office building and parking lot complex dubbed "The McEwan Building" at Railroad Plaza (site of the present-day law offices of O'Toole & Couch and Gibraltar Bank). In this photo, Hanover Township Mayor Sal Iannacone (left), M&E Chairman Andrew L. Cobb Jr. (center), and railroad president Andrew L. Cobb III ceremoniously break the ground at the start of construction on August 29, 1966. With this symbolic act, an era ended, and the only natural park in the center of Whippany was banished to memory. (Courtesy of Railroad Museum of Pennsylvania (PHMC) Collection.)

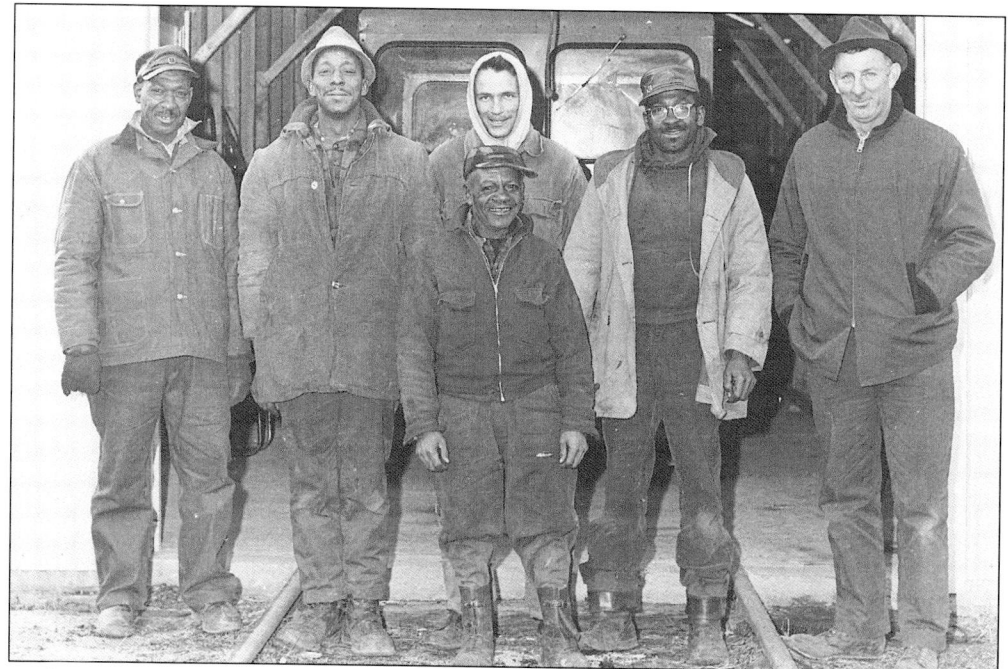

In the early 1960s, the track gang posed in front of the newly constructed Motor Car Shed at Morristown. From left to right are Theodore "T.D." Davis; David Morgan; Frank McKenna; Benjamin "Billy Goat" Eggleston; Harold "Willie" Sandure (maintenance foreman); and in front-center, Gilbert "Shorty" Watson. (Photo by Morristown & Erie Railroad; collection of Steven Hepler.)

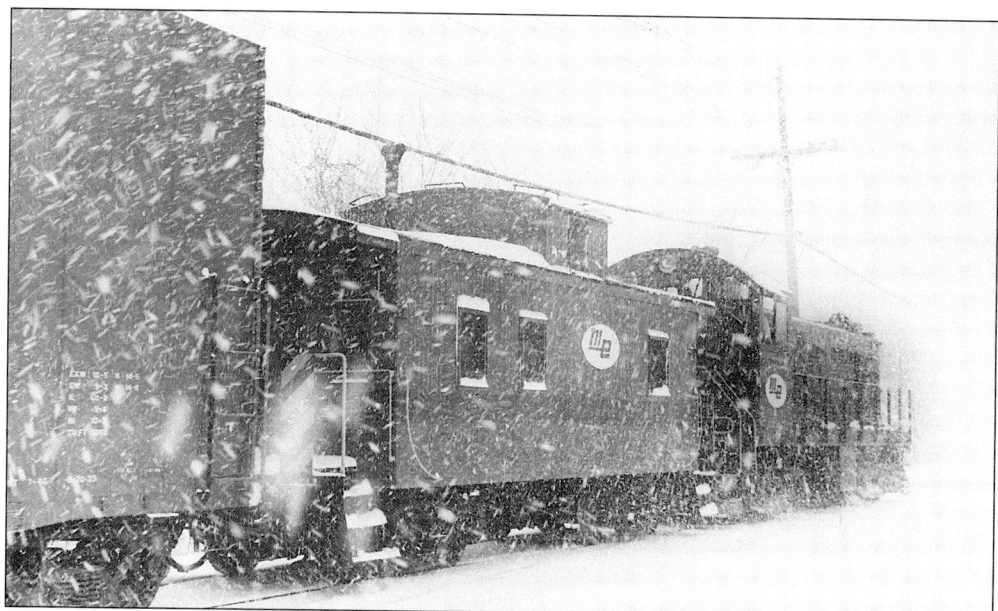

Easing its freight train out of Morristown, No. 14 will follow the course of the winding Whippany River as it makes its daily trek to Essex Fells on this snowy day in 1968. You can be sure the conductor has a fire burning in the caboose coal stove as the snow is piling up on the window sills and the crew has a long, cold day ahead of them. (Collection of Steven Hepler.)

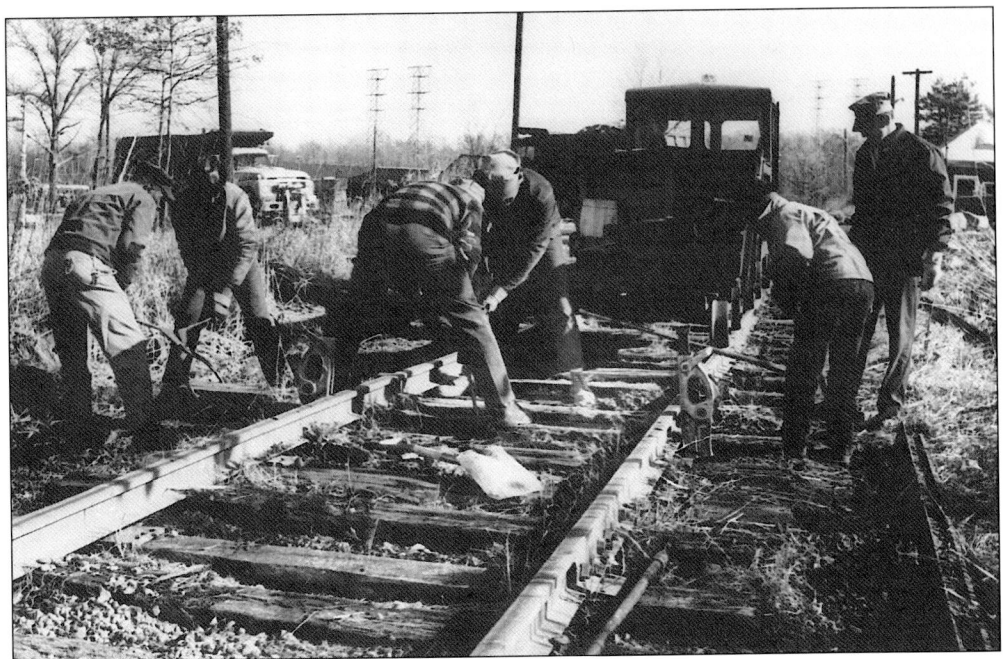

The track gang is hard at work replacing crossties on a section of track just west of the Beaufort Avenue (present-day Eisenhower Parkway) crossing and depot in this c. 1970 view. (Courtesy of Morristown & Erie Railway.)

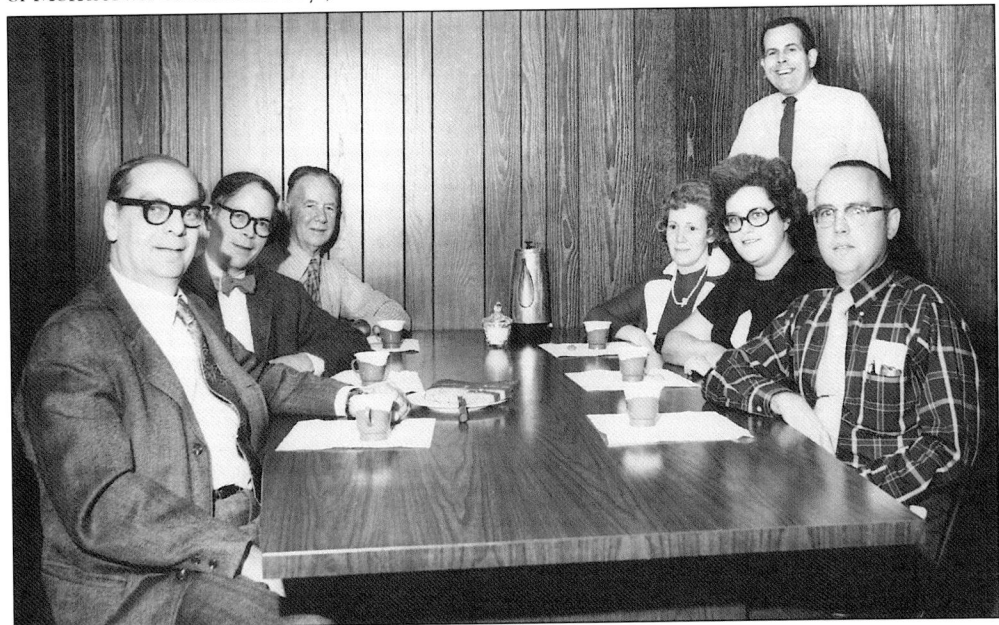

In the late 1960s at Whippany, Andrew L. Cobb III (standing) posed with, from left to right: (front row) Richard Cadmus, vice president and Daniel T. Lindo, secretary; (middle row) John D. McEwan, treasurer and Barbara Kopeck, clerk; (back row) Arthur Vreeland, auditor and Betty Herman, clerk. Later in Cobb's presidency, his management team of the 1970s began diverting earnings into unsuccessful, non-transportation business ventures. In 1977, the Morristown & Erie slipped into bankruptcy. (Courtesy of Morristown & Erie Railway.)

Eight
"Ride the Whippanong Trail":
The Morris County Central Railroad

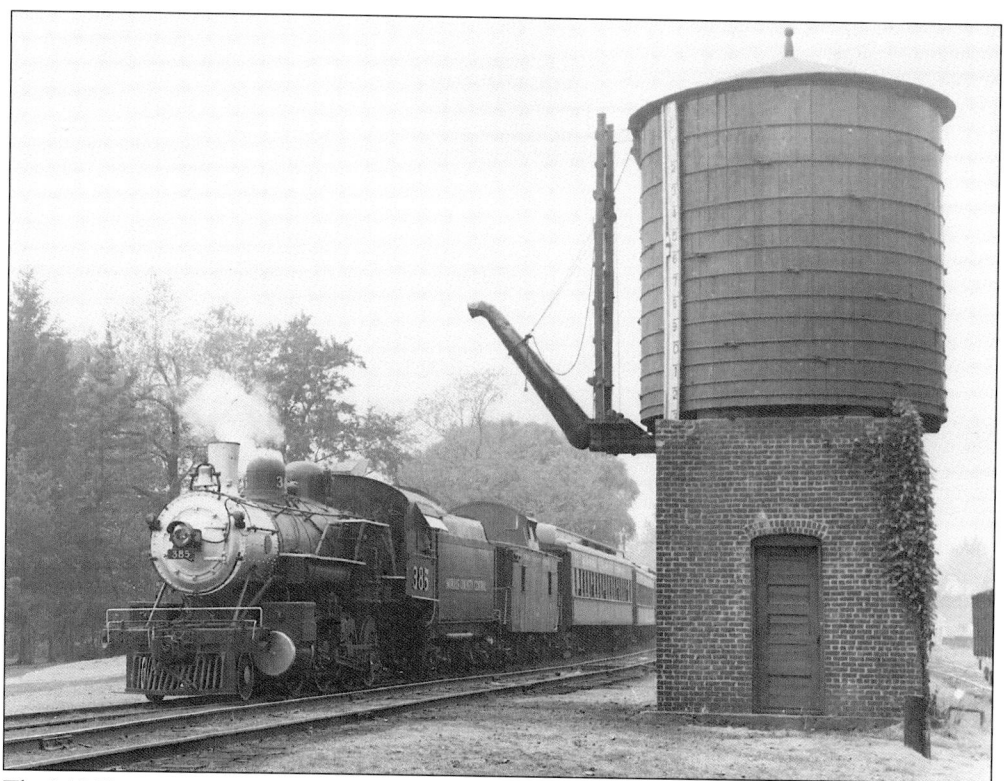

The M&E's steam era came alive again with the first run of the Morris County Central Railroad (MCC) on May 9, 1965. The antique train initially operated on Sundays only and quickly became a successful venture as thousands of passengers were carried back into railroading's colorful past. In this timeless scene, No. 385 passes the water tank at Whippany in June 1965. (Photo by Joe Schussman; courtesy of Railroad Avenue Enterprises.)

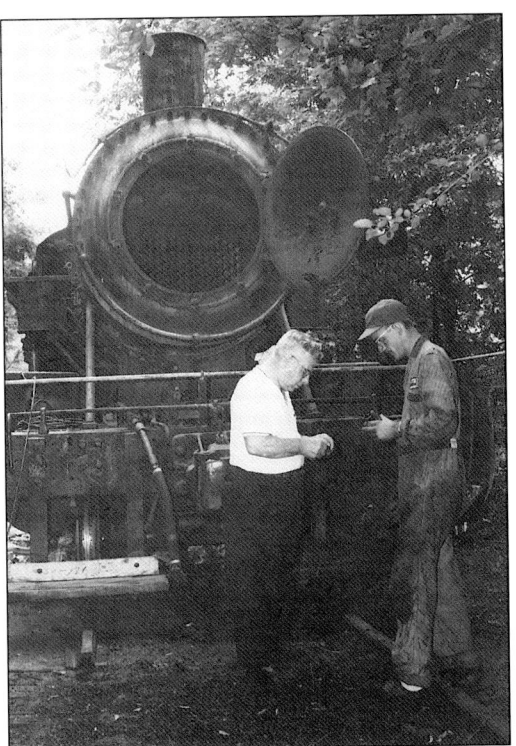

The Morris County Central began in 1963 when Parsippany, New Jersey resident Earle Gil purchased a former Southern Railway steam locomotive of 1907 vintage that he had discovered rusting away on the Virginia Blue Ridge Railway in Piney River, Virginia. Upon arrival at Morristown, Gil began restoration and, within three months, the 120-ton machine was back in operation. Here, Gil (right) is seen with Walt Avis discussing the overhaul. (Collection of Steven Hepler.)

Proudly posing alongside No. 385 on May 9, 1965, at Morristown are members of the Morris County Central crew. On the ground are, from left to right, Earle Gil, president; William Greenberg, treasurer; Charles David Visscher, vice president; John Hart, trainman; Richard Elhers, trainman; Art Bell, conductor; Carmen ?, fireman; and Henry Brown, engineer. Sitting up in the cab is Robert Robertson. (Collection of Steven Hepler.)

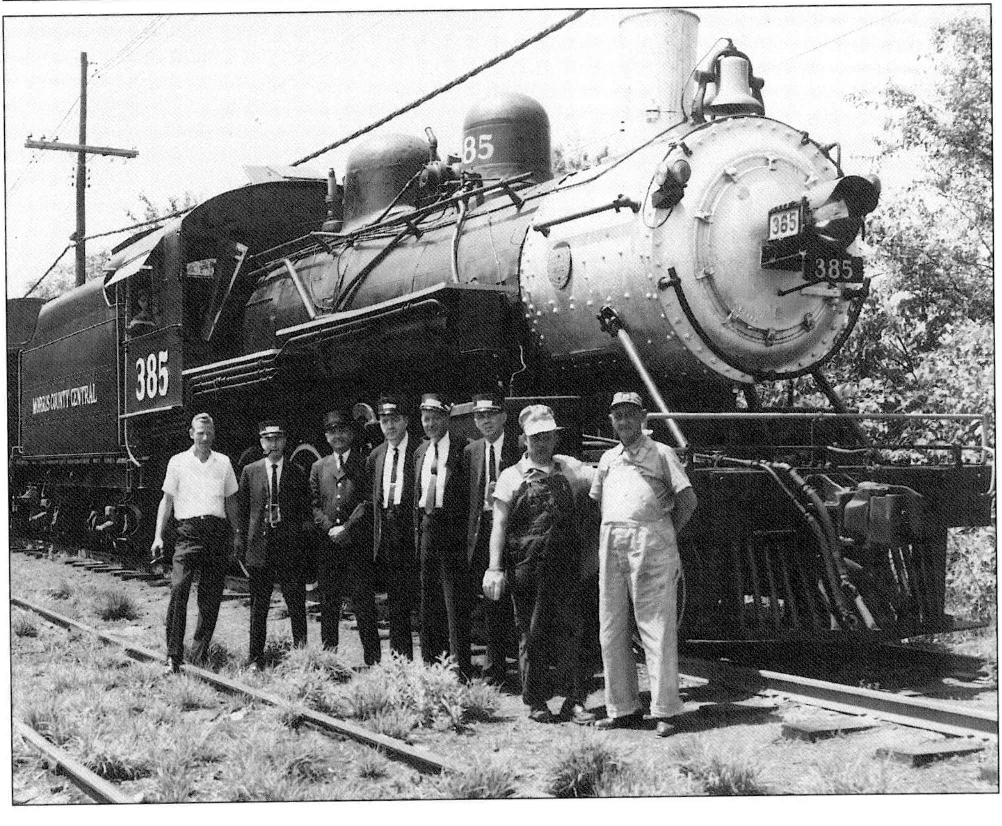

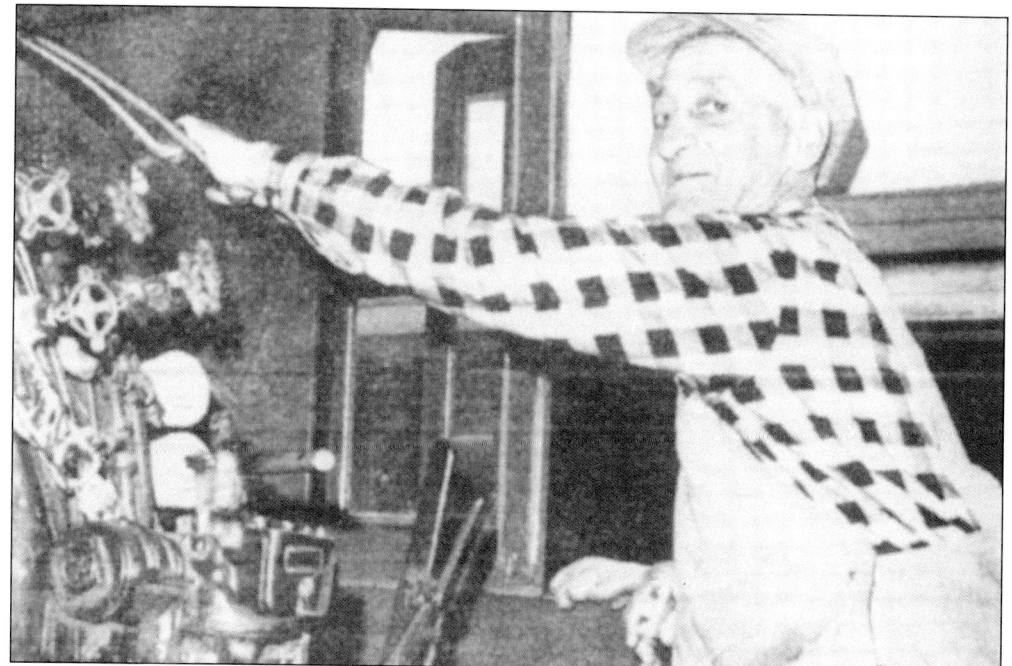

Retired M&E locomotive engineer Henry Brown is seen at the throttle of No. 385 on the Morris County Central's opening day, May 9, 1965. Engineer "Brownie" operated the final M&E passenger train some 37 years prior on April 28, 1928. For a look at "Brownie" in his younger years, refer to pages 46 and 60. (Collection of Steven Hepler.)

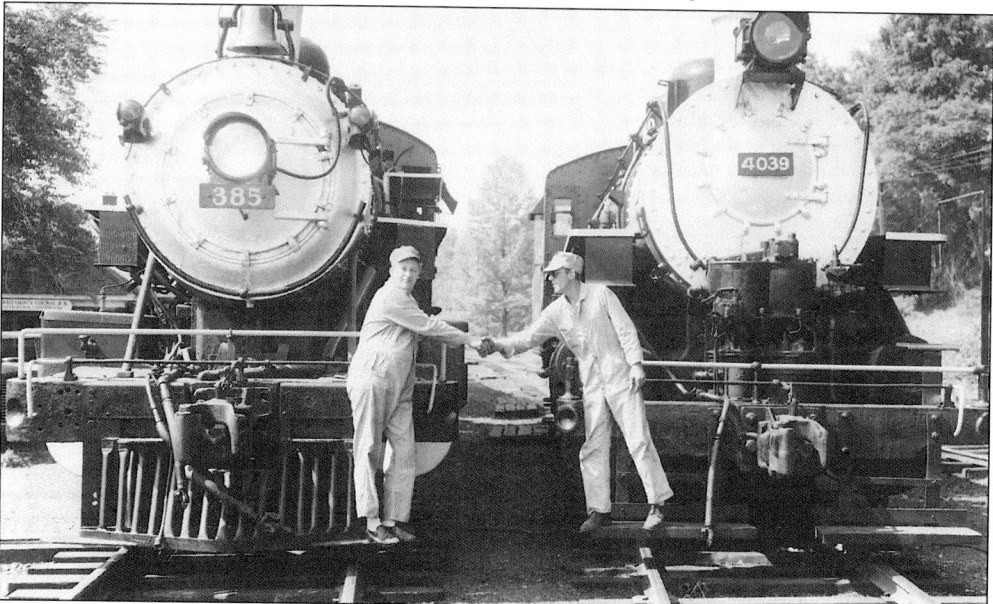

Bob Sutton (left, standing on No. 385) and MCC founder and president Earle Gil (right, on No. 4039) shake hands following their restoration of No. 4039 and its return to active service at Whippany in June 1966. Like No. 385, 4039 had been retired from the roster of the Virginia Blue Ridge. Gil purchased 4039 in late 1965, and it arrived at its new home shortly thereafter. (Collection of Steven Hepler.)

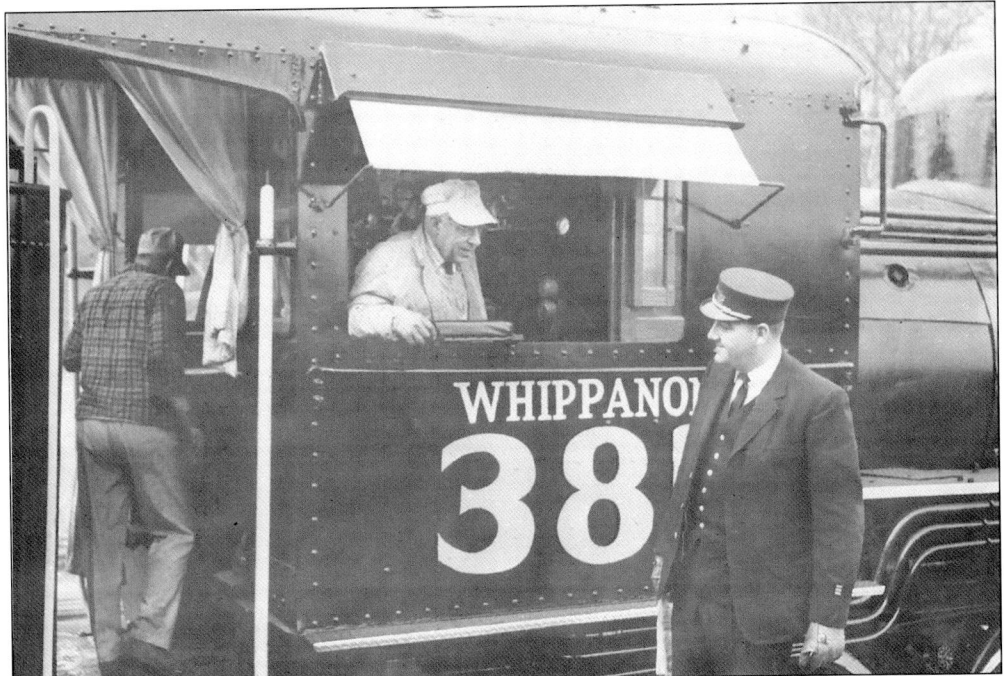

MCC locomotive engineer Andy Barbera and conductor John Hart share a few words at Whippany in 1966. Both men were full-time employees of the Erie Lackawanna Railroad at the time. Andy was the regular engineer of the famous *Phoebe Snow* streamliner, and John was a passenger conductor holding down a weekday run out of Hoboken. (Photo by Edward J. Ruland.)

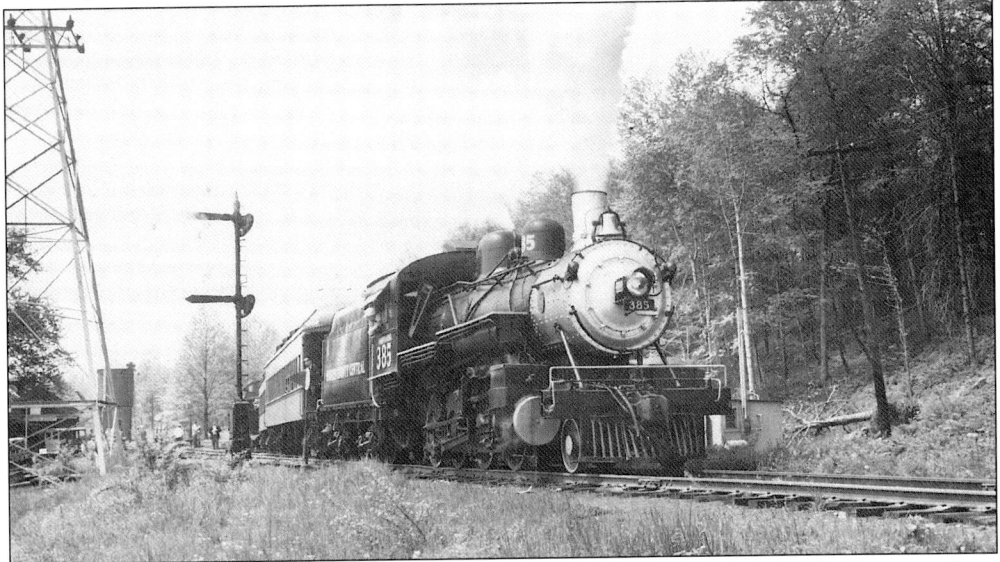

Photographer Ed Ruland captured No. 385 leading its excursion train out of Whippany for a scheduled run to Roseland in the spring of 1966. On board the vintage, former Jersey Central coaches and, in the old wooden ex-Pennsylvania Railroad caboose, hundreds of passengers are being treated to the nostalgic sights and sounds of a vanished American era. (Photo by Edward J. Ruland.)

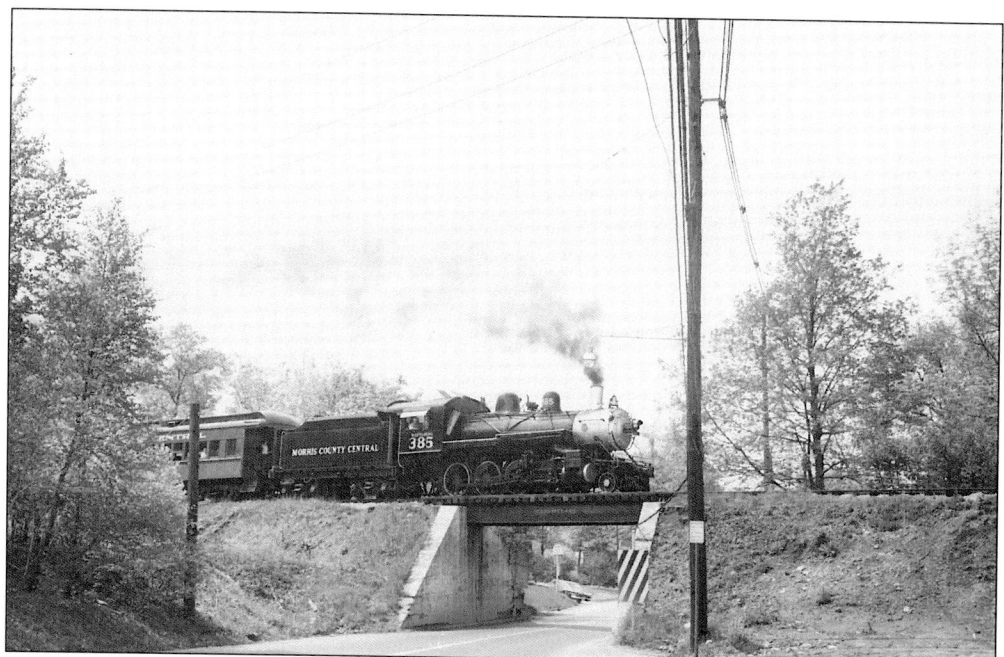

No. 385 rumbles across the M&E's Eagle Rock Avenue overpass at Roseland, New Jersey, in 1966. At the time, the overpass was wide enough for only two slim lanes of opposing traffic. By 1968, the roadway was widened to four lanes, and the rail overpass was replaced with a much larger structure. (Photo by Edward J. Ruland.)

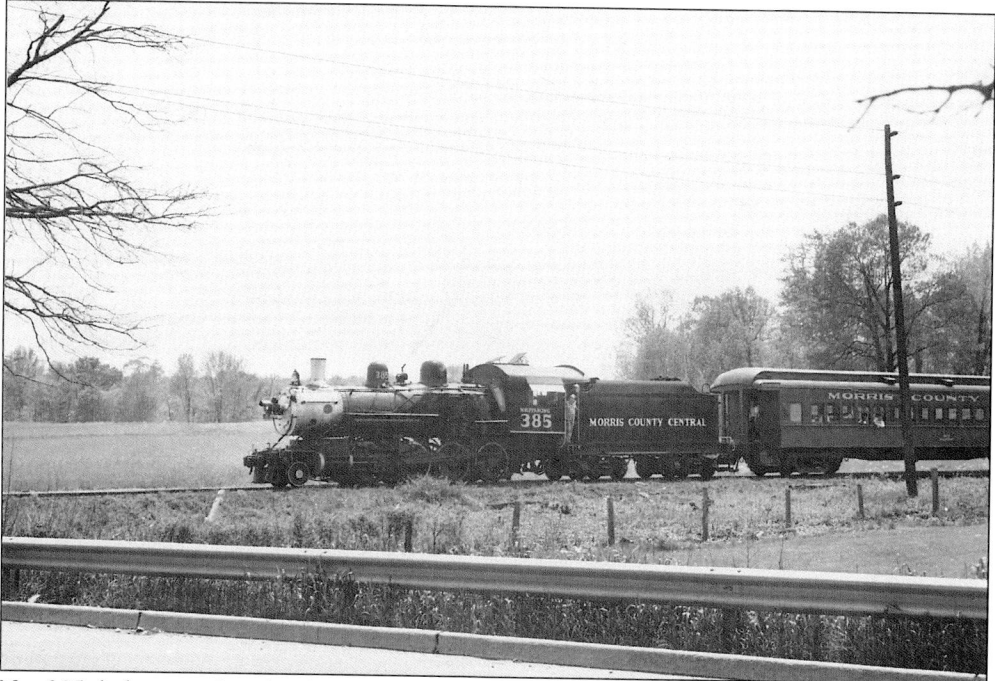

No. 385 drifts up to Roseland's Harrison Avenue in May 1966. Today, this pastoral scene has been obliterated by a suburban housing development, and the M&E rails through here have been abandoned. (Photo by Edward J. Ruland.)

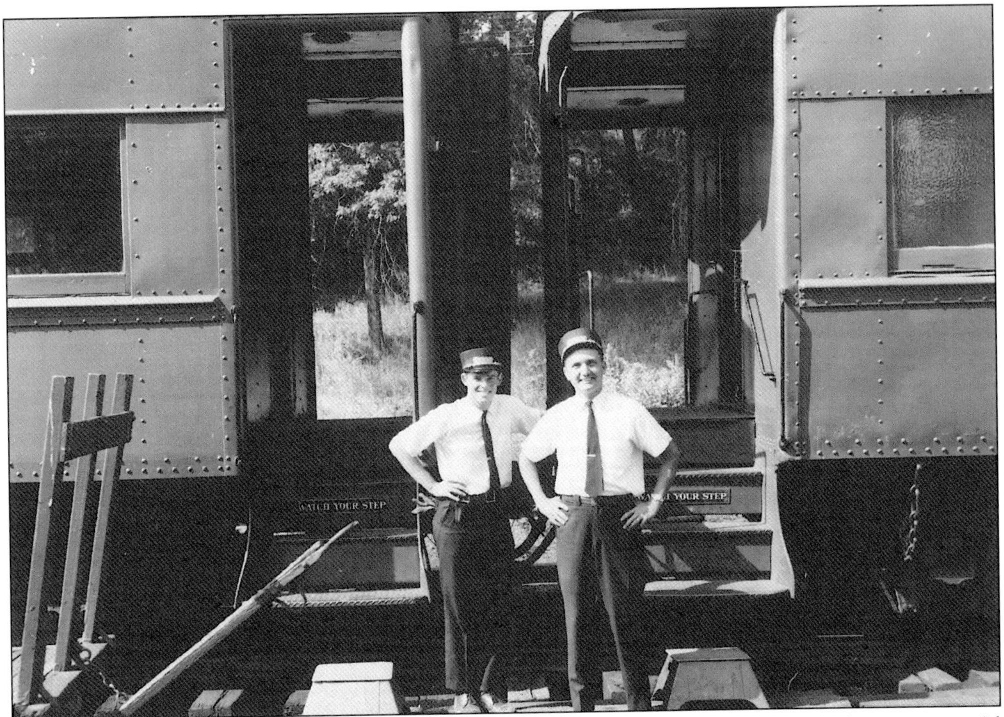

It is a warm day on July 17, 1966, and 19-year-old Morris County Central trainman Al Holleuffer (left) and conductor Dave Visscher prepare to greet passengers and help them board the excursion coaches at Whippany. The MCC's coaches were of 1915 vintage and were acquired from the Central Railroad of New Jersey. (Photo by Max Babinger; collection of Steven Hepler.)

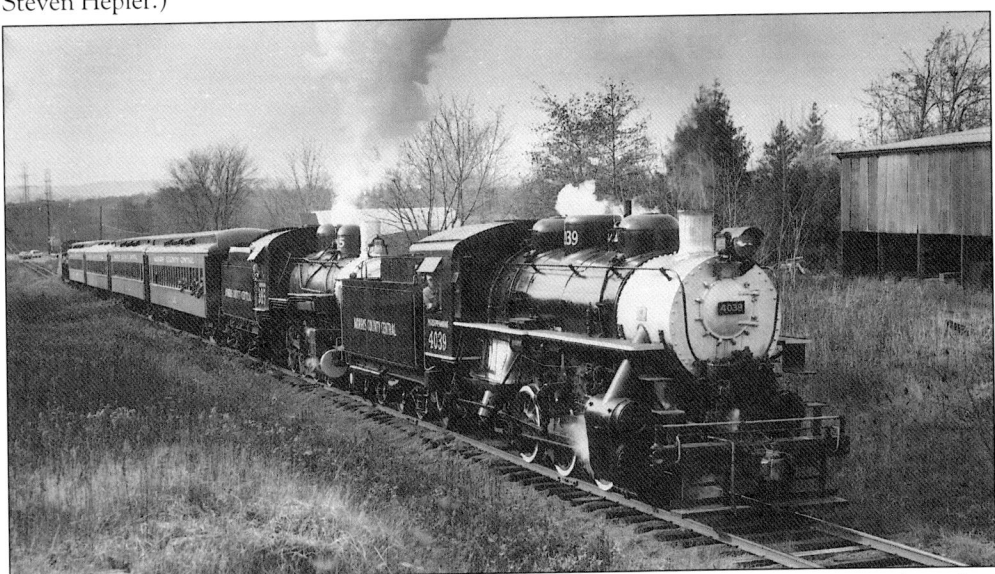

In a dramatic scene taken on November 6, 1966, MCC Nos. 4039 and 385 climb eastbound up the grade to DeForrest Avenue at East Hanover, New Jersey. The two engines were powering a special doubleheaded excursion to Roseland in commemoration of No. 385's 59th year. (Collection of Steven Hepler.)

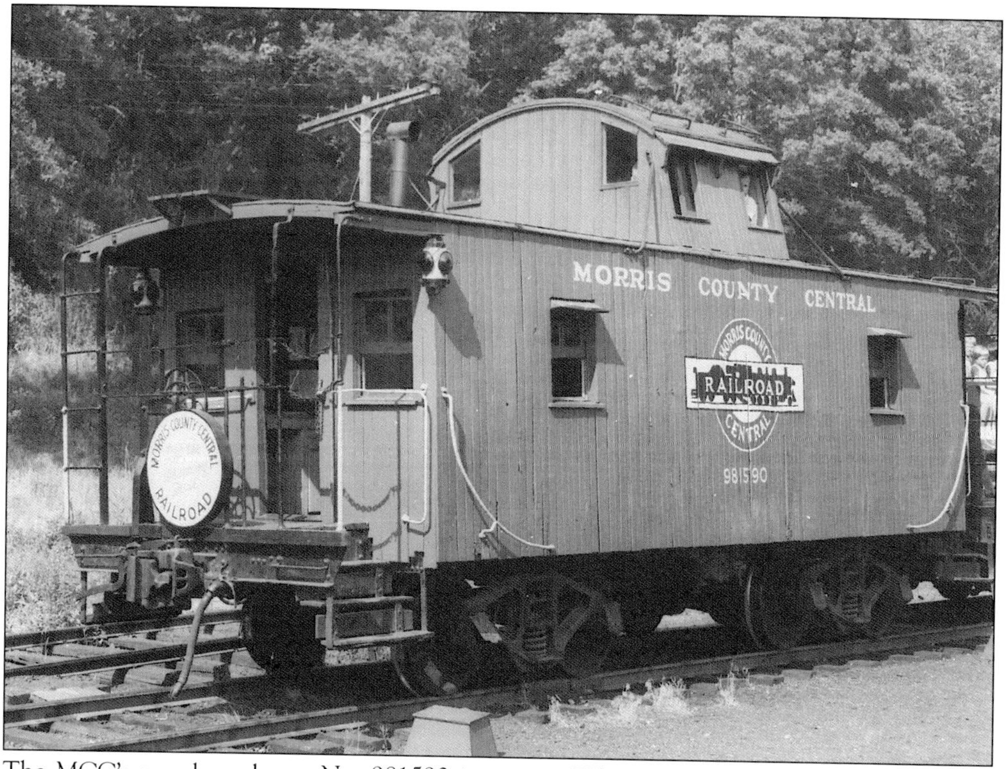

The MCC's popular caboose No. 981590 is seen at Whippany in 1966. Built in 1923, this former Pennsylvania Railroad wooden "cabin car" (alternative term for "caboose") was also nicknamed "Mae West" by PRR crews because of the very distinctive curve of the cupola roof. Old No. 981590 survives today, privately owned and displayed at Newfoundland, New Jersey. (Collection of Steven Hepler.)

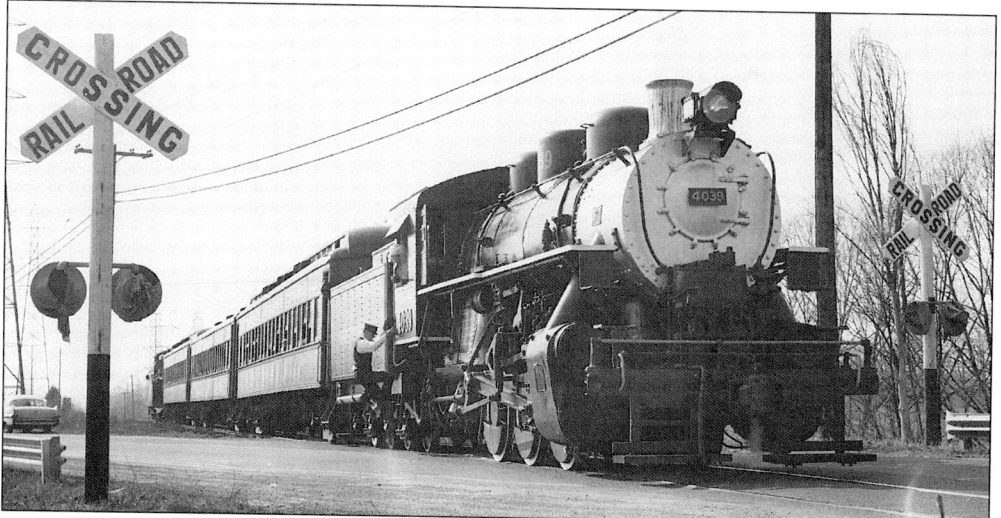

No. 4039 rolls across the M&E's Ridgedale Avenue, East Hanover grade crossing in April 1967. Engineer Andy Barbera widens out on the throttle as flagman Al Holleuffer climbs back onboard the locomotive after protecting automobile traffic against the passage of the train. (Photo by Edwill H. Brown; courtesy of Whippany Railway Museum Collection.)

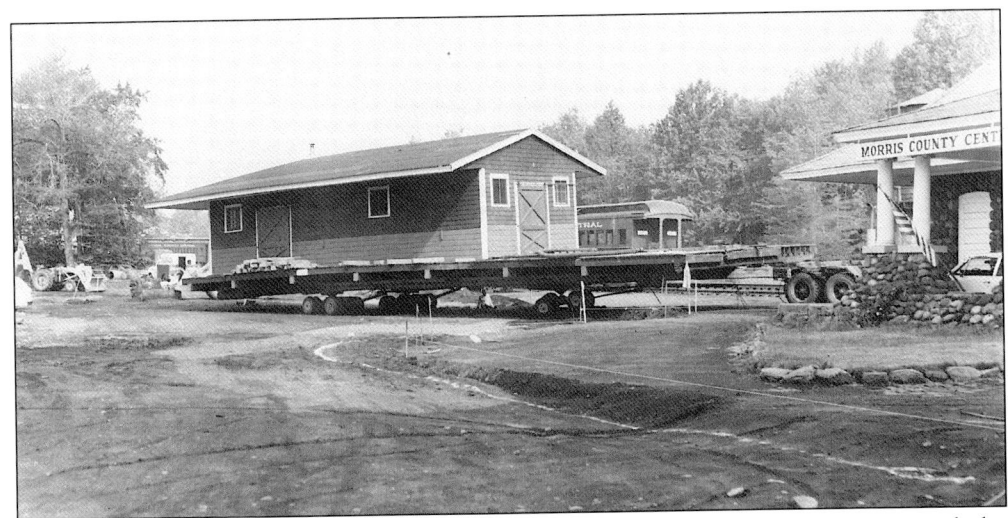

Threatened by the M&E's development of its Whippany property, the MCC saved the Whippany freight house from demolition in June 1967 by having it moved across four sets of tracks to a site opposite the station. Home to the Morris County Central Railroad Museum from 1967 to 1973, this classic railroad freight station is now the headquarters of the Whippany Railway Museum. (Collection of Steven Hepler.)

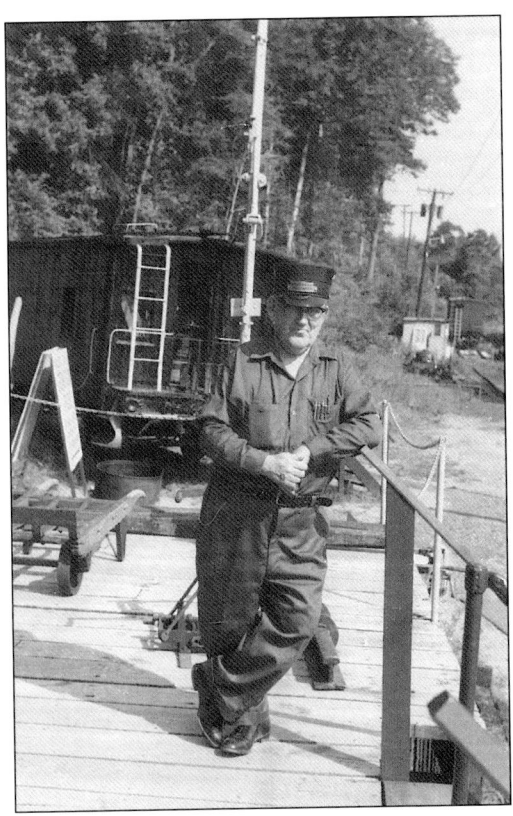

Max Babinger was a retired New York City trolley man who was the regular attendant at the Morris County Central Railroad Museum. Making the long trip to Whippany each weekend from his home in Long Island City, Max eventually moved into the M&E's Whippany and, later, Morristown stations. Max passed away in December 1973, not long after the MCC moved to a new location. (Collection of Steven Hepler.)

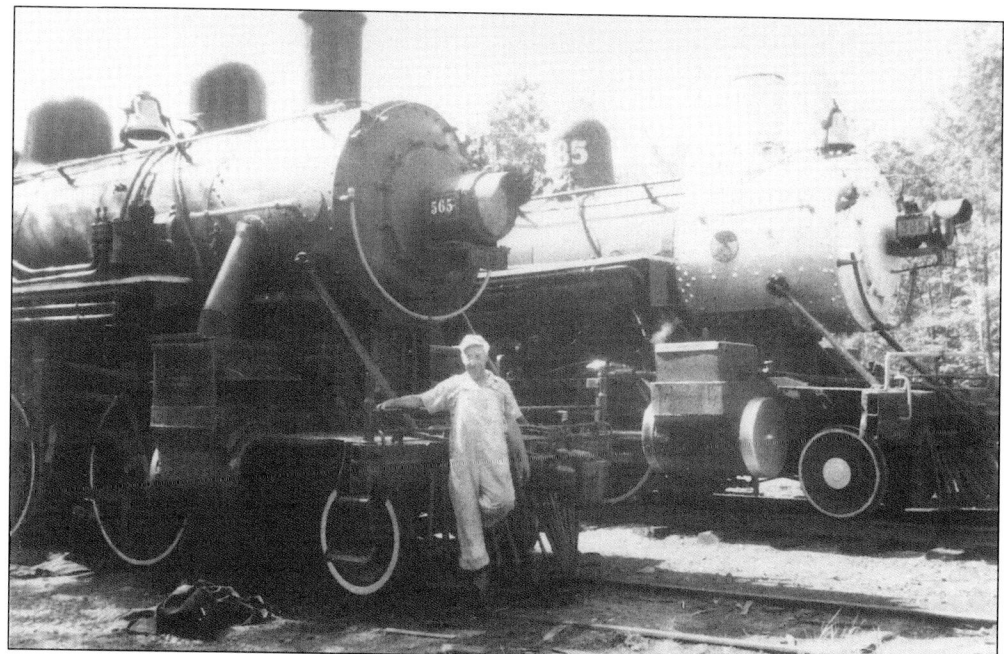

In July 1968, MCC engineer Andy Barbera posed with the railroad's "newest" addition, former Delaware, Lackawanna & Western RR 2-6-0 No. 565, built in 1908. One of only two remaining Lackawanna steam engines in existence, No. 565 was intended to be restored for operation at Whippany. Instead, 565 wound up being displayed at Citro's Restaurant in Wayne, New Jersey. Today, 565, in need of restoration, is at Steamtown USA in Scranton, Pennsylvania. (Collection of Steven Hepler.)

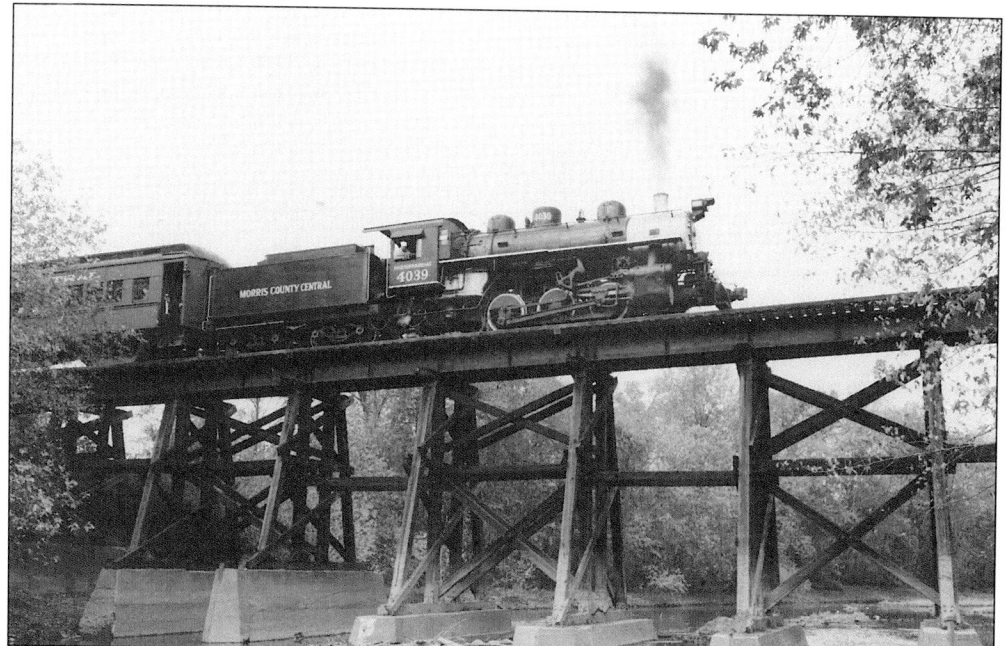

No. 4039 is flying high as it leads its train across the M&E's Passaic River trestle in Livingston in 1968. (Photo by Edwill H. Brown; courtesy of Whippany Railway Museum Collection.)

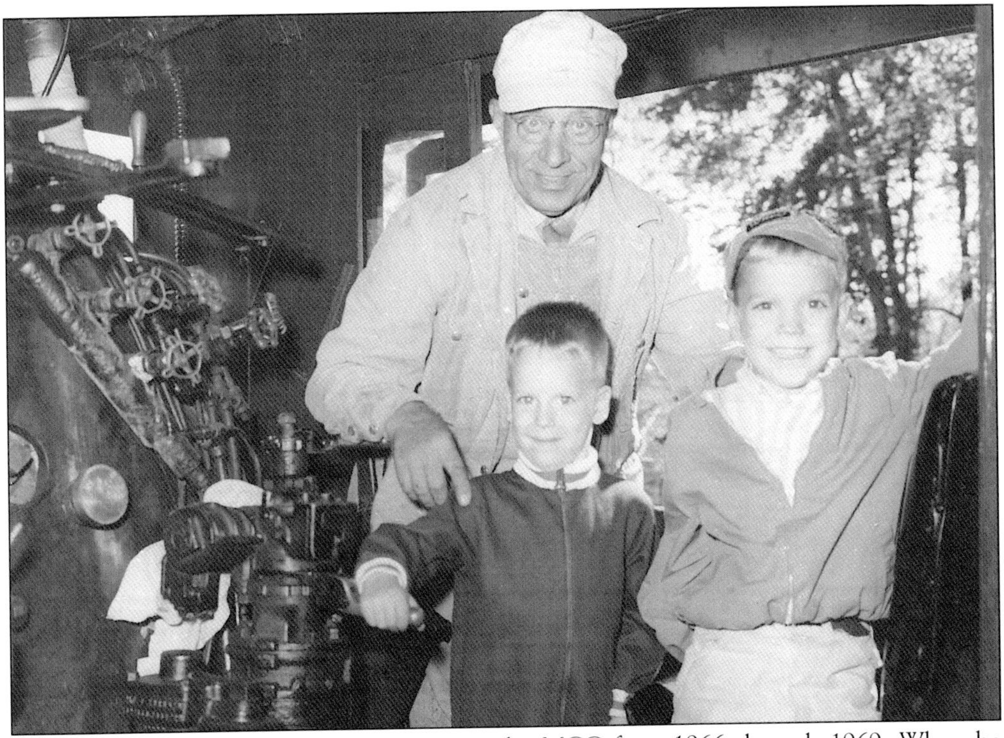

Andy Barbera was the weekend engineer at the MCC from 1966 through 1969. When he retired from the Erie Lackawanna on August 30, 1967, after 50 years, he made his final run at the throttle of the *Lake Cities Limited*. Andy is seen in the cab of No. 385 with John and Peter Maris in 1968 at Whippany. (Collection of Steven Hepler.)

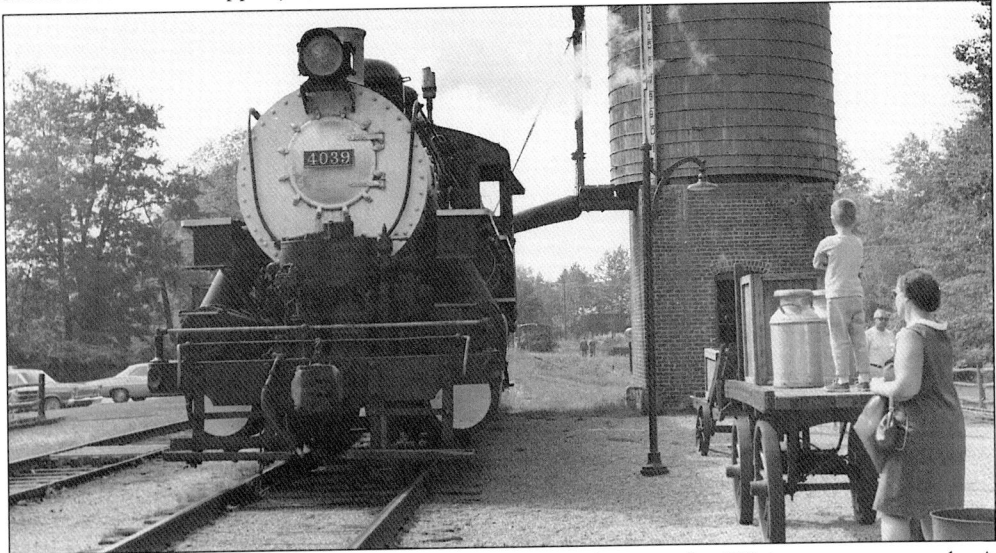

In the hot summer of 1969, No. 4039 quenches her thirst at the Whippany water tank. A young man, perched atop the baggage wagon, arms folded, watches intently. It would be nice to think that 30 years later, this youngster, now an adult, occasionally relives this timeless scene vividly in his childhood memories. (Photo by Edwill H. Brown; courtesy of Whippany Railway Museum Collection.)

Reviving memories of the past in the summer of 1973 and working hard on the vintage hand pump car are MCC employees, from left to right, Joe Krygoski, Bob Krygoski, George Hill, Roger Kruser, and Bob Kelly. (Courtesy of John Terry.)

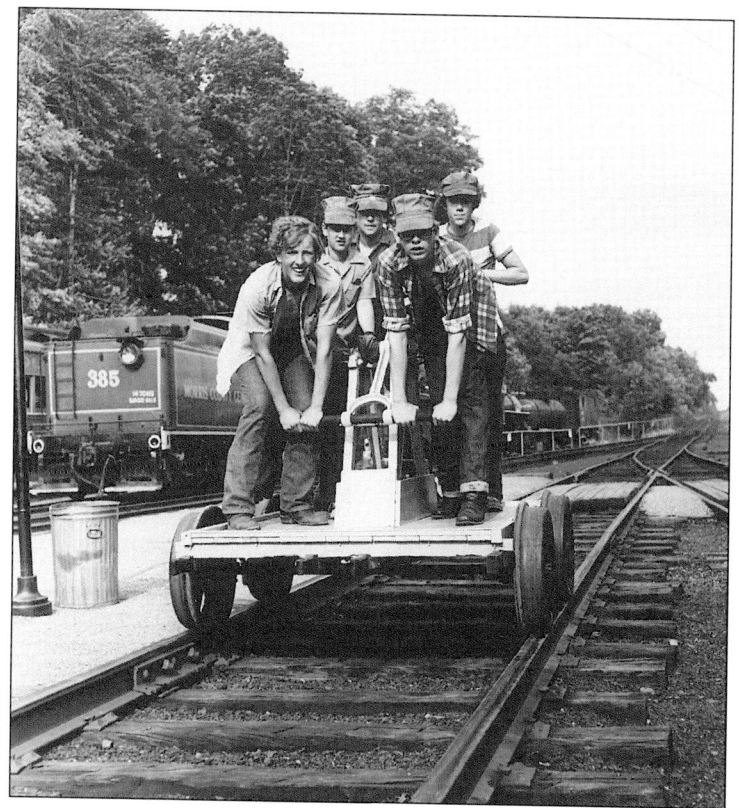

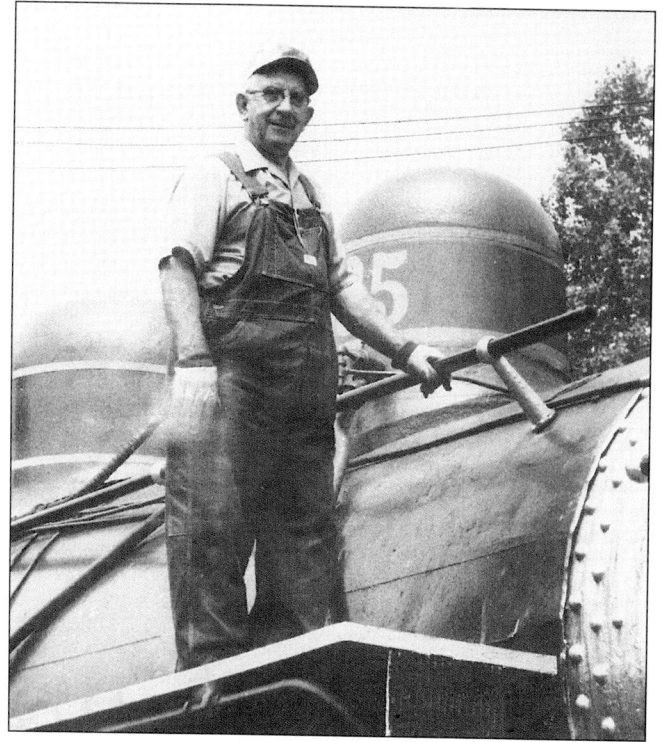

Retired Erie Lackawanna locomotive engineer Charles Barrett had 48 years of railroading under his belt when he came to the MCC in August 1969. As the regular engineer, he quickly earned the respect and admiration of all who worked with him. To show how much he was truly loved by everyone on the MCC, his signature was emblazoned on No. 385's cab in the grand railroad tradition. (Collection of Steven Hepler.)

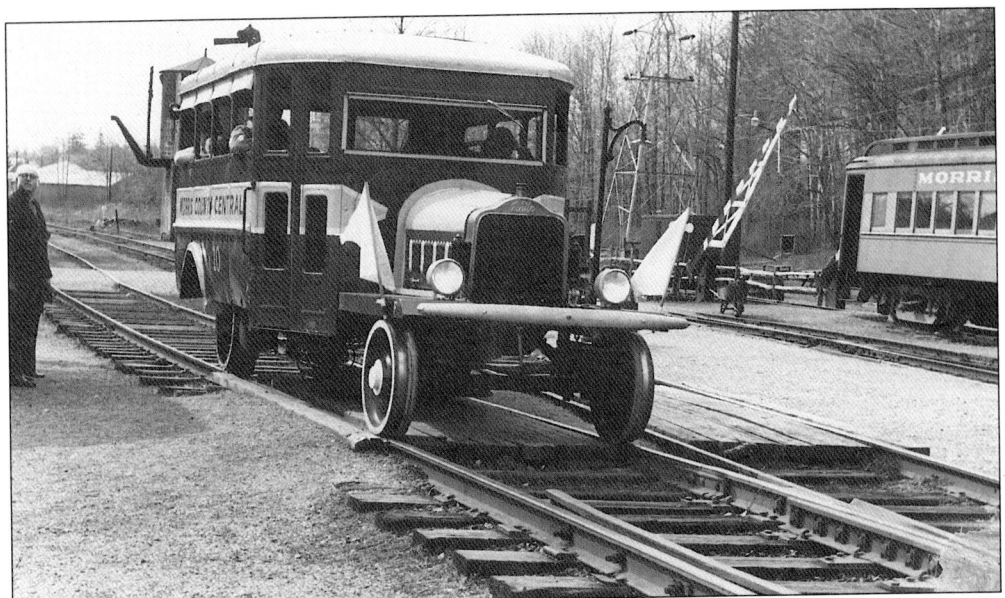

MCC Railbus No. 10, fashioned from the remains of the M&E's White Railbus, is seen departing the Whippany station in 1973. Rebuilt over a three-year period by MCC founder Earle Gil, the bus features a vintage replacement body and other antique components that help to recreate a very reasonable version of the 1918 original. The bus survives today as part of the Whippany Railway Museum collection. (Courtesy of John Terry.)

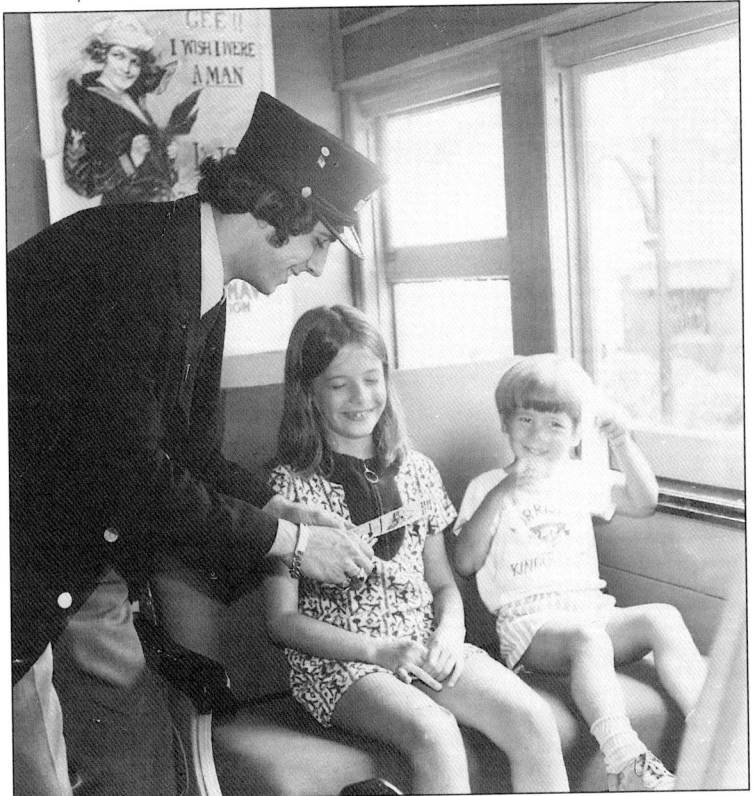

On board the train, Morris County Central conductor Steve Hepler collects the tickets of Kim and Adam Terry in 1972. The children grew up in a railroad family, so to speak, since their parents, John and Joan, operated the MCC's gift shop at Whippany and were officers of the excursion line. (Courtesy of John Terry.)

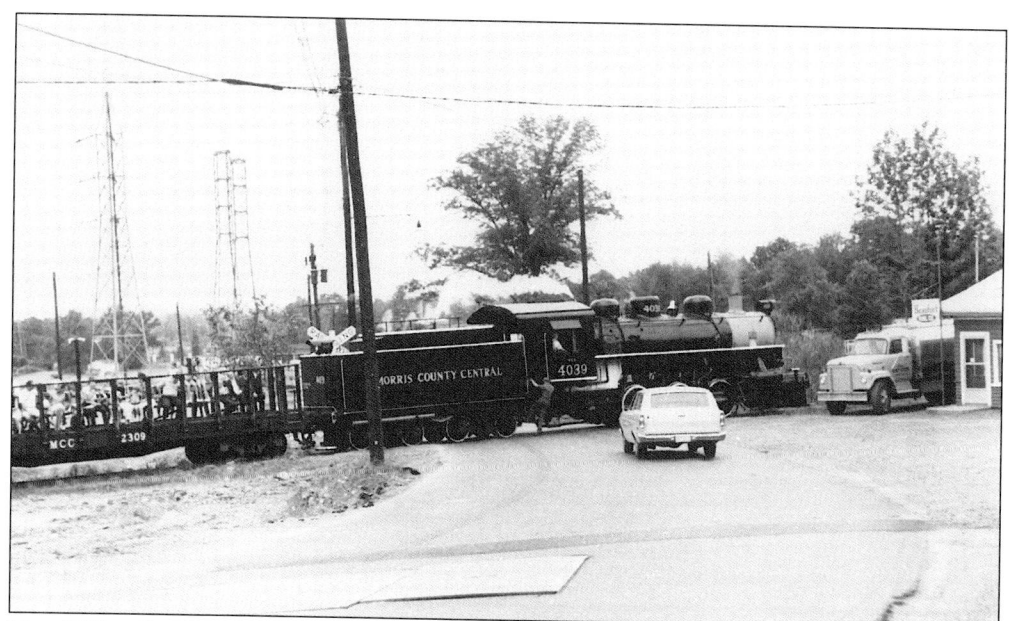

No. 4039 pulls its train across two-lane Beaufort Avenue in Livingston and past the old station on the right. This 1972 view is a far cry from the fast-moving four-lane Eisenhower Parkway of today. Where once only a pair of traditional wooden crossbucks warned motorists, today there are overhead gantry-mounted lights and bells to herald the approach of a train. (Courtesy of John Terry.)

Seen on the right-hand side of No. 385's cab is MCC engineer Charles Barrett in 1972. This true gentleman had a genuine love of railroading and a profound concern for the people around him. Whenever Charlie was at the throttle, timepieces could be set by his skillful handling of the train. He always operated in a safe manner and was consistently on time. (Courtesy of John Terry.)

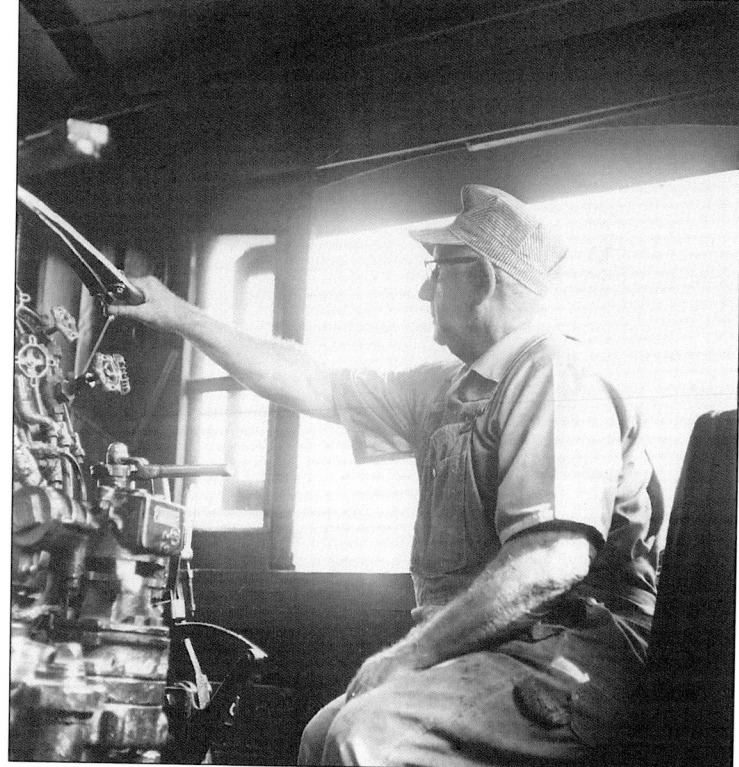

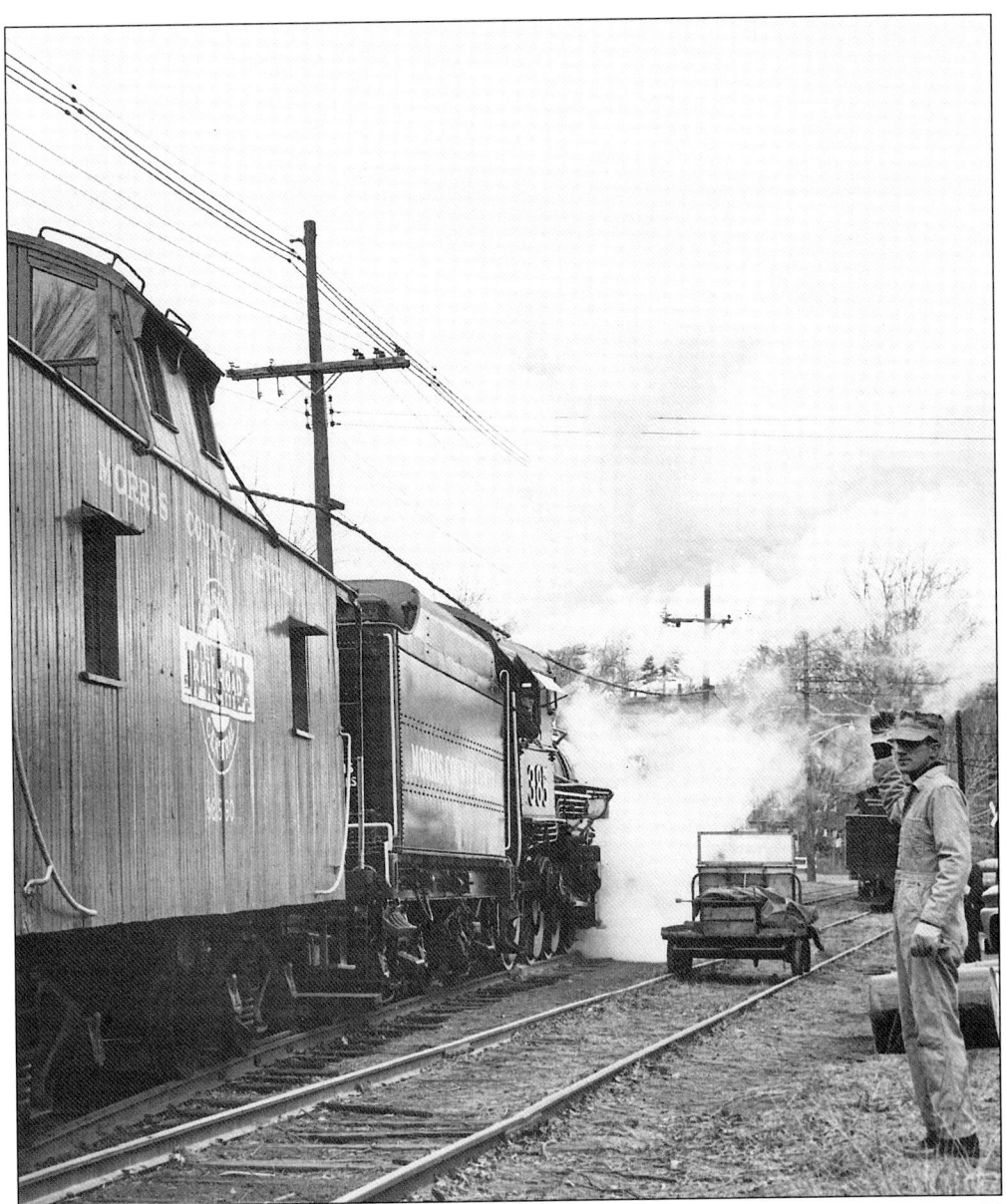

Any one of the thousands of passengers that boarded a Morris County Central train could not begin to imagine how much effort went into its operation. A founding father of the steam preservation movement, strong in the early 1960s, was Earle H. Gil, pictured here, waving to passengers as his restored locomotive No. 385 leads its train out of Morristown in a cloud of steam. This man literally put his heart and soul into the MCC and, because of him, untold numbers of children had their first train ride and encountered a live, fire-breathing machine, capable of transporting them back in time. The MCC moved its operations off the M&E to a new location at Newfoundland, New Jersey, at the end of 1973 and ultimately went out of business in December 1980. Today, the antique trains that Earle Gil and his dedicated crew managed to operate for 15 years are acknowledged as one of the pioneering American efforts to preserve the historic era of steam railroading, long after the lonesome whistles had faded from the scene. (Collection of Steven Hepler.)

Nine
REBIRTH...
THE MORRISTOWN & ERIE RAILWAY

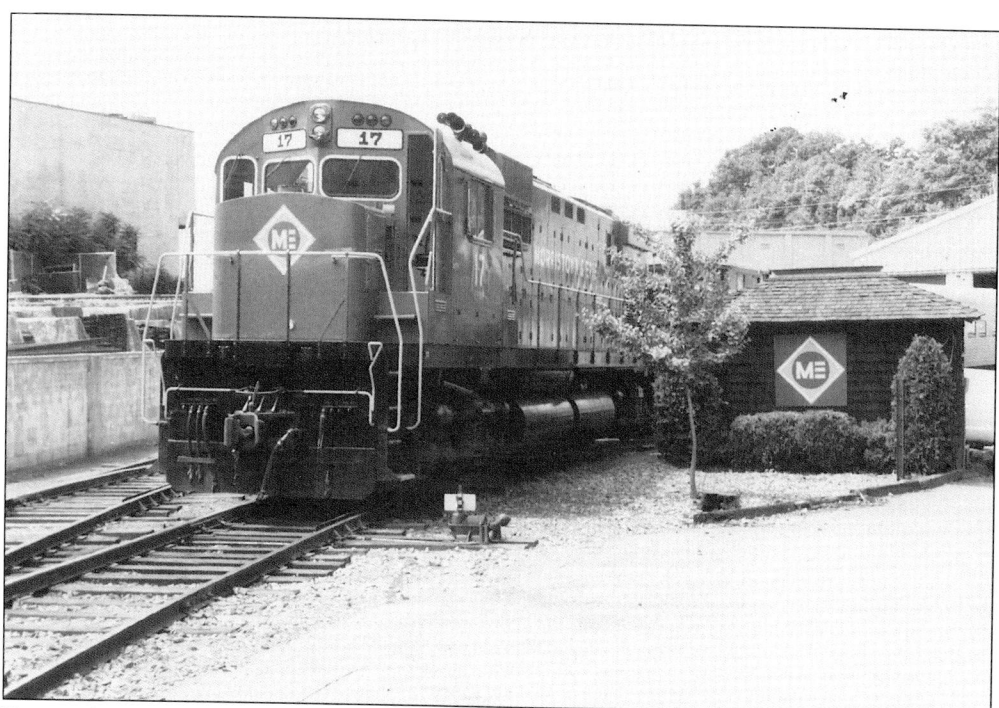

For nearly 75 years, the Morristown & Erie Railroad Co. operated profitably and successfully. However its fortunes changed drastically when the management of the mid-1970s caused the company to fall into bankruptcy in January 1977. Five years later, with a new owner, new image, and a new stable of locomotives, the Morristown & Erie Railway, Inc. was back on track and recognized as a true success story. (Courtesy of Morristown & Erie Railway.)

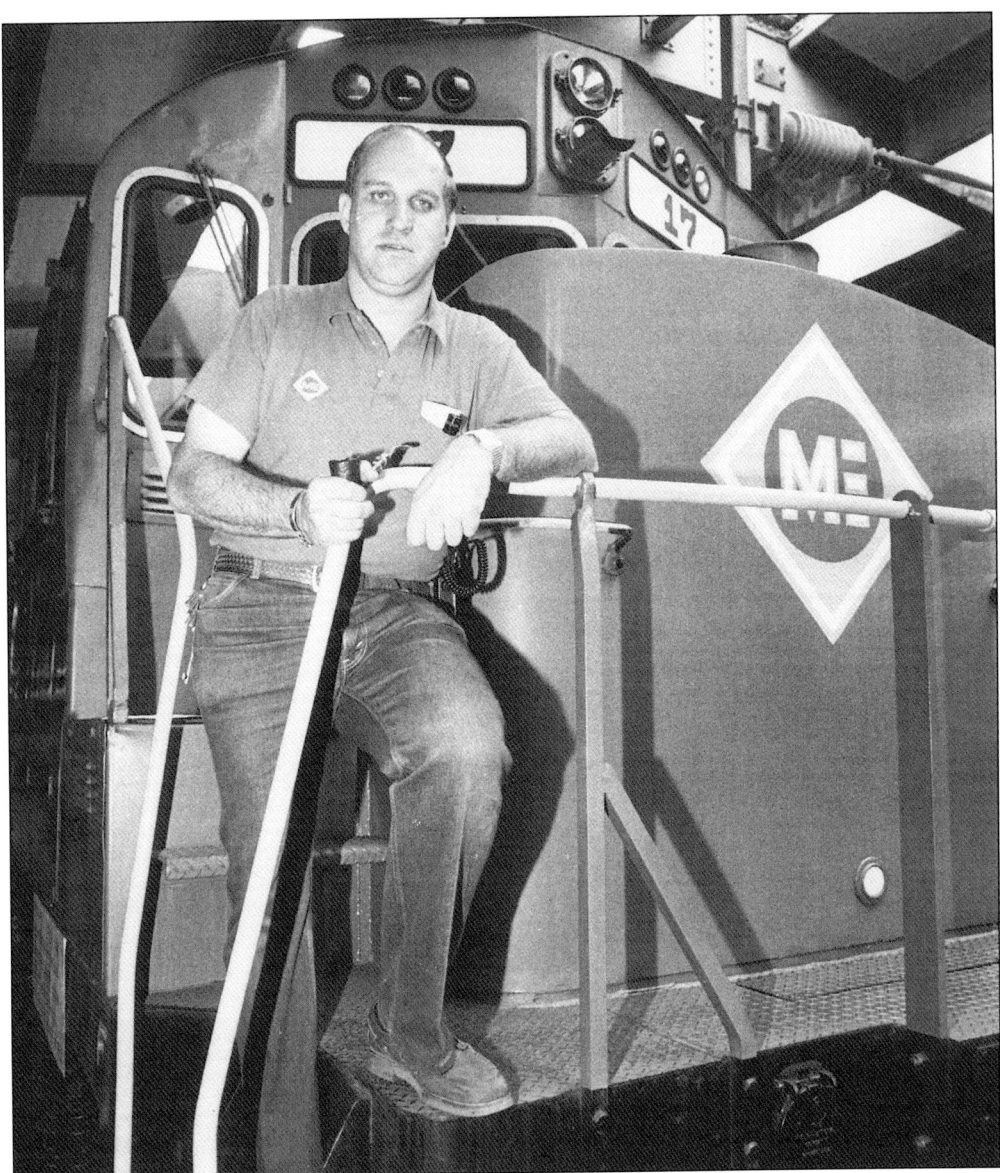

The Morristown & Erie Railroad continued to operate while in receivership through the efforts of a court-appointed trustee and General Manager Thomas G. Peterson. What the railroad needed was someone with experience in managing a business and a leader who was willing to invest heavily in both dollars and personal commitment. The M&E was very fortunate when Benjamin J. Friedland began negotiating to buy the railroad in 1980. For six months, he served as an unpaid advisor to the trustee as he became familiar with the railroad. On January 1, 1982, the company was reorganized as the Morristown & Erie Railway, Inc. Four additional locomotives were acquired, and the roadbed received its first maintenance in nearly a decade. Because of Friedland's dedication, the railroad was able to rise from the ashes of bankruptcy and become an important link in Morris County's transportation network. Ben led the M&E for nearly two decades, and, when he passed away on August 3, 1998, at age 55, his loss was a tremendous blow to his family, friends, and employees. (Courtesy of Morristown & Erie Railway.)

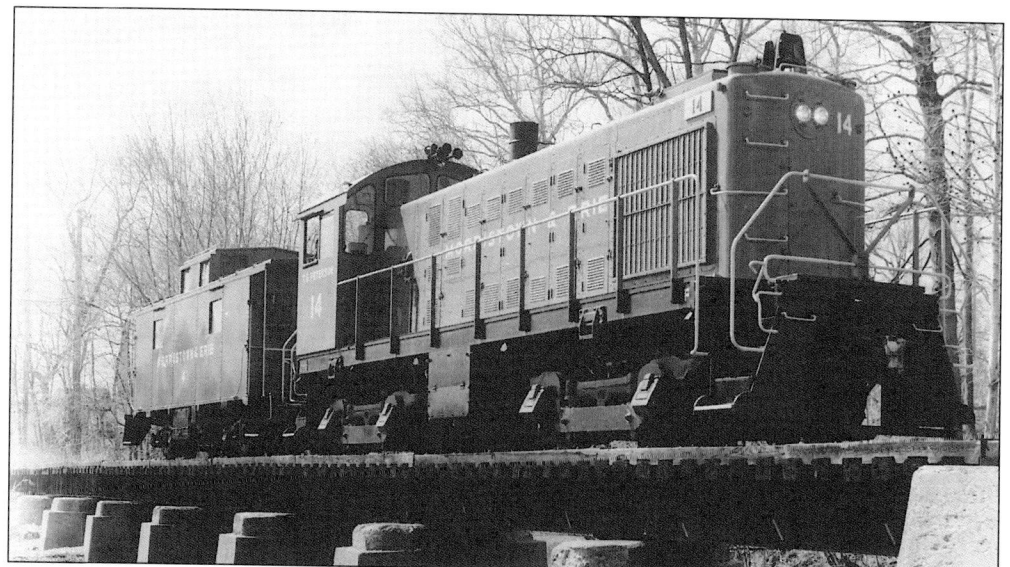

In 1981, Ben Friedland and M&E general manager Thomas G. Peterson decided that old No. 14 would get a new lease on life with a total rebuild at the Morristown shop. She was given a coat of bright red paint and rededicated on July 23, 1981, as the *T.G. Peterson* in honor of the faithful general manager who guided the railroad through its darkest days. This picture was taken in November 1981. (Photo by Benjamin J. Friedland.)

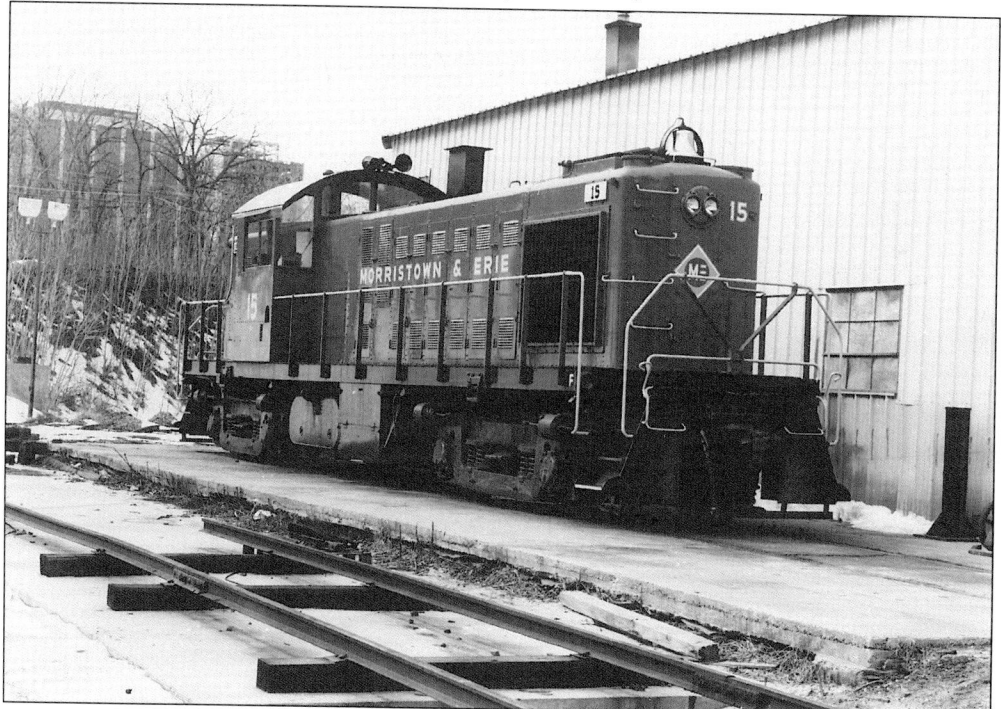

Out of service in late 1981, No. 15 was repainted in the new scheme in September 1982 and put back on the freight jobs. Taken out of service one more time in 1983, she was sold to the Connecticut Valley Railroad Museum and left the familiar M&E rails forever in July 1985. She is seen here at Morristown on February 24, 1983. (Courtesy of Bob Pennisi.)

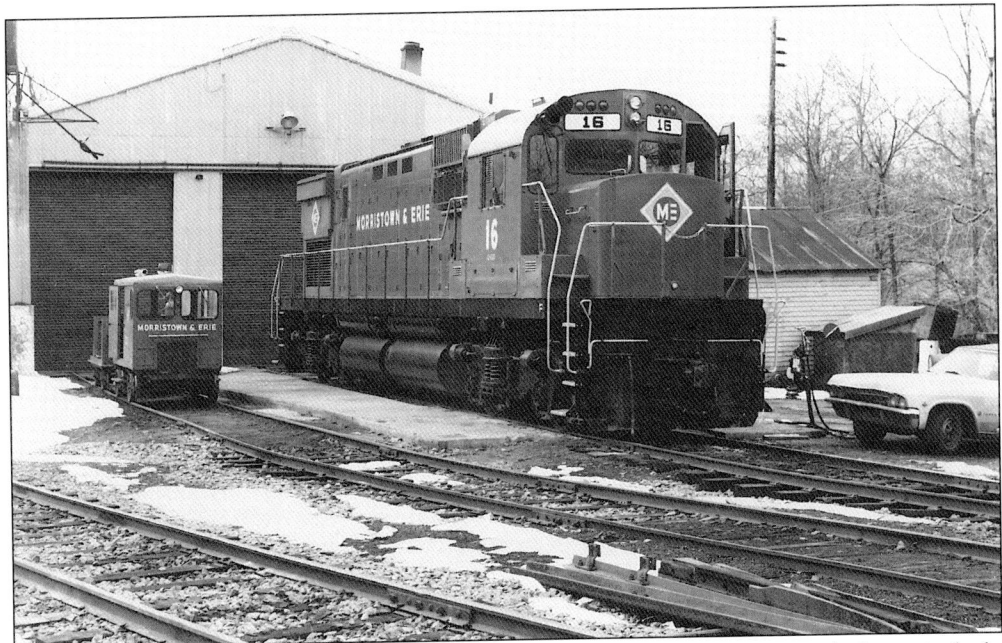

High-horsepower locomotives came to the M&E beginning in August 1982 with the arrival of a 3,000-horsepower, ex-Conrail "Century 430" unit. The M&E's "new" engine was originally built by ALCO in November 1967 for the New York Central System. Upon delivery at Morristown, the locomotive was sandblasted and painted in the railroad's tasteful red and black scheme with white and gold lettering and numbered "16." (Courtesy of Bob Pennisi.)

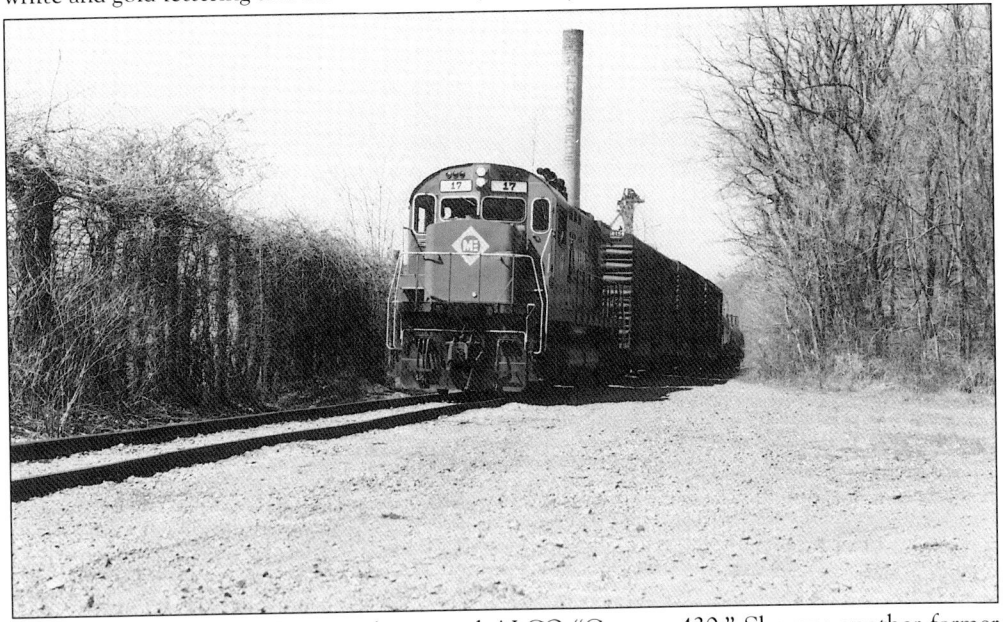

In July 1983, the railroad acquired a second ALCO "Century 430." She was another former New York Central engine constructed in November 1967. Both of the M&E's 130-ton "430s" worked on Penn Central and, later, Conrail. The new unit was placed in service as M&E No. 17 in March 1984 and is seen here passing the abandoned Eden Mill at Whippany on April 14, 1986. (Courtesy of Bob Pennisi.)

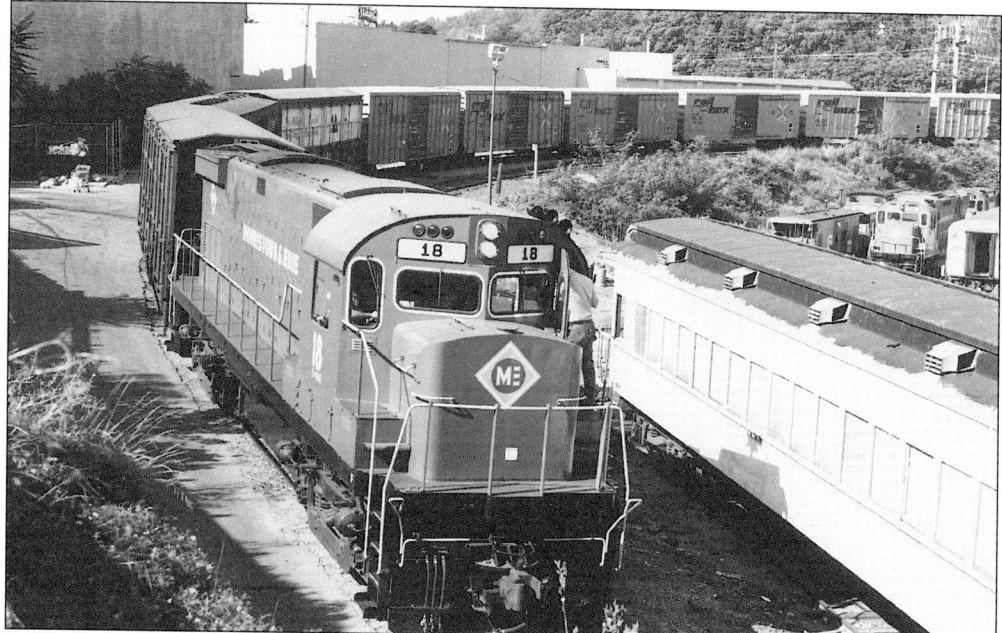

December 1983 saw the purchase of two ex-Toledo, Peoria & Western ALCO "Century 424" units, numbered 800 and 801, that had been built in 1964. When the 125-ton, 2,400-horsepower twins came to the M&E, they were given the numbers 18 and 19 and placed in service during the summer of 1984. No. 18 rounds the Morristown interchange on August 23, 1985, with the morning train. (Courtesy of Bob Pennisi.)

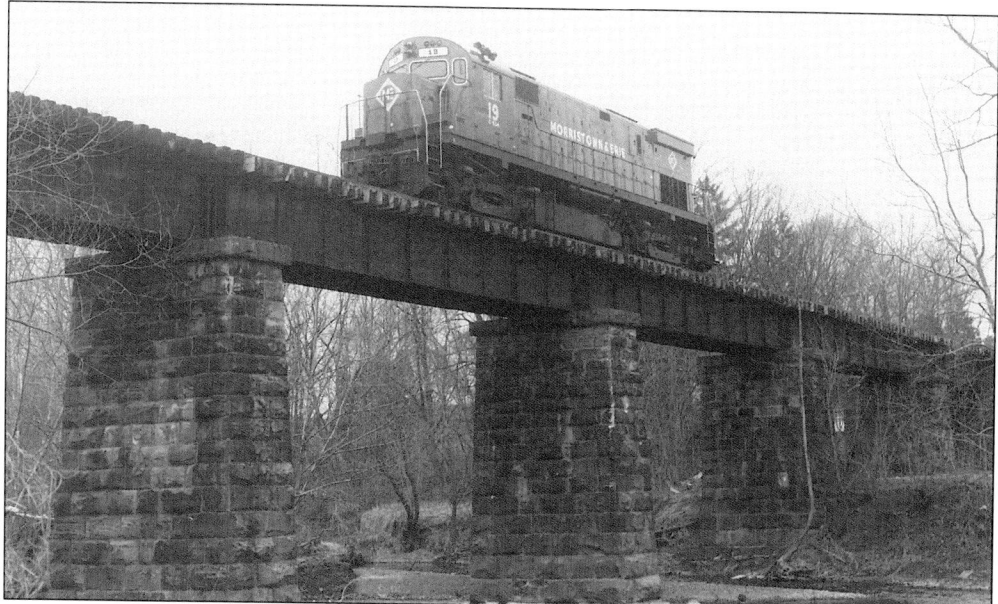

No. 19 crosses the New Hope and Ivyland's substantial bridge at Rushland, Pennsylvania, on February 25, 1991, during the period that the M&E was the designated operator of this former Reading Railroad branch line. This locomotive, along with sister unit No. 18, suffered heavy damage in 1965 when they were involved in a wreck while in service for their original owner, Toledo, Peoria & Western. Both units were later rebuilt by ALCO. (Courtesy of Bob Pennisi.)

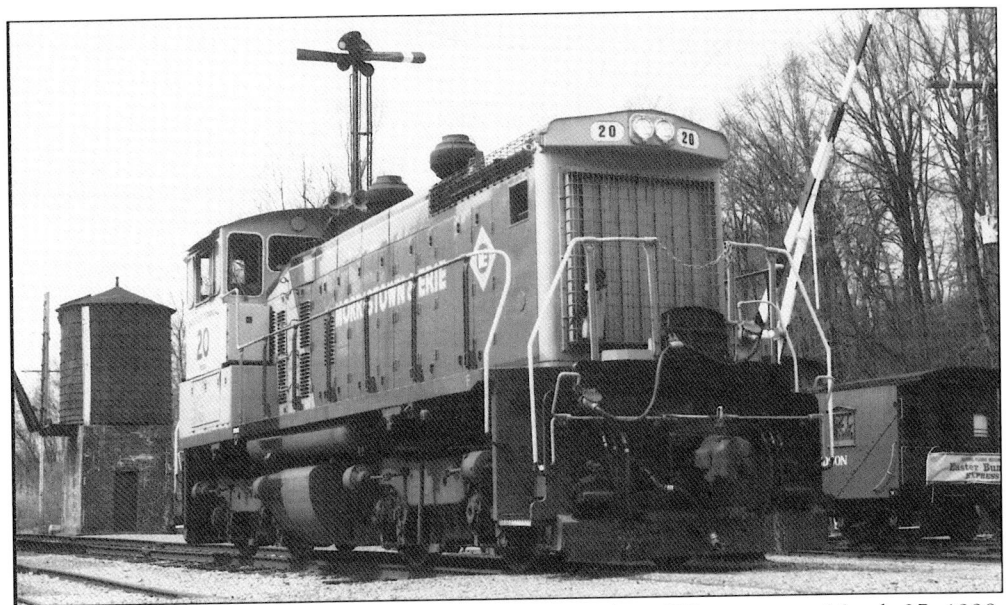

Morristown & Erie SW-1500 No. 20 pauses momentarily at Whippany on March 27, 1998. No. 20 was remanufactured by Conrail at Altoona, Pennsylvania, in 1996 for the M&E and was originally built by Electro-Motive Division, General Motors, in 1964 as Richmond, Fredericksburg & Potomac (RF&P) No. 91. It is the only one of the original batch of RF&P SW-1500s to have road trucks, dual controls, and full multiple unit capability. (Photo by Steven Hepler.)

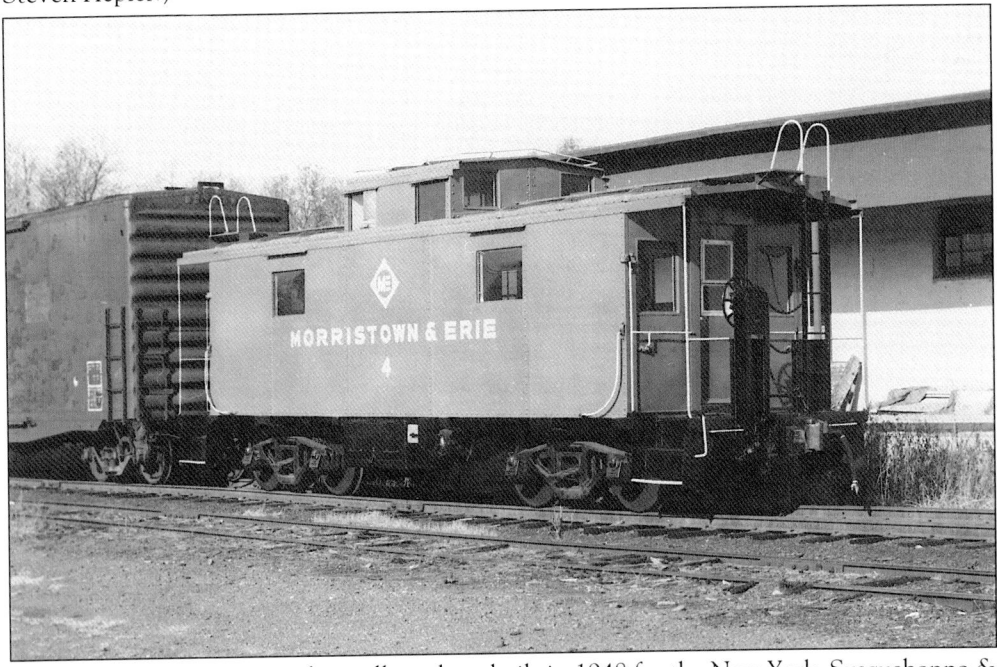

M&E caboose No. 4 is a modern, all-steel car built in 1948 for the New York, Susquehanna & Western Railroad and used on that company's freight trains until 1976 when it was retired. It arrived at Morristown in September 1979 and was then overhauled, renumbered, and placed in service by the M&E in October 1981. (Courtesy of Bob Pennisi.)

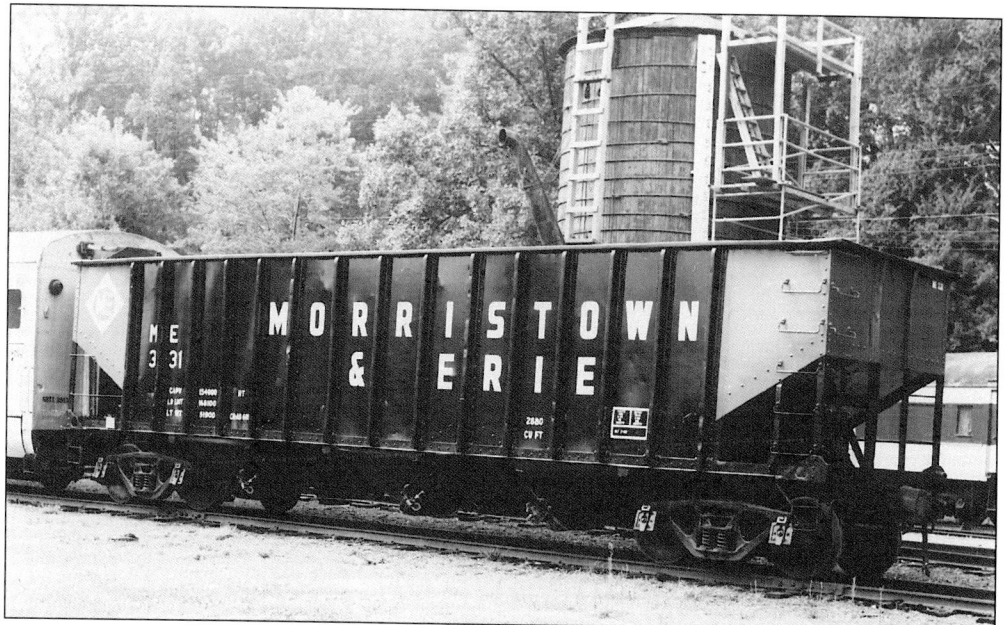

The railroad also owns two former Erie Lackawanna 77-ton-capacity hopper cars used for ballast laying. They were built in 1968 by the Greenville Car Co. and were acquired from NJ Transit in mid-1985. They are numbered 330 and 331; the latter is shown here at Whippany on July 19, 1986. (Courtesy of Bob Pennisi.)

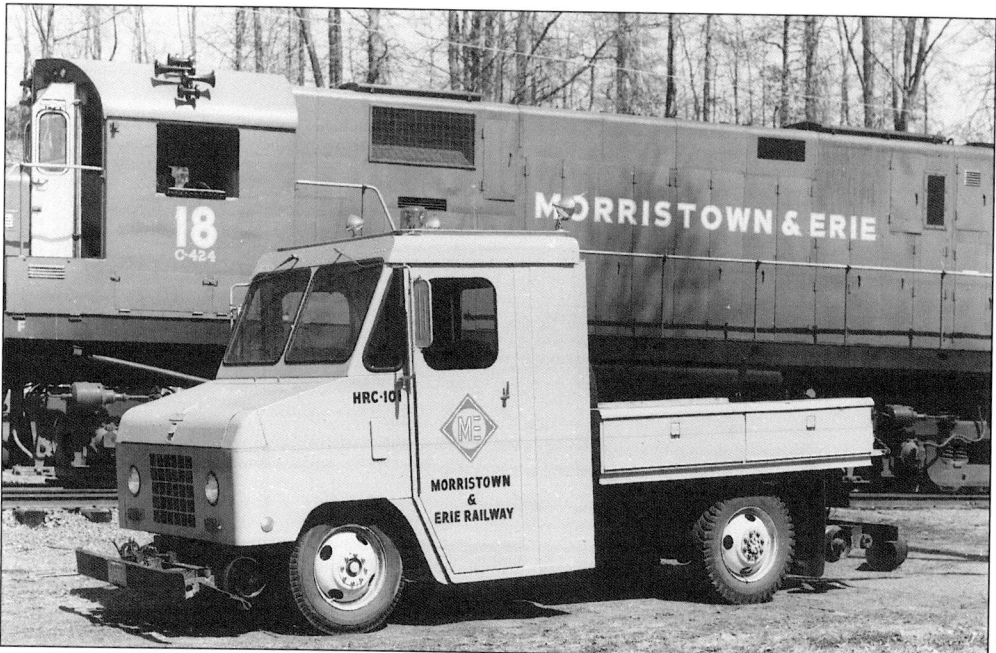

A former Conrail Chevrolet Hi-Rail pick-up vehicle, with both rubber tires and flanged wheels that permit it to travel over highways or railroad tracks, was acquired in April 1985. In addition to carrying men and materials directly to a work site, it is also used for inspecting sections of the M&E's right-of-way. High Rail Car-101 is seen at Whippany on March 26, 1986. (Courtesy of Bob Pennisi.)

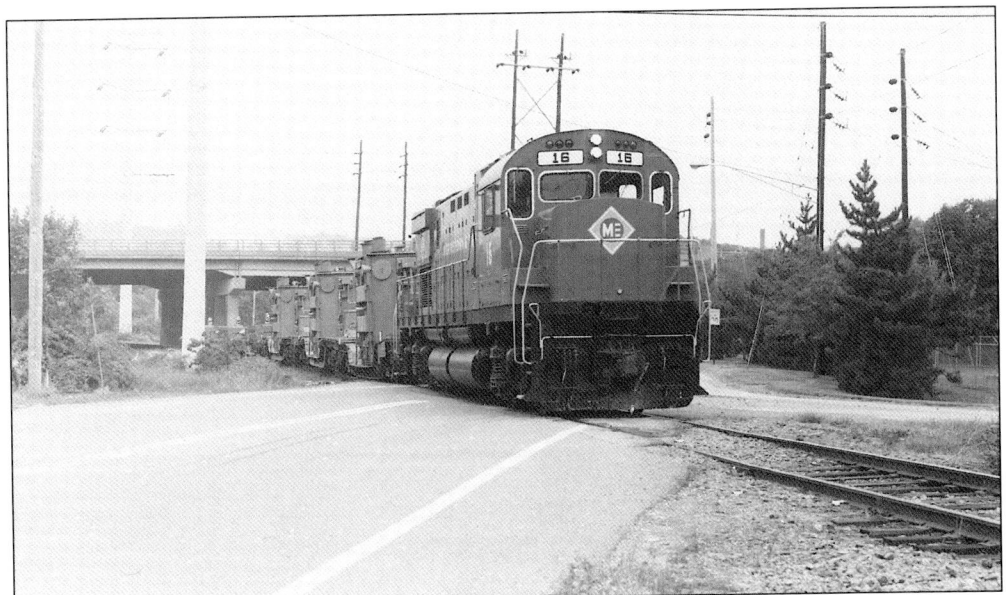

No. 16 rolls across Eden Lane on September 20, 1985, as it makes its way east through Cedar Knolls and Whippany on its way to the Public Service power station in Livingston. Included in the consist are three huge transformers and several trailing cars loaded with assorted electrical supplies for the power plant. (Courtesy of Bob Pennisi.)

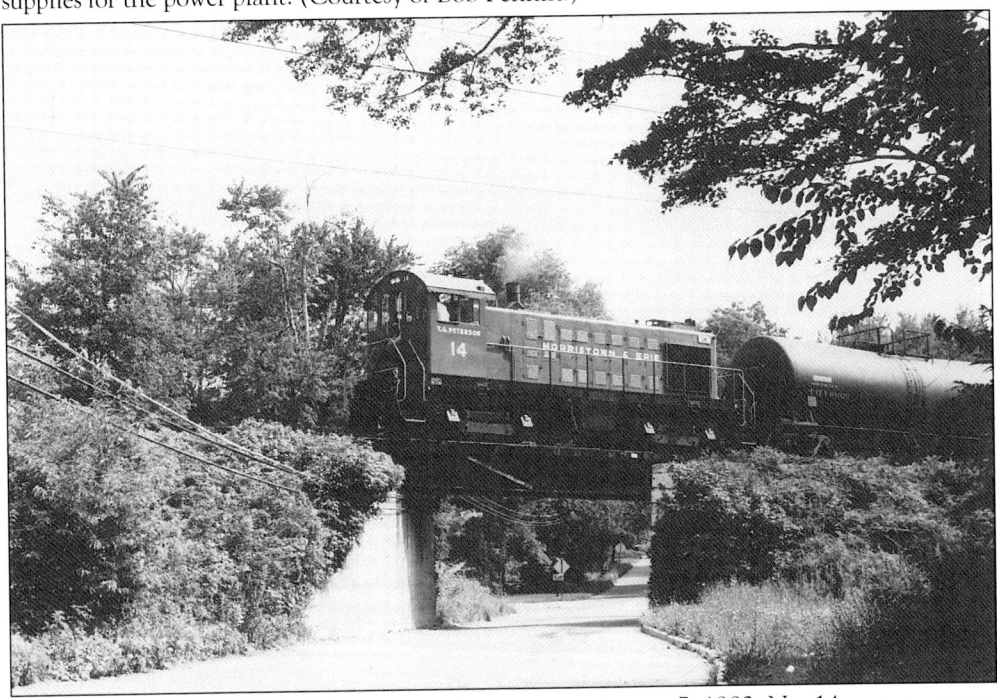

Heading west to Morristown after a run to Roseland on August 7, 1982, No. 14 tows an empty tanker which has just been picked up from Royal Lubricants in East Hanover. The train is crossing the bridge at River Road in East Hanover. The trees lining the roadway beyond the bridge help to provide shade to the small farm off to the left of the photo. (Courtesy of Bob Pennisi.)

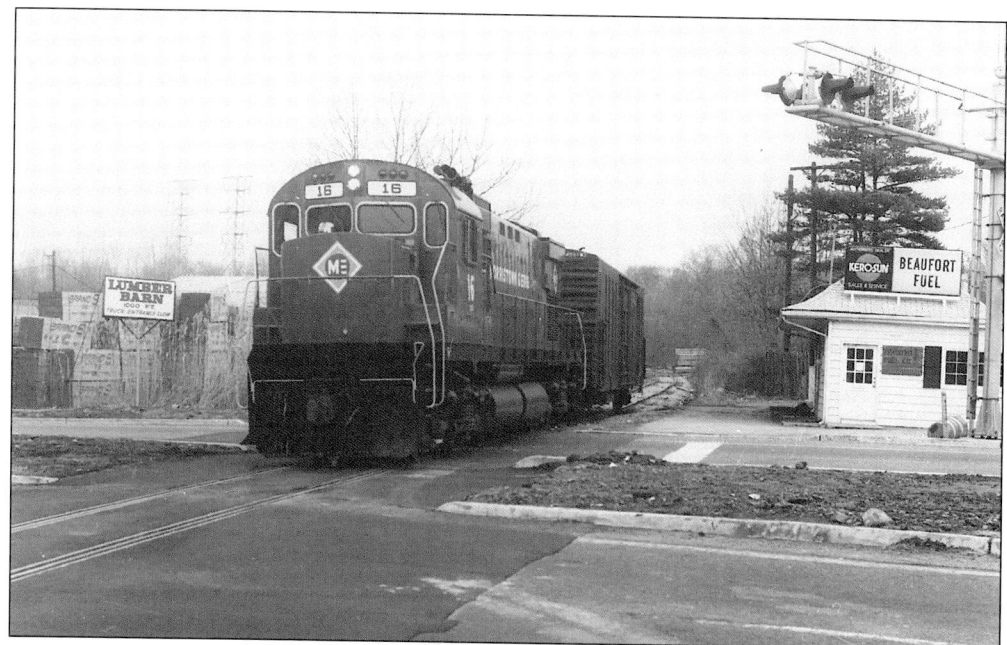

On Tuesday, December 22, 1987, No. 16 is caught by the camera as she tows a lone boxcar past the old Beaufort Avenue station and rolls across four-lane Eisenhower Parkway. Today, the small depot, one of two remaining on the M&E, stands vacant, its future uncertain. (Courtesy of Bob Pennisi.)

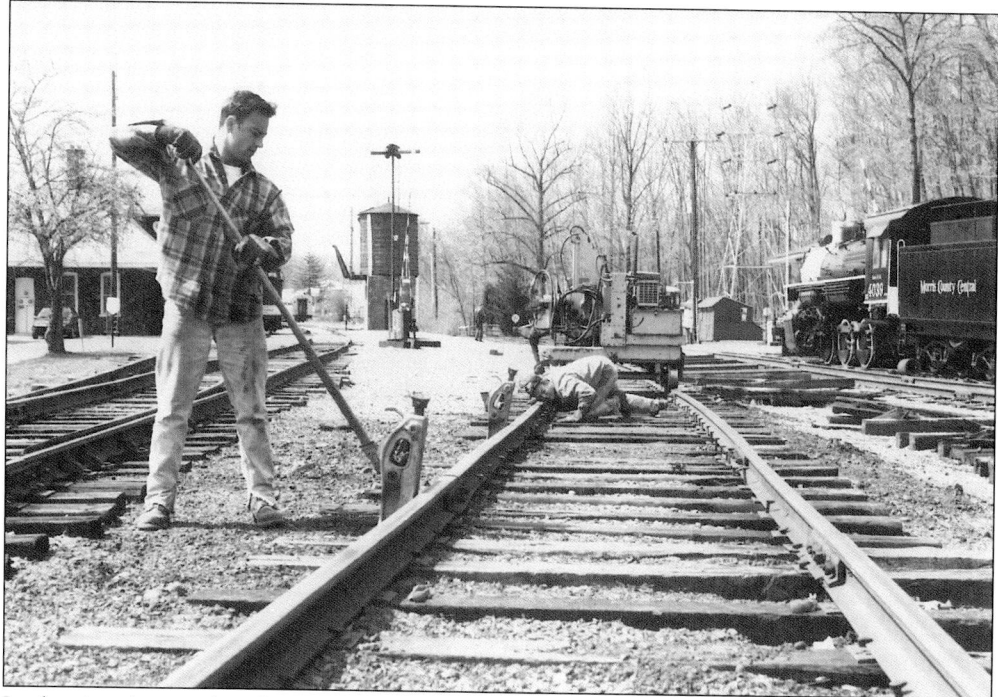

In the time-honored tradition, track supervisor Gerald Smith (background) takes a sighting as track worker Todd Senise (foreground) uses a lining bar to level up one of the rails on the runaround track at Whippany on April 3, 1998. (Photo by Steven Hepler.)

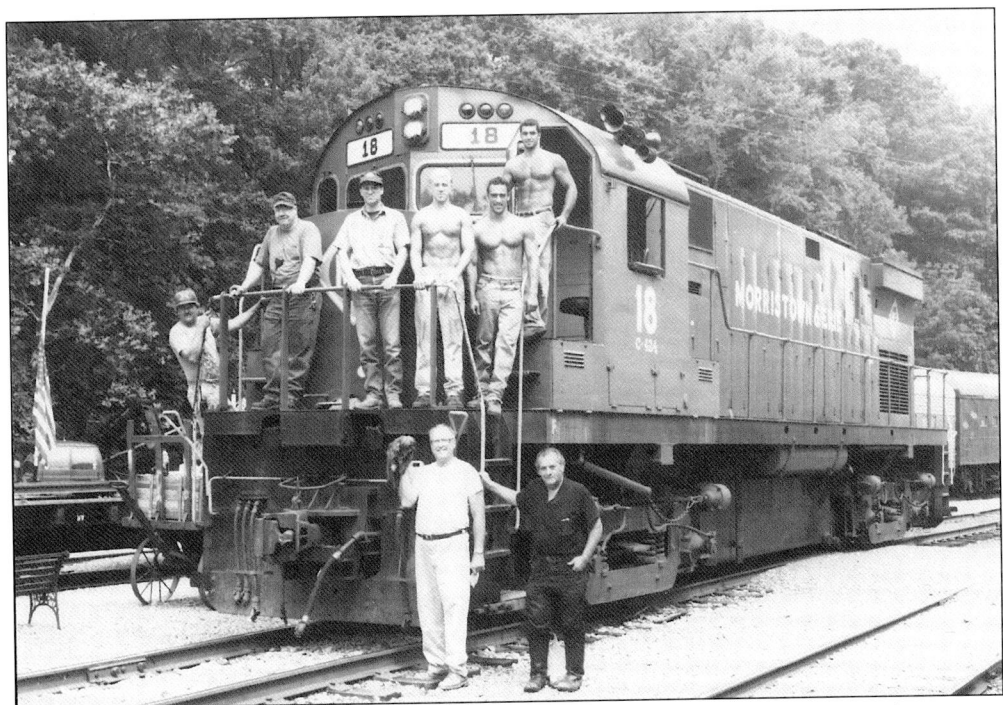

On August 14, 1998, No. 18 doubled as a stage for the crew as they posed for the camera at Whippany. From left to right are track supervisor Gerry Smith; superintendent Bill Myers; engineer Rich Campana; and track workers Sean O'Neil, Todd Senise, and Lee Stark. On the ground are Ed Kruckeberg (holding his dog, Gabby) and Art Jones. (Photo by Steven Hepler.)

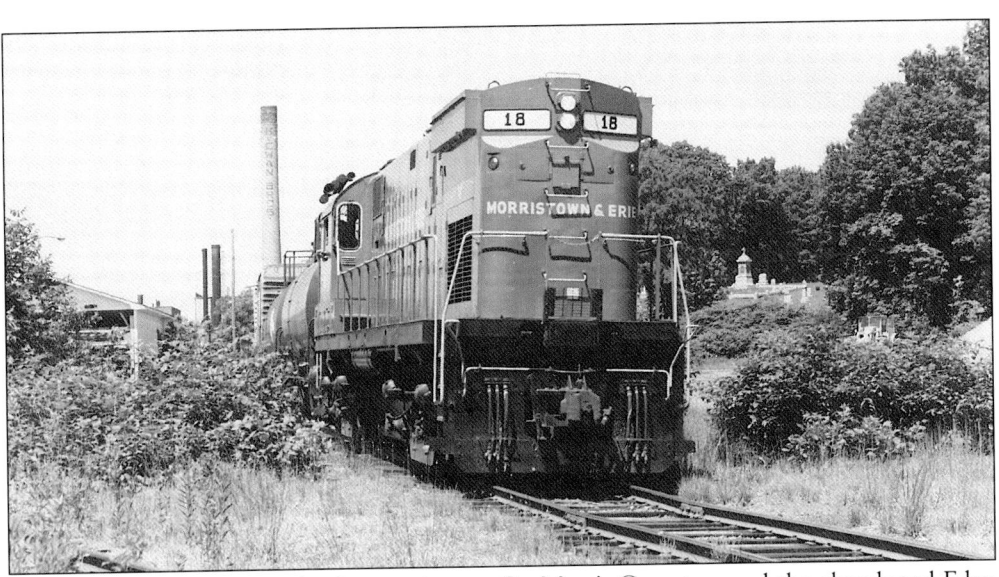

Morristown & Erie No. 18 leads its train past St. Mary's Cemetery and the abandoned Eden Mill in Whippany on June 9, 1986. It was at this exact site that construction began on the Whippany River Railroad on Monday, April 22, 1895. Over 100 years later, the railroad and its people continue to provide essential and friendly service to the many communities along the "Whippanong Trail." (Courtesy of Bob Pennisi.)

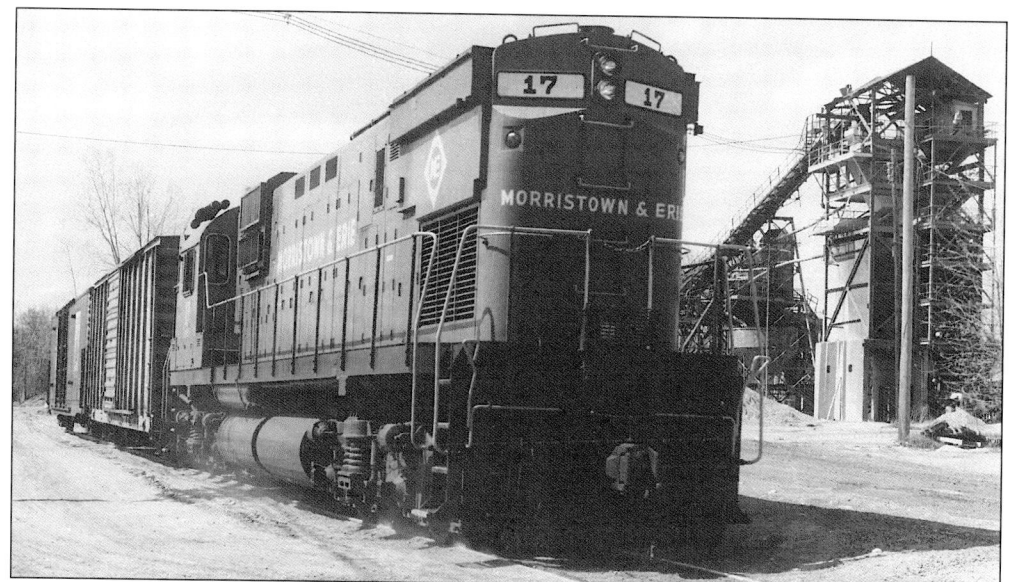

The Morristown & Erie is the operator of the privately owned, former Chester Branch of the Delaware, Lackawanna & Western. The line runs from its connection with NJ Transit at Lake Junction near Wharton to Randolph, a distance of about 4 miles. With No. 17 in charge, a "Chester Division Local" passes the County Concrete plant at Kenvil, New Jersey, on April 21, 1987. (Courtesy of Bob Pennisi.)

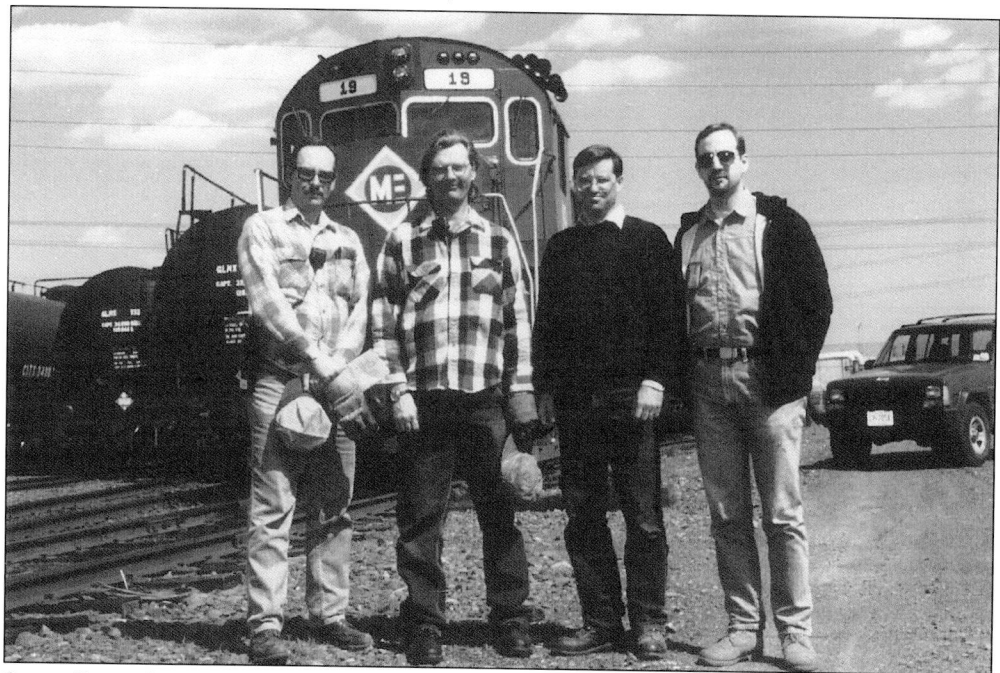

Since December 1995, the M&E has been performing switching duties at The Oil Shale Company (TOSCO) Bayway Petroleum Refinery in Linden, New Jersey. Service is provided all day, Monday through Friday, and half a day on Saturday. On May 14, 1996, from left to right, Walt Switz, Paul Yanosik, Rich Campana, and John DeStephanis gathered around No. 19 before starting the days work at the huge complex. (Courtesy of Mike Del Vecchio.)

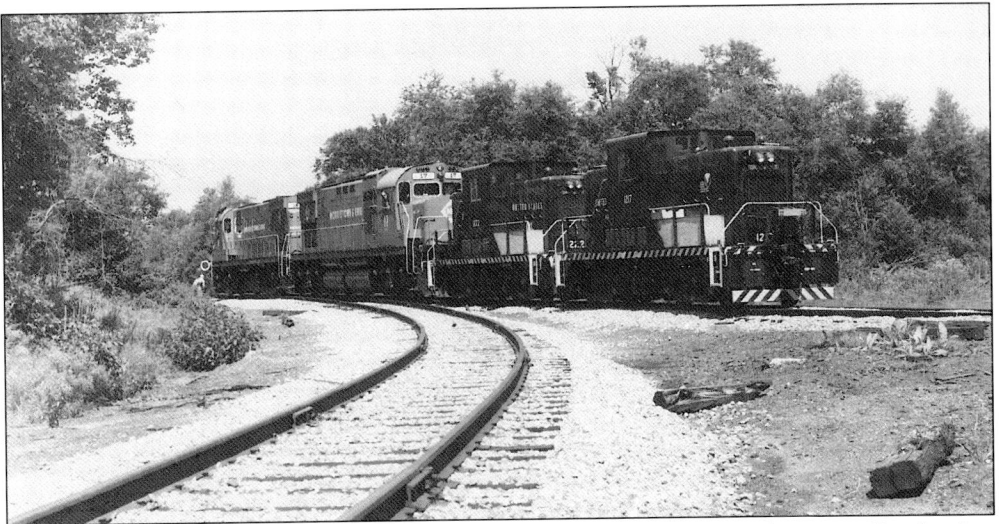

Unusual equipment moves are a regular part of the present-day M&E's business. On this hot August 14, 1987 day, two of the M&E's big ALCO "Century" units have two relatively tiny Army switching locomotives from Picatinny Arsenal in tow at Ferremont Junction near Kenvil, New Jersey. The Army units were on their way to a midwest base via the M&E's Conrail connection at Lake Junction. (Courtesy of Bob Pennisi.)

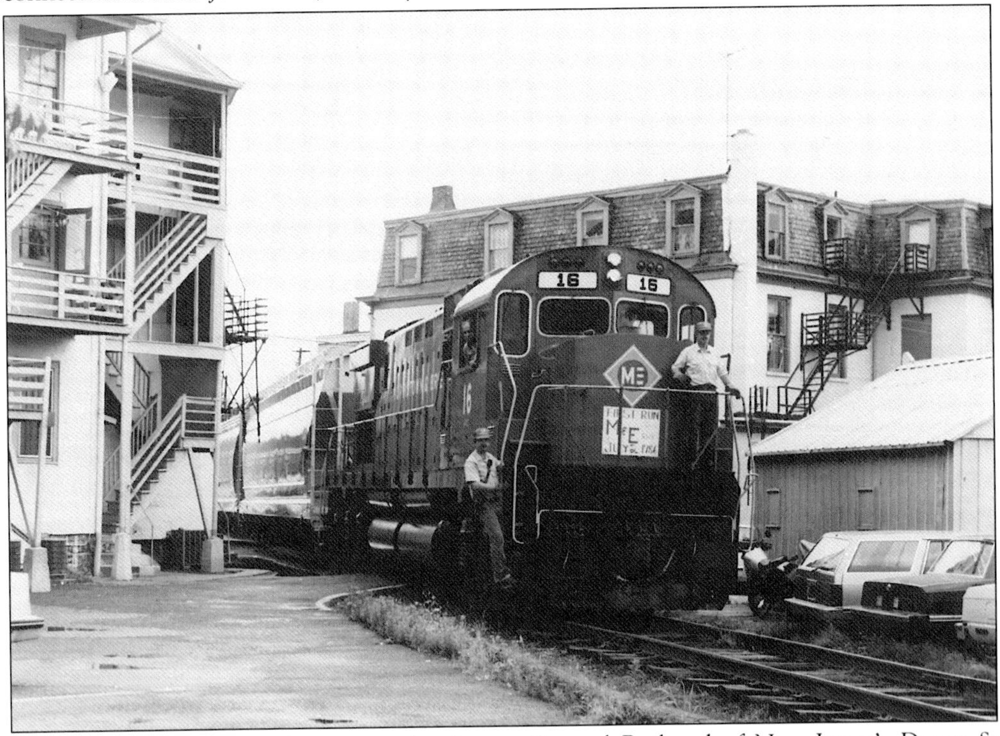

The M&E also leases and operates the former Central Railroad of New Jersey's Dover & Rockaway Branch from Morris County. The M&E operated its first train over the branch on July 2, 1986, and it is seen here cautiously passing through the back streets of Dover with Ben Friedland at the throttle. Trainman Steve Kay (left) and conductor Al Holleuffer keep a watch on the track ahead. (Photo by Bob Pennisi; courtesy of Alan J. Holleuffer.)

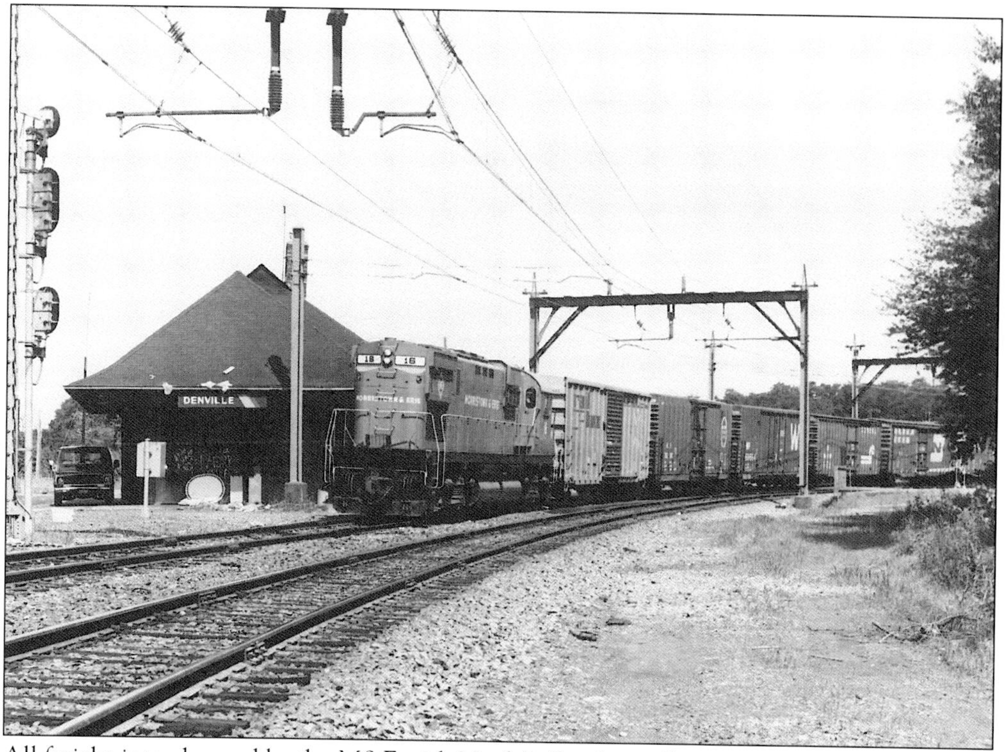

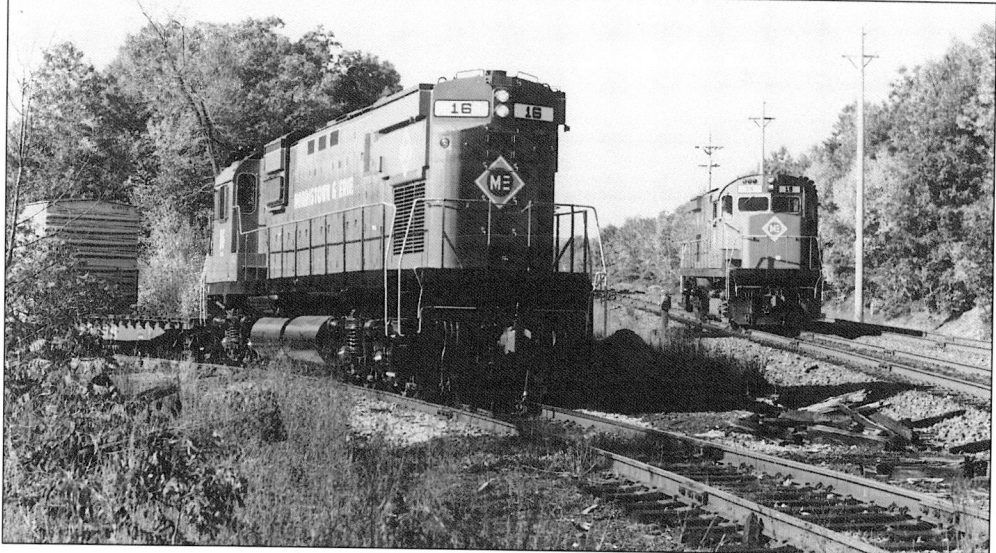

All freight interchanged by the M&E with Norfolk Southern (formerly Conrail) is received at Lake Junction in Wharton. The Morristown interchange was closed, ending the confusion of having two interchanges only a few miles apart. Here we see the M&E exercising its trackage rights agreement with New Jersey Transit as one of its freights travels west past the (no longer standing) Denville depot on July 1, 1986. (Courtesy of Bob Pennisi.)

M&E No. 18 waits on the NJ Transit (ex-Delaware, Lackawanna & Western) main line at Lake Junction near Wharton, as No. 16 pulls onto the main after completing a run over the Chester Division on October 19, 1987. (Courtesy of Bob Pennisi.)

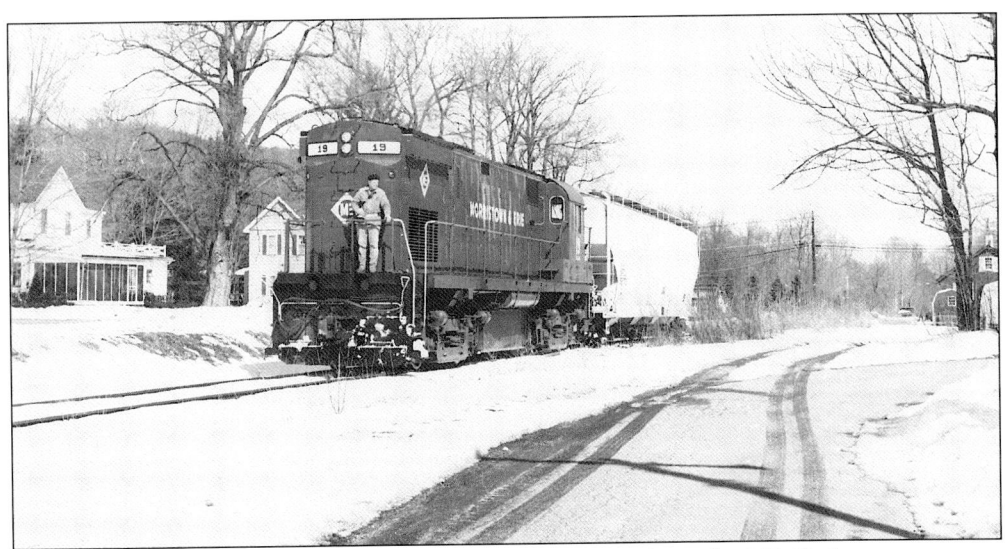

Conductor Al Holleuffer is bundled up for a cold day of work on the M&E's first revenue run over the former Central of New Jersey High Bridge Branch on February 25, 1993. The train is seen passing through Flanders, and that mantle of freshly fallen snow adds a nice touch to this rural scene. (Photo by Bob Pennisi; courtesy of Alan J. Holleuffer.)

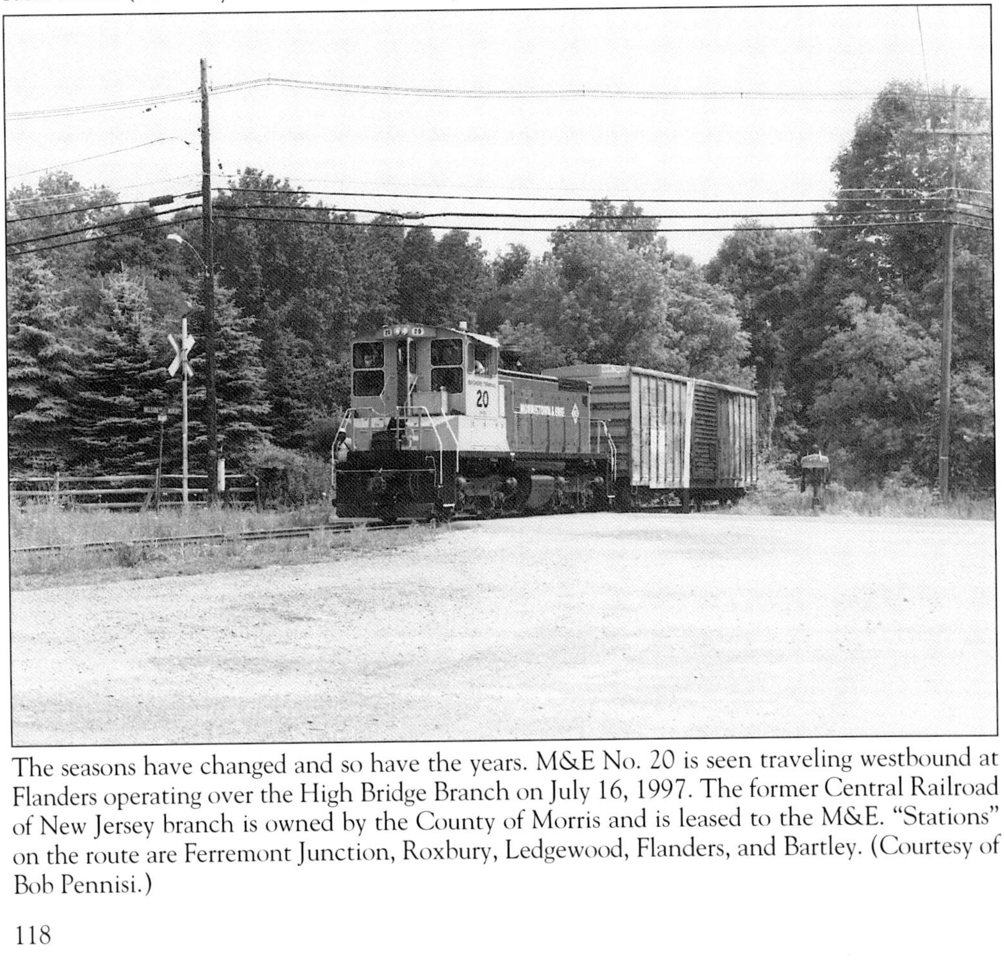

The seasons have changed and so have the years. M&E No. 20 is seen traveling westbound at Flanders operating over the High Bridge Branch on July 16, 1997. The former Central Railroad of New Jersey branch is owned by the County of Morris and is leased to the M&E. "Stations" on the route are Ferremont Junction, Roxbury, Ledgewood, Flanders, and Bartley. (Courtesy of Bob Pennisi.)

Ten
Historic Preservation at the Whippany Railway Museum

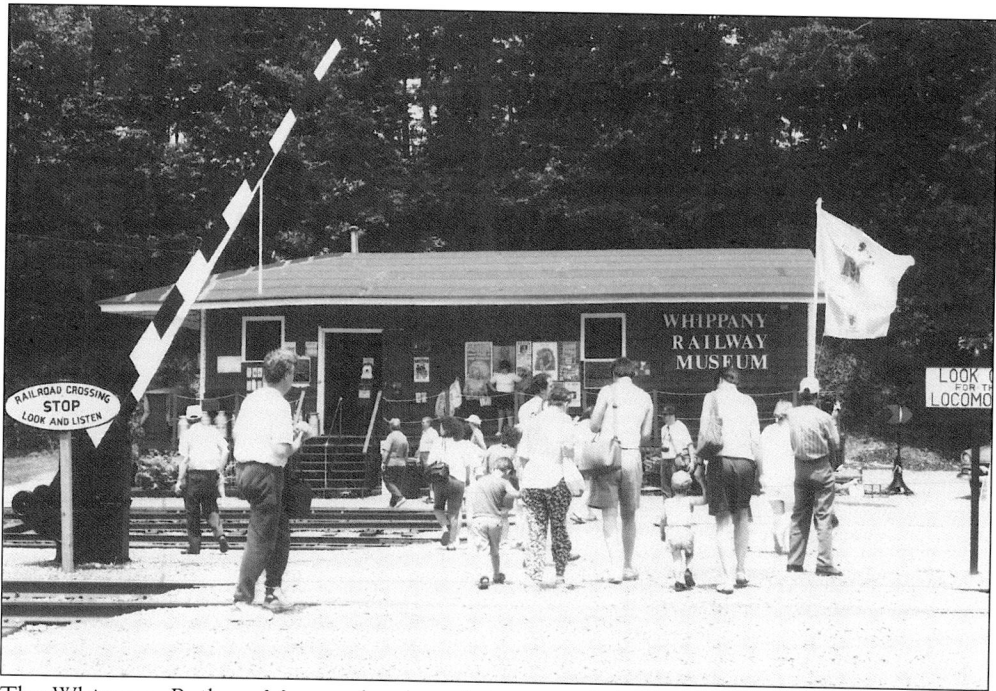

The Whippany Railway Museum has been bringing to life the saga of New Jersey's railroads to the public since 1985. Displays tell the story of the railroad through representative models, historic photographs, and rare paperwork. Other exhibits highlight a variety of railroad china, tools, and appliances, such as bells, whistles, and headlights. The memories of railroading's past live on within the walls of the Whippany freight house for all to enjoy. (Photo by Steven Hepler.)

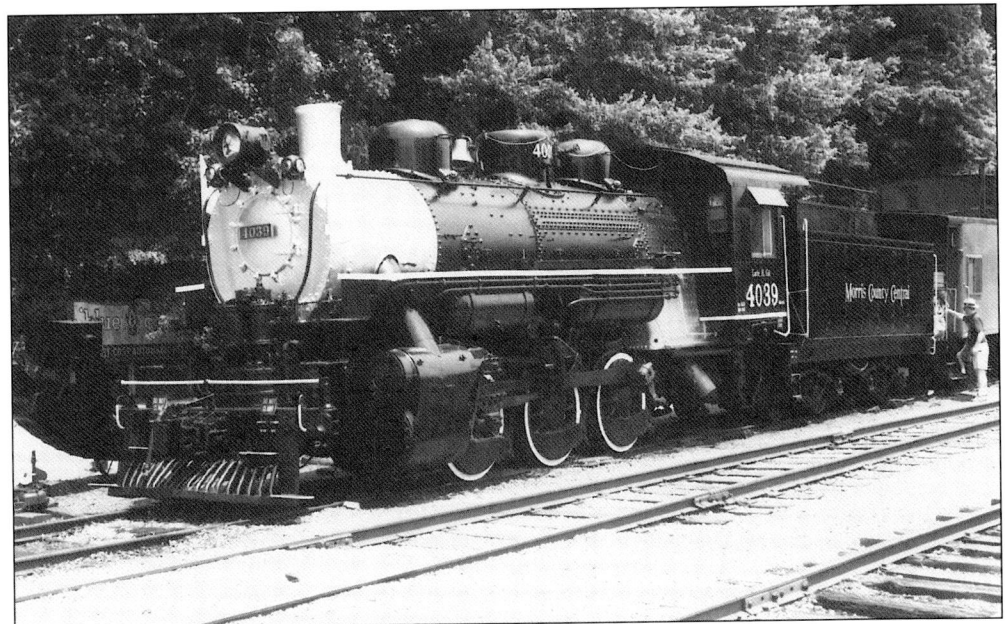

Morris County Central steam locomotive No. 4039 is a 135-ton 0-6-0 switching engine built for the U.S. Army in November 1942 by the American Locomotive Company. Now owned by the museum, a restoration to operation is the nonprofit organization's ultimate goal for 4039. The thrilling sights and sounds of steam railroading may once again become commonplace in Hanover Township. (Photo by Steven Hepler.)

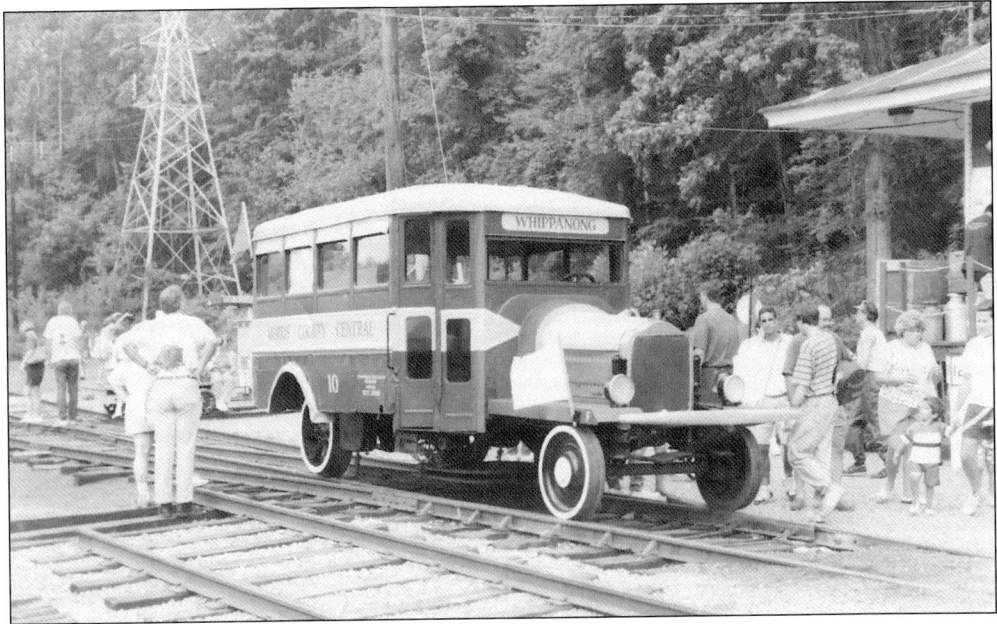

Former M&E Railbus No. 10 is admired by the crowd at the Whippany Railway Museum in September 1996. As this is written, the railbus has just celebrated its 80th birthday on the Morristown & Erie. President McEwan's purchase of No. 10 in 1918 has proven to be a hardy and historic one indeed, as new generations continue to experience this unique New Jersey transportation artifact. (Photo by Steven Hepler.)

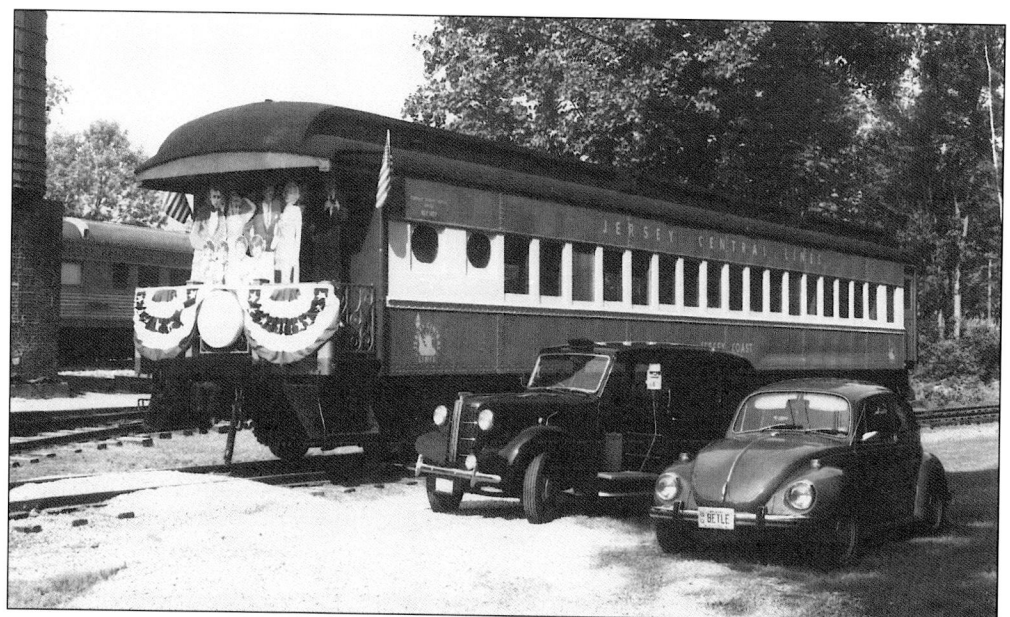

The *Jersey Coast* was built as a standard coach in 1927 for the Central Railroad of New Jersey (CNJ). In 1948, the CNJ converted it into a Commuter Club Car. The museum has painted the exterior of the car in the CNJ's *Blue Comet* colors of Packard Blue and Jersey Cream. The *Blue Comet* was the CNJ's crack passenger train of the 1930s, running between Jersey City and Atlantic City. (Photo by Steven Hepler.)

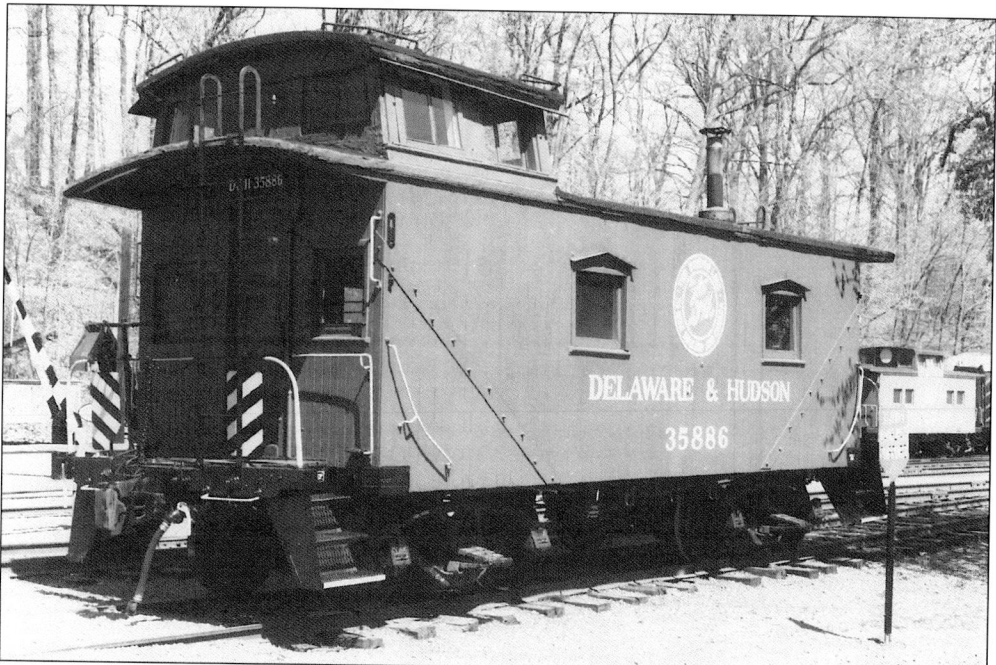

The author's classic, all-wood, 1913-vintage Delaware & Hudson (D&H) caboose No. 35886 was used in regular freight service on the D&H for over half a century. Today, it is enjoyed by countless visitors who are lucky enough to ride aboard it during the museum's special passenger excursions. (Photo by Steven Hepler.)

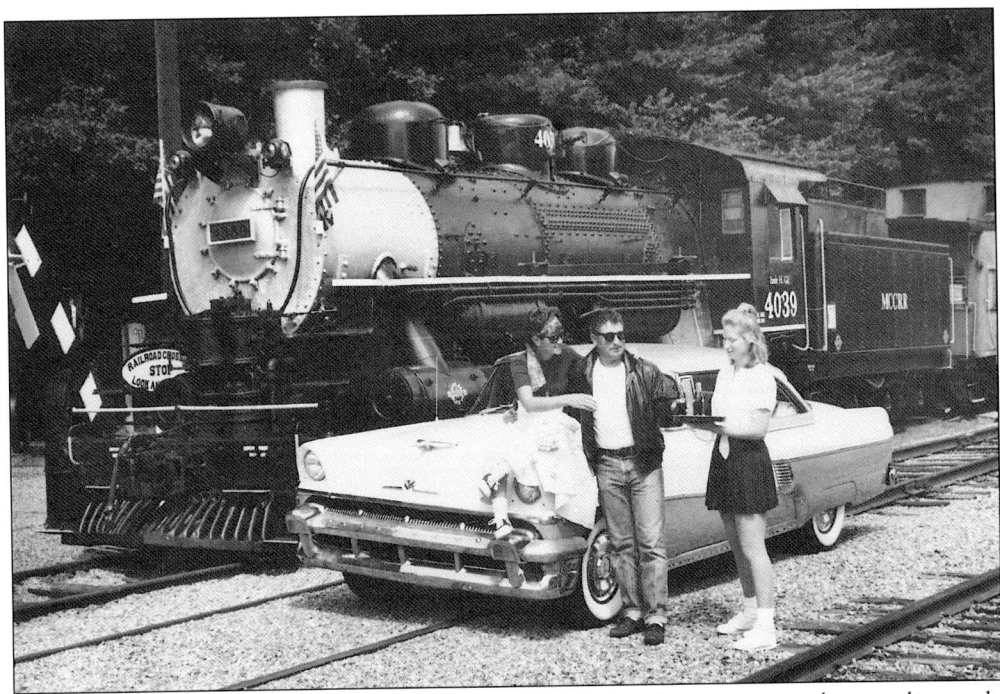

In a scene reminiscent of the Fab Fifties, a car hop serves the young couple a cooling soda pop as they enjoy a summer's outing in their restored 1956 Mercury. The Whippany Railway Museum's steam locomotive No. 4039 provides an impressive background. (Photo by Steven Hepler.)

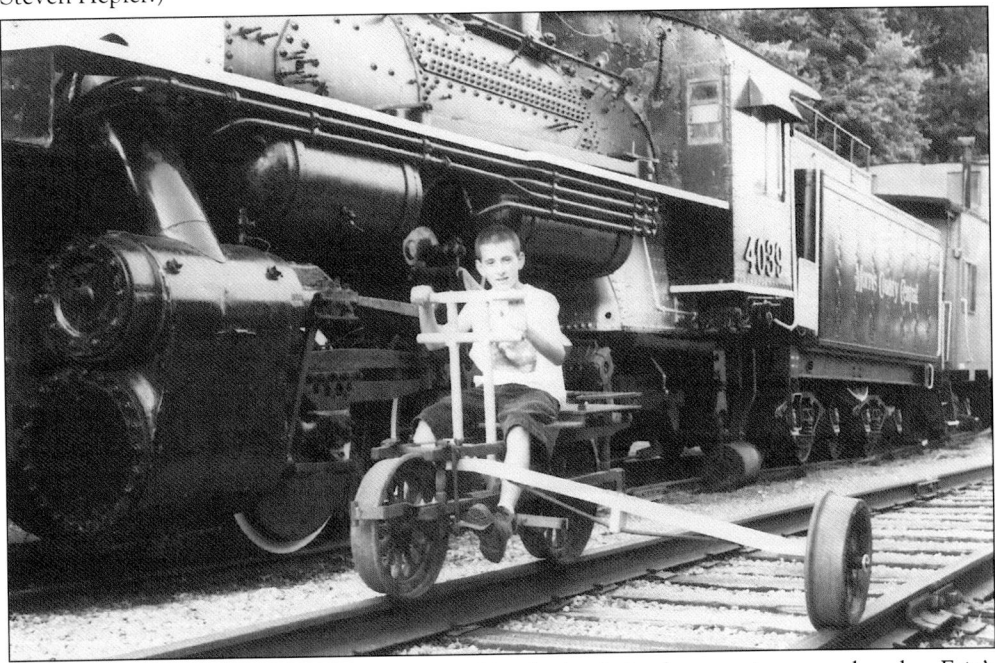

Eric Krygoski gives the museum's 100-year-old velocipede its first run in many decades. Eric's grandfather, Earle Gil, restored this unusual 19th-century three-wheel vehicle in 1998. (Photo by Steven Hepler.)

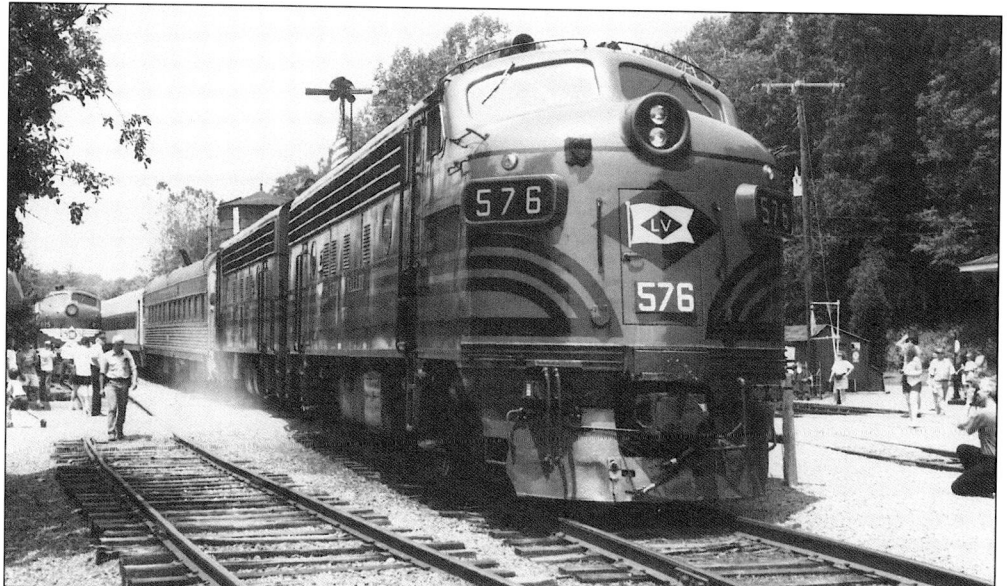

Excursion trains depart from the historic Whippany station during special events at various times of the year. In this scene, Lehigh Valley diesel No. 576 arrives from the west with a trainload of happy passengers. The locomotive is owned by the United Railroad Historical Society of New Jersey and is usually displayed at Whippany. (Photo by Steven Hepler.)

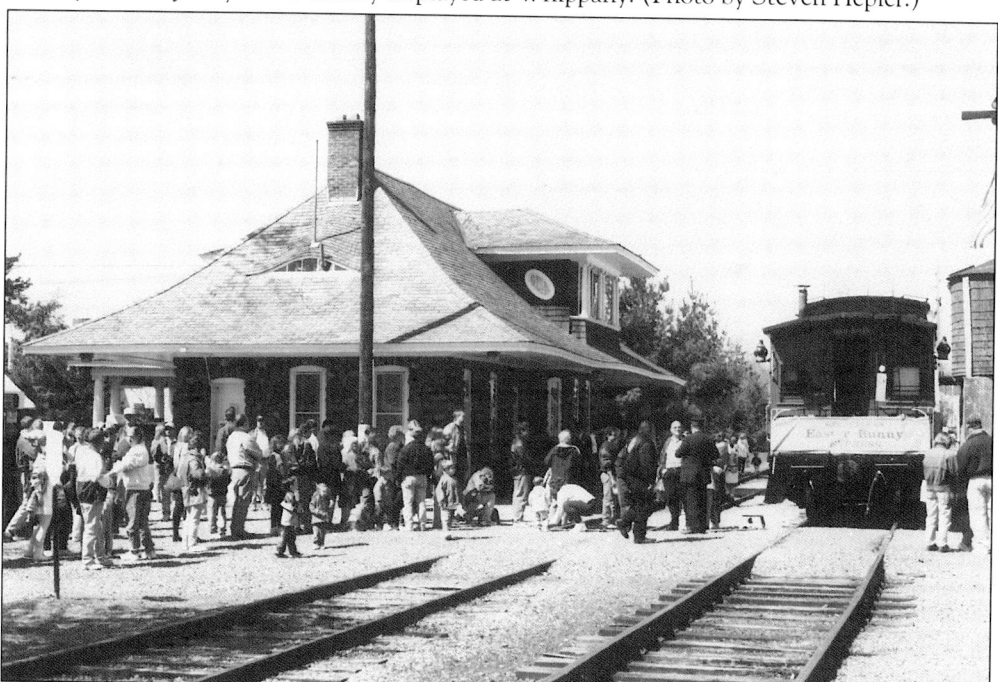

It's train time at Whippany! The museum's special excursions afford an opportunity for families to join in the fun, thrill, and excitement of riding a shortline passenger train. These trips have a unique educational value as well, since they give today's generation a chance to experience the glory of railroading, something that we cannot afford to lose to the past. (Photo by Steven Hepler.)

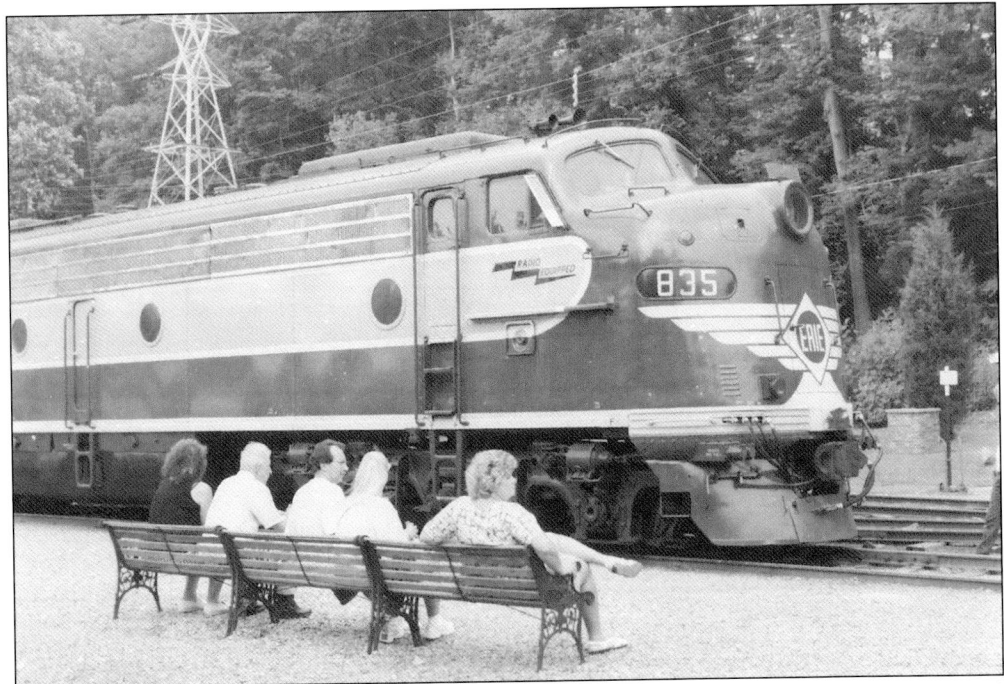

United Railroad Historical Society of New Jersey owns a pair of restored E-8-type diesel locomotives, which they have painted in the classic two-tone green passenger colors of the Erie Railroad. A group of visitors relax on the platform benches at the Whippany Railway Museum as they look over the lead unit of a recreated "Erie Limited" arriving at the station on September 8, 1996. (Photo by Steven Hepler.)

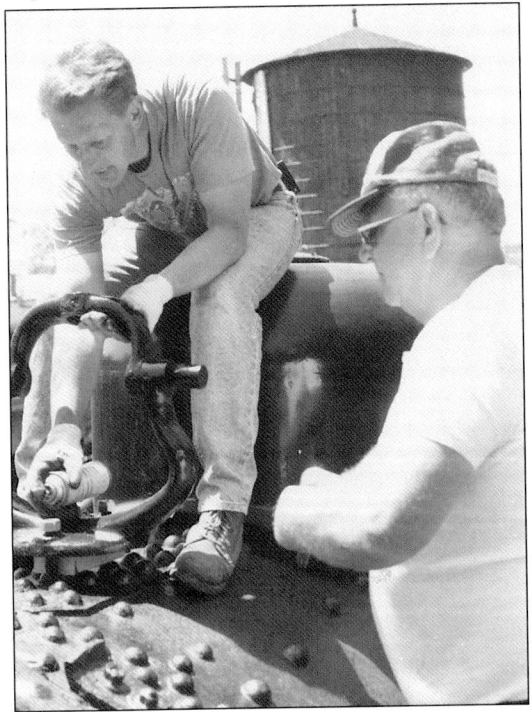

Up on the boiler of No. 4039, museum vice president Joe Krygoski (left) and trustee Charles Berkemeyer adjust the engine's bell bracket prior to installing the bell itself in the yoke. The majority of the museum's collection of artifacts are restored by museum members, all of whom are unpaid volunteers. (Photo by Steven Hepler.)

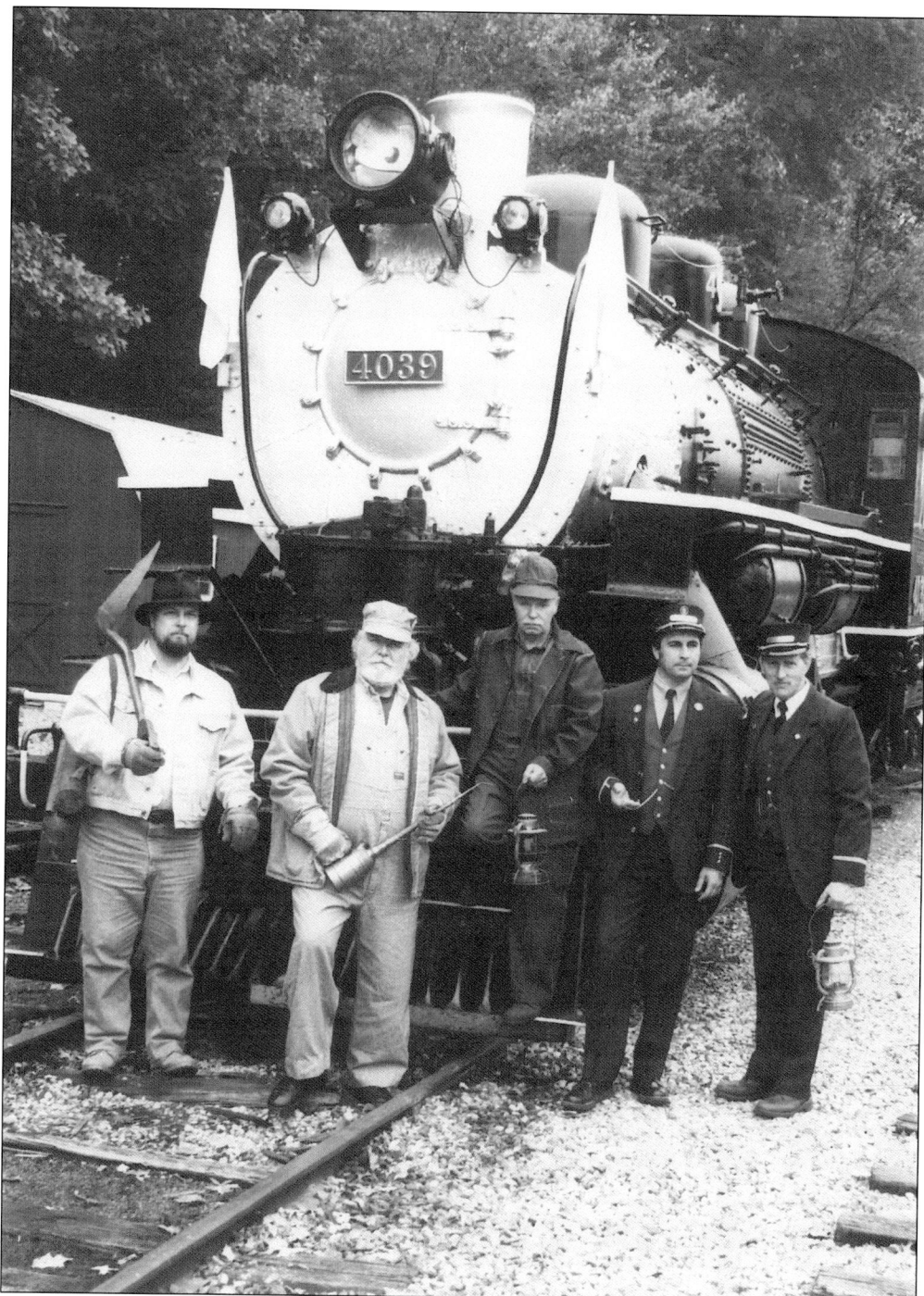

This nostalgic scene, similar to the one on page 58, shows Whippany Railway Museum members posing with their locomotive at Whippany on October 19, 1997. From left to right are Gerard Geisler, treasurer; Charles Berkemeyer, trustee; Paul Bartholomew, trustee; Steven Hepler, president; and Joseph Krygoski, vice president. (Photo by Paul Tupaczewski; courtesy of Whippany Railway Museum Collection.)

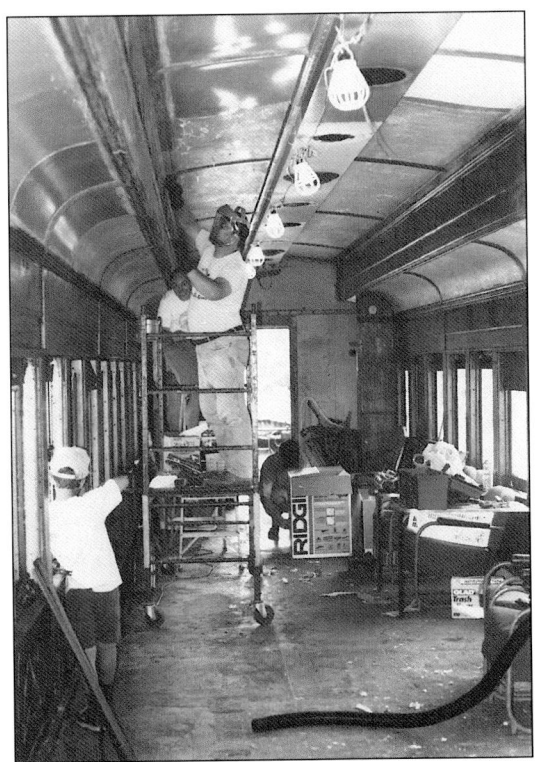

Museum members Christian Geisler (foreground), Gerry Geisler (on scaffold in front), Vin LiBrizzi (behind Gerry), and Ib Pedersen (kneeling in background) are busy at work inside the *Jersey Coast*, stripping off decades of old paint and varnish from the interior of the car. Restoration of antique rail equipment requires constant maintenance to protect these relics from the elements and the ravages of time. (Photo by Steven Hepler.)

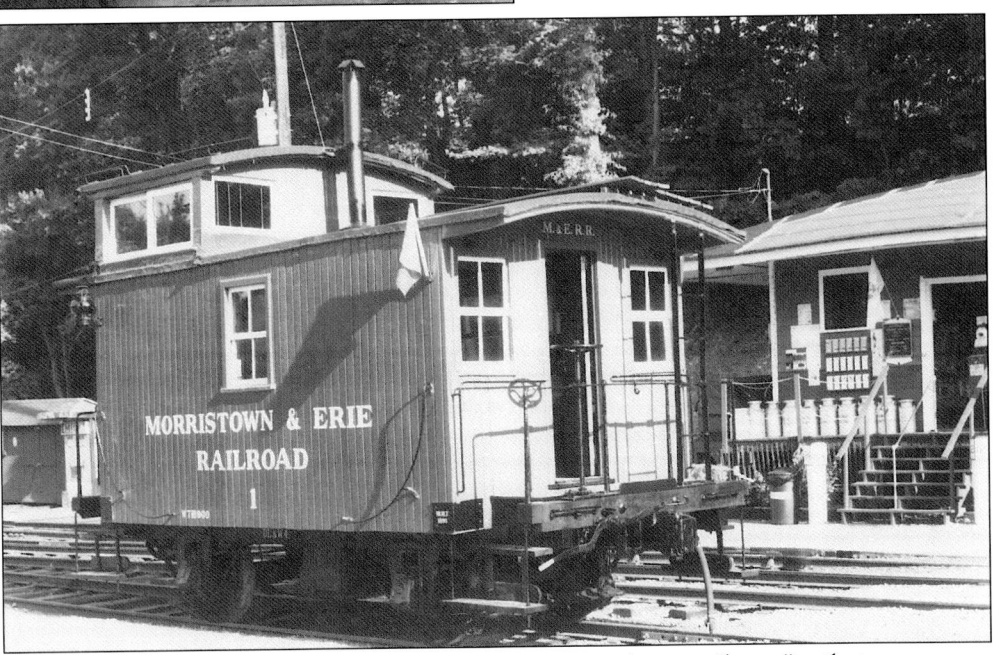

After a 38-year absence, "bobber" caboose No. 1 returned to its "home" rails in very poor condition on July 29, 1998. Owned by the United Railroad Historical Society of New Jersey and leased to the Whippany Railway Museum, the 100-year-old artifact was restored to its late 1930s M&E appearance by museum members and is seen posing proudly at Whippany on September 13, 1998. (Photo by Steven Hepler.)

Each year the museum celebrates the return of spring and the start of a new operating season by running the popular "Easter Bunny Express." Thousands of families are greeted by the famous rabbit, and candy Easter treats are handed out to passengers by friendly, costumed attendants. (Photo by Steven Hepler.)

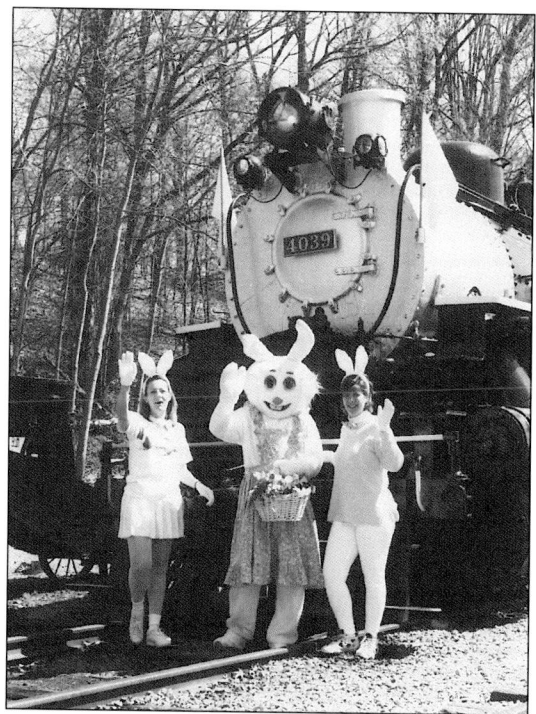

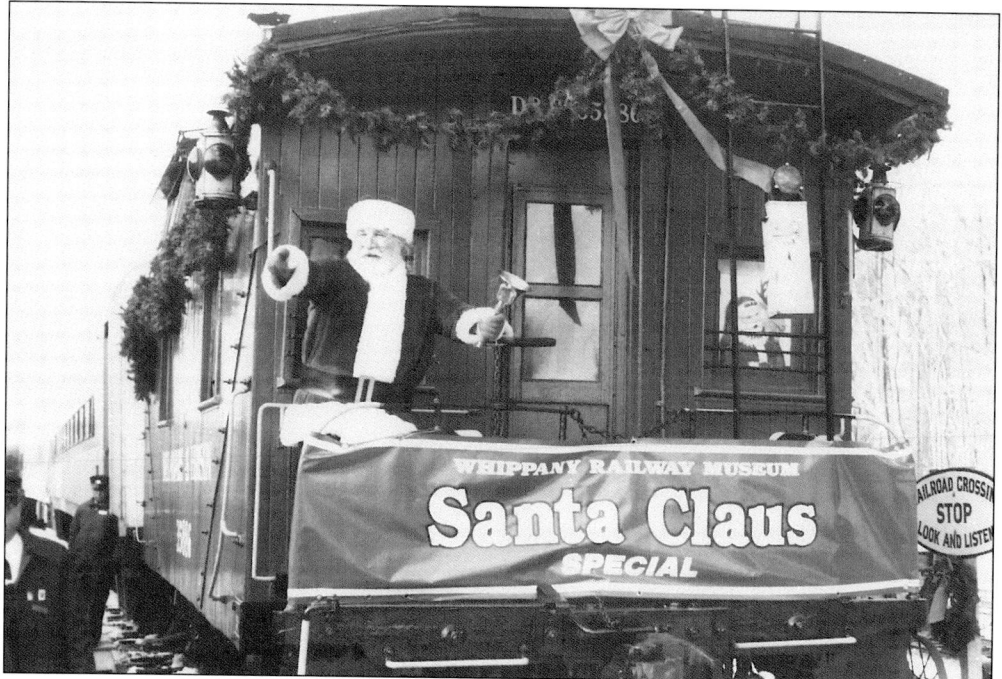

During the Christmas season, the museum is fortunate to have the services of a man who is known to all and needs no introduction. As he makes his way through the train, he brings holiday cheer to each and every passenger. From the steps of the caboose, Jolly Old Saint Nick waves to the crowds on the depot platform just before the departure of the "Santa Claus Special." (Photo by Steven Hepler.)

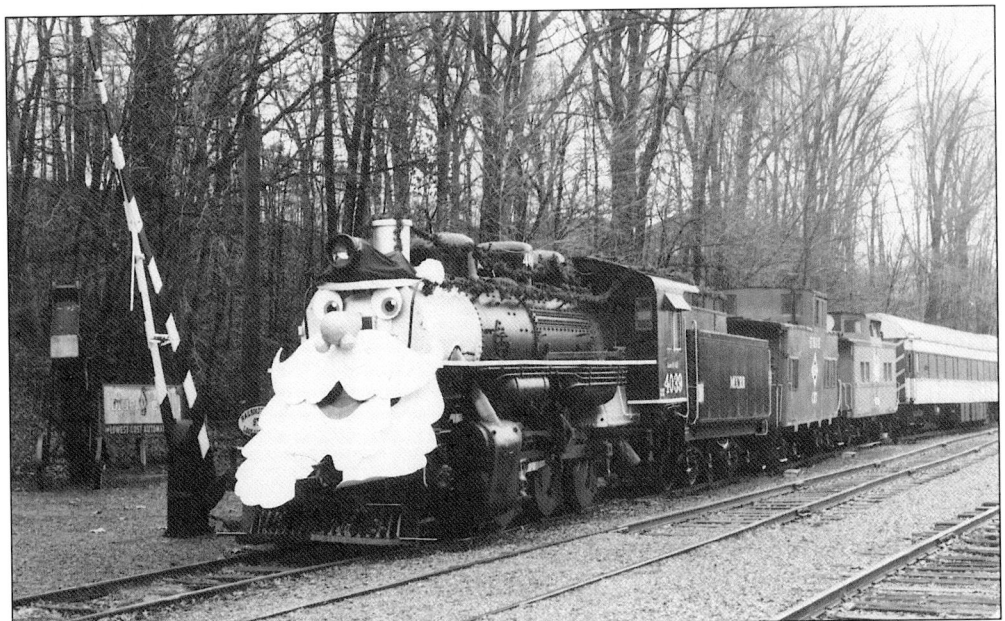

Steam Locomotive No. 4039 can be found posing as a 135-ton Santa Claus during the Christmas season at the Whippany Railway Museum. Young and old alike delight in this whimsical, giant, jolly Kriss Kringle. (Photo by Steven Hepler.)

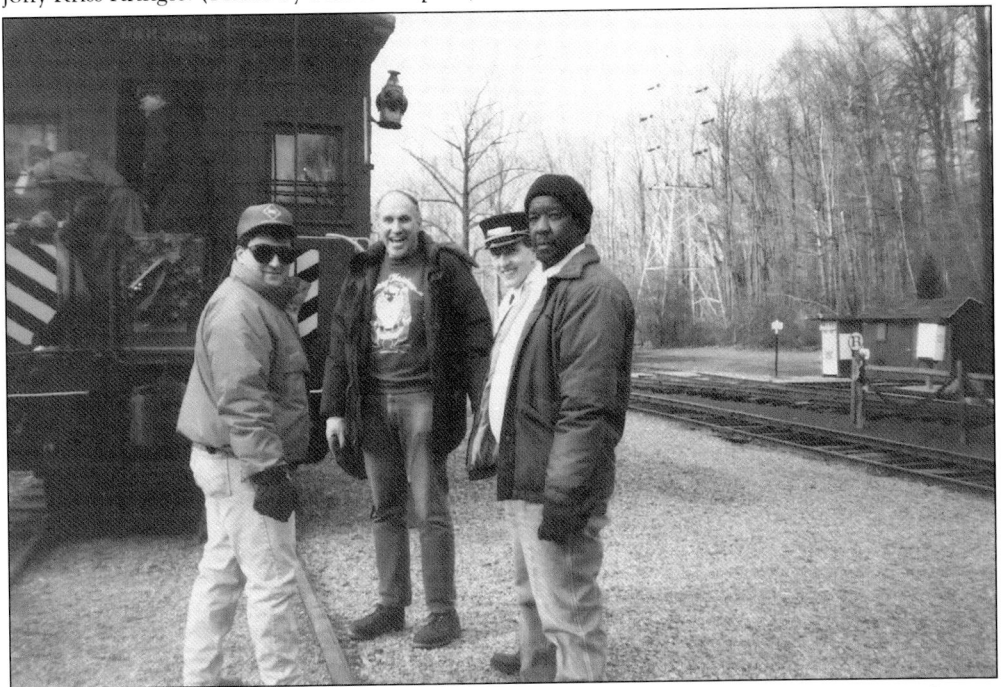

The late Ben Friedland (center), president of the Morristown & Erie, breaks into a wide grin as the shutter clicks. Steve Friedland (left), Whippany Railway Museum vice president Joe Krygoski, and M&E brakeman Roger Cozart (right) look on. Ben's dedication to historic railroad preservation enabled the museum to prosper. His passing was untimely, and he will be deeply missed by all who benefitted from his generosity. (Photo by Steven Hepler.)